CU00797214

EARL SCRUGGS

Roots of American Music
Folk, Americana, Blues, and Country

June Skinner Sawyers, series editor

In recent decades American roots music has experienced a revival in popular performance and critical attention. Rowman & Littlefield's series Roots of American Music: Folk, Americana, Blues, and Country seeks to explore the origins of these musical genres as integral parts of cultural experience and shared musical history. With dynamic biographies of musicians responsible for enduring traditions in these genres, the series introduces accessible scholarship to expose the significance of these musicians to a wide audience. Stylistic and cultural investigations into the genres provide contextual anchors for broader understanding of trends that continue to influence music today. Just like the musical traditions investigated, this series looks to music's past in order to understand its future. The series welcomes projects that seek to explore the reaches of folk, Americana, blues, and country traditions as they were formed in the past and as they continue to evolve in the contemporary music scene.

Published Titles

John Lee "Sonny Boy" Williamson: The Blues Harmonica of Chicago's Bronzeville by Mitsutoshi Inaba (2016)

The Americana Revolution: From Country and Blues Roots to the Avett Brothers, Mumford & Sons, and Beyond by Michael Scott Cain (2017)

Earl Scruggs: Banjo Icon by Gordon Castelnero and David L. Russell (2017)

EARL SCRUGGS

Banjo Icon

Gordon Castelnero
David L. Russell

ROWMAN & LITTLEFIELD
Lanham • Boulder • New York • London

Published by Rowman & Littlefield
A wholly owned subsidiary of The Rowman & Littlefield Publishing Group,
Inc.
4501 Forbes Boulevard, Suite 200, Lanham, Maryland 20706
www.rowman.com

Unit A, Whitacre Mews, 26-34 Stannary Street, London SE11 4AB

British Library Cataloguing in Publication Information Available

Library of Congress Cataloging-in-Publication Data

Names: Castelnero, Gordon, 1965– | Russell, David, 1960, July 5–
Title: Earl Scruggs : banjo icon / Gordon Castelnero, David Russell.
Description: Lanham : Rowman & Littlefield, [2017] | Series: Roots of American music: folk,
    Americana, blues, and country | Includes bibliographical references and index.
Identifiers: LCCN 2016050166 (print) | LCCN 2016050662 (ebook) | ISBN 9781442268654 (hard-
    cover : alk. paper) | ISBN 9781442268661 (electronic)
Subjects: LCSH: Scruggs, Earl. | Banjoists—United States—Biography. | LCGFT: Biographies.
Classification: LCC ML419.S38 C37 2017 (print) | LCC ML419.S38 (ebook) | DDC 787.8/
    81642092 [B]—dc23
LC record available at https://lccn.loc.gov/2016050166

Printed in the United States of America

To my wife, Amy, and daughter, Cassandra,
both of whom I am blessed to have by the grace
of our Lord and Savior Jesus Christ.
—Gordon Castelnero

With deep devotion to my wife, Sherry; my children,
Kurt, Sandra, Weston, and Veronica; and my mother,
Virginia, each of whom are a blessing from God, and to
my father, Ken, who passed away during this project.
—David L. Russell

CONTENTS

SERIES EDITOR'S FOREWORD

This is the third volume in the Roots of American Music: Folk, Americana, Blues, and Country series. Each book in the series examines the influences on and of the music from a cultural context. Moreover, the books are written by authors who are knowledgeable and authoritative in their field but who are still able to communicate to the general reader. The series examines the body of work by particular artists in folk, Americana, blues, and country and their offshoots; explores the various influences and roots of these artists, both major and lesser-known, who warrant closer examination; and studies musical trends within these genres in an attempt to both understand and reveal their historical influences.

Earl Scruggs was a pioneer and an innovator. By popularizing the three-finger banjo-picking style, a defining characteristic of the bluegrass sound, he revolutionized bluegrass and helped establish the foundation of the music as we know it today. Scruggs first came to fame in 1945 as a member of Bill Monroe's Blue Grass Boys. His singular style transformed the banjo, then dismissed as an instrument best used for comedic effect, into a lead voice. He performed as a duo with guitarist Lester Flatt from 1948 to 1969, creating an exciting and highly syncopated style of bluegrass that appealed to generations and crossed musical genres.

The phenomenal success of "The Ballad of Jed Clampett," the theme music from the popular 1960s television series *The Beverly Hillbillies*, and "Foggy Mountain Breakdown," which appeared on the soundtrack of the classic and groundbreaking 1967 film *Bonnie and Clyde*, made him a household name. In 1969, he teamed up with his sons to form the Earl Scruggs Revue, a band that fused rock and folk with bluegrass, which earned him even greater cachet with the younger generation. But Scruggs was always ahead of his time and open to new ideas. Everyone seemed to want to work with him, and he, in return, welcomed and encouraged their input.

As Gordon Castelnero and David L. Russell make clear in *Earl Scruggs: Banjo Icon*, a loving homage to the bluegrass legend, Scruggs's legacy lives on. Béla Fleck, Sonny Osborne, and J. D. Crowe are perhaps his best-known successors, but countless others have been influenced by Scruggs and have followed in his footsteps.

Earl Scruggs earned many awards and received numerous accolades during his long life: induction into the Country Music Hall of Fame, multiple Grammys, a National Medal of Arts, even a star on the Hollywood Walk of Fame. In early 2014, the Earl Scruggs Center: Music & Stories from the American South opened in Shelby, North Carolina, in a restored courthouse just a few miles from the place where Scruggs was born and raised. The Center examines Scruggs's career while exploring the history and cultural traditions of the surrounding region.

Earl Scruggs was a great musical ambassador. In fact, his music changed lives. He played a style of bluegrass banjo that epitomizes American roots music at its best and most uplifting. This book is a testament to his ongoing legacy and influence.

June Sawyers
Series Editor

FOREWORD

Béla Fleck

I first heard Earl Scruggs's banjo in *The Beverly Hillbillies* theme song in Queens, New York, when I was about five years old. My big brother, Louie, and I were enjoying the rare privilege of watching Grandpa's TV during the day, unsupervised. When that theme came on, I couldn't breathe or think; I was completely transfixed. As it finished, I turned to my brother and said, "Did you just hear that?" He replied, "Hear what?" I said, "Wait, it will come back at the end of the show," and it did, for a short reprise under the credits. "Isn't that amazing?" I asked, and he responded without enthusiasm, "I guess." It had no impact on him whatsoever, but my life had just been changed irrevocably and forever.

Over the many years since my first exposure to "that sound," I've found that nearly every serious banjoist has had his or her Earl Scruggs "come hither" moment. Some were behind the wheel listening to the radio and had to pull over because they simply couldn't drive anymore. For some it was "Foggy Mountain Breakdown," for some *The Beverly Hillbillies* theme, for others the *Grand Ole Opry* or the Flatt and Scruggs TV shows. But once that sound stopped, they were left with an incredible compulsion to go find a banjo and learn to play it.

One of the most profound things about Earl is *that* impact. There have been a lot of great banjo players since who have all expanded the language, but no one so far has had the effect of Earl. I believe that there are banjo people and non-banjo people, and it's not usually based on personal choice. It's hard to believe, but some folks just don't like the banjo, while for the true banjo person it's a deeply embedded pre-disposition. It's just in there, and when they hear Earl Scruggs they are awakened and activated.

Once activated, the next step is to learn to play, and once they have spent some time doing that, they find themselves even more blown away by Earl. One of the most fascinating properties of his playing is the apparent effortlessness of it all. But it takes an awful lot of skill to make it look so effortless.

Now the advancing banjoist must dig deep into the Scruggs instruction book. A focused enough disciple will discover every mistake in the tablature. These mistakes appear to have been put in there intentionally, to separate the serious people from the hacks. Even this seems perfect.

Next, one should study all the different live versions of the songs to truly understand how Earl varies the songs in subtle ways with every performance. You'll start to realize that his banjo parts are not "set pieces" but melodies that he can express in various ways based on how he is feeling that day. It's his own personal language, and naturally he does not choose to say things the same way every time.

And finally, the highest level a banjo player used to be able to aspire toward was to actually meet the man.

I want to tell you how I got to meet Earl Scruggs. When I came onto the scene, he didn't seem to be out playing, so hearing him in person wasn't possible. Folks figured it was a low-ebb period for him health-wise, and sure enough a few years later he had a quintuple bypass that left him feeling much better and ready to get out and play some music again.

When I moved to Nashville to join New Grass Revival in 1981, I was hoping I'd eventually get to meet him, but it wasn't happening. Over the course of several years, I did meet and become warm friends with John Hartford, who was very close to Earl. One day John told me that he was getting together with Earl regularly and encouraging him to get out his banjo, which was exciting for me to hear. He asked me if I'd ever met Earl, and I confessed that sadly I had not. He scratched his head or his chin, and said, "Let me think about that."

Sometime later, I got a call from John and he said, "I'm going to pick with Earl; grab your guitar and come to my house." He didn't want me to overcome Earl with a bunch of modern banjo antics, so I played rhythm guitar with Earl while John played fiddle and Randy Howard played mandolin. Earl kept nodding at me to play guitar solos, and I tried with limited success, but what was amazing was getting to play rhythm for him.

As we finished our jam, John said, "Earl, Béla plays a little banjo too." Earl said, "Well, pick us one!" The pressure was on! I remember bravely playing a Charlie Parker jazz tune for him. He responded, "And they said it couldn't be done!" in that understated drawl he had. Far from being intimidated or put off by this fancy-pants New York kid, he was curious and encouraging.

From then on we were friends. We had various jams, usually instigated by John. A few times Earl, John, and I went to Bobby Thompson's house to jam. Bobby was laid low by MS and couldn't play anymore, but he sure loved having us over there playing for him, and we loved it too.

It was there that Earl grabbed my late-1930s Style 75 flathead Gibson banjo with the loose head and big arched fingerboard, and he wouldn't give it back to me all night. I was perfectly thrilled to be playing his amazing Gibson Granada for the evening, and I do believe we played "Foggy Mountain Special" for twenty minutes. That night, he played a bunch of stuff I had never heard him do, on my banjo!

It was exciting to find that the Scruggs language was far from completely documented, and that there was plenty of fresh stuff happening all the time in his playing, just like there always had been. Perhaps it's the egotism of youth to think that after a certain age the story is pretty much told, and that was certainly the rap on Earl at the time, especially among people who didn't have personal contact with his playing. The conventional line was that you had to hear Earl in the fifties to hear the real stuff. It was great to understand that none of that essence had gone away. He just didn't play as much as he did back then.

An important thing to understand about those amazing early periods was just how much he was playing his instrument. The banjo was in Earl's hands all the time. From my own experience, I have learned that when I am out on tour, playing nearly every night for weeks, with the added lengthy sound-checks in the afternoon, my playing becomes super solid. I can play with very little effort, and the language I use becomes a flow. In other words, I can direct the proceedings in my playing with gentle, mental nudges the way you would if you were communicating with words. When I'm not playing, I have a lot of fresh ideas, but less of that super solidness.

I noticed when I jammed with Earl that he was turning his lack of playing time into a strength. He wasn't playing much those days, but when he did, he was super fresh and relaxed, enjoying the fluidity of his language but not attempting to drive it or play in the way that we all like to imitate from the old days.

I learned a lot of lessons while sitting with him about what it means to be a musician for your whole life, that other people's ideas about how you should play should not be your guide. He was blowing me away with his sheer natural talent just as much in those years. My practice, practice, practice mantra was irrelevant for someone like him; especially at the stage of life he was in when we became even better friends.

Some years later, his wife, Louise, had passed away, and Earl was not playing out very much. He deadpanned to me, "I played one show last year but I'm thinking about cutting back a bit." At this point I had become pretty good friends with the Scruggs family, and I could come over and visit him when I was home off the road, a development I treasured and took advantage of often.

During this period, I found myself strangely afraid to play my own language in the fear that it would put him off somehow, but he kept encouraging me to go for it. Gradually I let the cat out of the bag, and he would get so excited. My role changed, and now when I came to visit I would try to entertain Earl by playing the most far-out things I could imagine. He loved it and responded in kind, often playing something I had never heard him do before in response. While John Hartford (now long gone) used to always pull out a recorder when he jammed with Earl, I never felt that it was appropriate to even ask to do so, and these precious experiences reside in my memory alone now, undocumented.

Earl honored me near the end of his life by coming to my home and allowing me to play my banjo concerto *The Impostor* for him. He also came to the premiere concert with the Nashville Symphony Orchestra. I had the opportunity at the end of the performance to dedicate the piece to Earl in person from the stage, and the standing ovation that ensued was deafening and lasted for several minutes. Gary Scruggs tells me that this was the last concert Earl went to see, and six months later, he was gone.

With Earl gone, I can feel his impact on me and the entire banjo community even more strongly. There is a beginning and an ending to his story now, but his legacy continues, carried on by the many thousands of banjo people, like myself, who would never have been activated were it not for hearing "that sound," finding themselves a banjo, and trying to play just like Earl, which of course was impossible for anyone but him.

PREFACE

Almost all of the material used to construct this book was derived from seventy-one interviews we conducted. Our purpose is to present an oral history of Earl Scruggs's life and musical influence from the collective memories of the family, friends, acquaintances, and musicians/entertainers inspired by him. This is our way of ensuring that Earl's legacy is depicted with a freshness that's personable and conversational. Interviewee contributions appear in direct quotes.

Our use of existing quotations from Earl and Louise Scruggs were granted to us by the copyright owners. We wanted to include their voices, as they are relevant to the content of this book. All of the preexisting interview material is clearly identified.

Research for Earl's Gibson banjos was supplied by Jim Mills and used by permission of Jim Mills Banjo Inc. The balance of contributory material not provided by our primary sources but crucial to the continuity of the story is either identified in the text or listed in the notes at the end of the book.

ACKNOWLEDGMENTS

Of all the people who helped turn this book into a reality, we would like to express our sincerest thanks to Gary Scruggs for his enthusiastic participation and support. We are very grateful to him and his family members—Grace Constant, Elam Scruggs, and J. T. Scruggs—for allowing us to interview them. Our appreciation cannot be expressed enough for their faith in trusting us to preserve the memory of Earl Scruggs, whose musical genius brought so much joy to countless people around the world.

In addition to the Scruggs family, we would like to thank all of the musicians, entertainers, and media professionals who took time away from their busy schedules to share their personal accounts of the banjo man with us. Their excitement for this project validated all our reasons for writing this book. Listed alphabetically, they are Jay Adams, Tom Adams, Eddie Adcock, Bobby Atkins, Max Baer Jr., Terry Baucom, Kristin Scott Benson, Byron Berline, Norman Blake, Ron Block, Don Bryant, Sam Bush, Greg Cahill, Ryan Cavanaugh, Roy Clark, Stephen Cox, J. D. Crowe, Charlie Cushman, Charlie Daniels, Steve Dilling, Bill Emerson, Silvio Ferretti, Béla Fleck, Vince Gill, Tom T. Hall, Willie Hall, Colonel Bruce Hampton, John Hickman, David Hoffman, Doug Hutchens, Kenny Ingram, Bob Johnston, Vic Jordan, Chris Keenan, Bill Keith, Jens Koch, Jens Kruger, Pete Kuykendall, Doyle Lawson, Bernie Leadon, Sam Lovullo, Jody Maphis, Steve Martin, Haskel McCormick, Roger McGuinn, Curtis McPeake, Matt Menefee, Jim Mills, Alan Munde, Willow Osborne, Herb Pedersen, L. Leon Pendarvis, Bob Piekiel, Marc Pruett, Butch Robins, Peter Rowan, Leon Russell, Sammy Shelor, Takashi Shimbo, Tim Stafford, Ralph Stanley, Roni Stoneman, Tony Trischka, Saburo Watanabe, Eric Weissberg, Pete Wernick, and Mac Wiseman.

We also want to extend our gratitude to the following individuals for their efforts in coordinating interviews, photographs, and other miscellaneous services that were valuable to us (in alphabetical order): Denny Adcock, Katie Altman, Carol Anderson, Fred Bartenstein, Cindy Baucom, David Bendett, Nancy Cardwell, Miss Cathy, Amanda French Clark, Mary Ann Clayton, Brenda Colladay, Leo Coulson, Joe DePriest, Maria Drummond, Emily Epley, Al Evers, Danny Forbes, Ben Hershman, Albert Ihde, Joy Johnston, Bryan Jones, Allie Kandell, Annette Kelley, Kitsy Kuykendall, Scott Lawson, Les Leverett, Matthew Lutts, LeRoy Mack, Natalie Mandziuk, Camilla McGuinn, Tom Mindte, Mike Moore, Erin Morris, Adrienne Nirde, Beth Odle, Scott O'Malley, Jay Orr, Gale Osborne, Penny Parsons, Susan Quatresols, Victor Robinson, Virginia Russell, June Sawyers, Susan Scruggs, Bob Stinson, Paula Szeigis, Santosh Tawde, and Tim Timberlake.

An extra special thank-you to Tom T. Hall for his gracious generosity in sending us to visit the Earl Scruggs Center in Shelby, North Carolina, through the Dixie Hall Fund. His thoughtful consideration was truly unexpected.

INTRODUCTION

Earl Scruggs was the most influential and most imitated banjo player
in the world. He helped give birth to bluegrass music when he joined
Bill Monroe's band and introduced his innovative and exciting three-
finger style of playing five-string banjo on the Grand Ole Opry.
—Gary Scruggs, musician and son of Earl Scruggs

In 1959, *New York Times* music critic Robert Shelton compared Earl
Scruggs to Niccolò Paganini by writing, "Earl Scruggs bears about the
same relationship to the five-string banjo that Paganini does to the
violin." As a natural virtuoso who was self-taught without reading music
(or tablature), Scruggs perfected and popularized the three-finger
method of banjo picking that was already in existence throughout the
region where he grew up in North Carolina. His endless hours of practicing around his childhood schooling and chores on the family's cotton
farm resulted in syncopated rhythms and a clarity of notes emphasizing
melody lines that refined the more "raw" picking styles of his predecessors. The rapid speed and precise timing of his various roll patterns also
contributed to a distinctive technique that became the standard by
which all five-string banjo players after him learned, called "Scruggs
style."

A shy man of few words, Earl expressed himself through his banjo.
The communication from his head to his hands was superb, as many of
those interviewed have referenced—they could detect his feelings
through the notes he played. And like many musical geniuses, Scruggs
brought a unique quality to his instrument that had never existed before

him but will continue to live long after. Crucial to this understanding is knowing the right-hand roll patterns that he put forth, which are tantamount to an entirely new language. This unheard vocabulary for the five-string banjo was carved out of a series of patterns that he invented. Even though he believed that the forward roll pattern, used exclusively, was limiting (or at least he came to know this as he gained more experience playing banjo), he never ceased to use it or variations of it in his own particular style. He merely thought you didn't have to be limited to one type of roll.

Any new banjo student has to contend with an array of Scruggs roll patterns like the forward roll, alternating thumb pattern, backward roll, forward-reverse roll, and Foggy Mountain roll (which is prominently featured in Earl's signature composition, "Foggy Mountain Breakdown," but is also a standard in other tunes). Another characteristic in his musicianship is the way he separated his notes when he played. Musicians will often talk about the proper distance between the notes (the separation of notes) as a necessary component of playing with consistent timing. "With Earl it was not about playing more notes or playing more complicated notes," professes multigenre banjoist Jens Kruger. "But it was about how you play them. The first time I heard Earl Scruggs, I thought he was so amazingly precise—that was my first impression. Every note was in time and good tone. I mean, that was the first thing I instantly knew."

Good tone is a key element that Scruggs aficionados often mention when talking about his musical abilities. He developed a tone quality that demonstrated the attention he paid to the notes he picked, giving them the importance they deserved within the context of any given tune. The tone he created was the result of what he felt within himself, which corresponds with the idea that it also has a connection to the feeling, or emotional component, of the musician. Earl's sound was pleasant to the ears due in large part to the unequaled touch he had on the strings of his banjo. It was not something he could really explain to people when asked how he pulled tone the way he did; he just simply picked and didn't think too much about it.

"Earl was one of a kind, and he did it his way; he was a three-finger genius," admits veteran bluegrass banjoist J. D. Crowe. "There will never be another Earl Scruggs. Nobody has ever come close to Earl in tone and sound. He had that special something that no one else had. He was the first and he couldn't have done it any better." This sentiment is fairly widespread. Progressive banjo player Matt Menefee plays a style today that includes a great deal of jazz, fusion, blues, and various other forms of contemporary music, yet his first exposure to the five-string was through old Flatt and Scruggs records. The impact of Earl's banjo for him was "like a deluge of truth, soul, and tastiness flooding into the parched ears of the listener. I could feel every note. Like a bomb going off inside of me and the feeling of shrapnel being broadcast throughout my bloodstream and embedding itself under my skin. He found the sweet spots in rhythm that defined bluegrass banjo."

Timing concerns itself with the consistency of the beat. In a band scenario, the timing goes awry when a player either speeds up and rushes the beat or slows down and drags the beat. In such a situation, you're only as good as your weakest link. The relentless timing with which Earl Scruggs played was made possible by the other members of his two primary bands: the Foggy Mountain Boys and the Earl Scruggs Revue. They, in essence, created the rail system upon which Earl's "timing-drive" train could ride. "Earl had the extreme luxury of playing with the same guys all the time for many years, and when you can depend on the guys who are backing you up, as he could, drive takes on many different definitions," echoes bluegrass banjoist Charlie Cushman. "Earl had that luxury of being able to spontaneously put drive anywhere he wanted to, real sweet, or real laid back, or right dead on the beat. His vocabulary and the way he set up his solos, and all his backup, is what really defined Earl Scruggs."

The disciples of Earl each have their own take on the definition of timing and drive, yet there is very little disagreement that he played it better than anyone else. "His drive and his power, and if you've seen videos of the old Martha White shows, the power he played with is just amazing, just the drive, it was like an explosion when Earl played," notes seasoned banjoist Bill Emerson. "Earl didn't have anyone to go by or copy like we did, and I just think that's the way he felt it, and the way he heard it; it was something he was born with, and he just developed that himself." Legendary banjo player Kenny Ingram further explains, "Earl gave the banjo a voice that it never had before, an actual voice, you know. The banjo was singing while he was playing, and that's my best description of Earl's drive and timing. It's so simplistic sounding that it fools most people and most people are not even close."

There is something appealing about an instrument played with what seems to be a perfect separation of notes. When you combine that with drive, you've created something that's long lasting in the ears of the listener. "All the old guys always talked about timing," comments bluegrass banjoist Butch Robins. "As far as Earl is concerned, he played five to ten milliseconds in front of the beat and he didn't rush it." Concurringly, Blue Highway guitarist Tim Stafford predicates, "It's as close to rushing as you can get, and Earl was the master at it. Like he's almost rushing, but he's not, he's still inside the groove of the band."

Drive is not only confused with the idea of playing good timing, but often there is an expressed misunderstanding that drive is equal to a fast tempo. "Drive is not speed, drive is not necessarily a high-paced tempo, and that's where a lot of people get it confused," remarks bluegrass mandolinist Doyle Lawson. "They think if it's fast, it's drive. There's an emotion in the picker and the picking, and you can feel it whether or not it's a fast song or a slow song. [An] example is the song 'Before I Met You' by Lester and Earl. Listen to Earl's break, that's drive."

Scruggs's musical talent was an instinct to know exactly where to place a given phrase, lick, or note, whether he was playing lead or backup. It's what he didn't play that stands out, which is another way of saying that he didn't upstage the music but kept it simple. "He was a genius at backing up other instruments," insists Ron Block, banjoist for Alison Krauss and Union Station. "I love what he does behind the fiddle; it adds so much tension and excitement. Earl 'got with' whatever was playing and played to it, and played for it. He didn't overplay. He didn't distract from the fiddle, or Dobro, or the other instruments, and especially the vocals."

Earl Scruggs was a stickler for playing the melody and not doing anything to distract from what the other musicians were attempting to accomplish onstage. "Earl was the best at creating a mood with the solo, and with his backup, and with everything," says Lonesome River Band banjoist Sammy Shelor. "He was one of those guys who could play backup while the singer was singing, but he never got in the way. There's only been a few musicians who can do that. I can't do it; I have to display my fills during the breaths, then I'm a rhythm instrument while the singer's singing." Earl's breaks were always focused on the melody, and his backup playing was crafted around complementing what the vocalist was singing. "When he played a melody note, the melody note stood out. It just reached out and touched [you]," adds professional banjoist Steve Dilling. "It's kind of hard to describe, it was just head and shoulders above anything else. He was the greatest melody player to ever come along."

The manner by which Earl Scruggs picked the five-string banjo stemmed from a basic philosophy coupled with subtle nuances that contributed to his unique style. In his *Banjo Newsletter* column "Earl's Way," Bob Piekiel describes the final ingredients in detail:

> When you looked at Earl from the front, if you watched him play, it looked like his fingers weren't moving much at all, but if you looked at him from the side, most of the picking motion he was getting was coming from his fingertips plucking up toward his palm. In other words, the fingertips and the first two joints of his fingers from the tip back, that's where he was getting most of his picking motion from. So between the length of his fingers and the way his fingers curled, he was almost picking the strings from the bridge, up and away from the head in a vertical motion towards his palm, not picking the strings horizontally. That snap is what gave him the crisp, driving tone, coupled with the fact he had a very strong thumb he learned to use in the early days.
>
> Earl had a bunch of subtle little movements and tricks that he would do that he wouldn't even think about to embellish certain sounds like sliding with his fingernail, or lifting his hand off the [banjo] head when he picked certain notes. Sometimes he would brush the strings sideways versus picking them like I was describing. Sometimes he would stroke down with his thumb across two or three strings rather than just picking one. There were a bunch of things that he did that you couldn't identify unless you saw him do it.

When it came to Earl Scruggs's most acclaimed works, two songs and one album rank at the top of the spectrum (among many) in both popularity and influence. Almost everyone who watched the 1960s hit sitcom *The Beverly Hillbillies* can sing the catchy theme song and even try to mimic the banjo solo (with something like, bang-da-da-bang-da-da-bang). "The Ballad of Jed Clampett" introduced Earl Scruggs and his three-finger style of banjo picking to mainstream Americans who had yet to hear bluegrass music. Some of the best banjoists in the world, like Béla Fleck and Terry Baucom, received their introduction to the instrument via the *Hillbillies*. "That really made an impression on me,"

Baucom confesses. "That really hit me. Like, man, this is something, and I would love to do that as well."

"Foggy Mountain Breakdown" is Earl's other Hollywood connection and took his 1949 composition to levels that seemed unattainable when it was originally recorded at a radio station in Cincinnati, Ohio. Though Scruggs played his signature tune for many years, it was Warren Beatty's fondness for the vintage recording that persuaded him to insert it into his 1967 blockbuster film *Bonnie and Clyde*. What was once old had become new as the talent of Earl Scruggs was solidified into American pop culture.

Even more so than "The Ballad of Jed Clampett," "Foggy Mountain Breakdown" spawned a host of disciples who were enamored by the energy they heard coming from him in just two minutes and forty seconds. "The sound of his playing was so exciting and also mind boggling to me at eleven years old," cites Blue Highway banjoist Jason Burleson. "The original '49 version of 'Foggy Mountain Breakdown' stands out in my memory. I remember listening to that over and over and over. It still can't be beat in my opinion." The general feeling about this particular cut among Scruggs enthusiasts is that it couldn't be duplicated by anyone else, including Earl himself. "He recorded 'Foggy Mountain Breakdown' a number of times," says bluegrass banjoist Haskel McCormick. "But the first recording was the best one to me, the 1949 recording. He didn't put in too much, but put in exactly what it needed. It was perfect, simply perfect."

Of all the albums that Earl Scruggs recorded, *Foggy Mountain Banjo* (1961) is hailed as his instrumental masterpiece. Virtually every tune on this album is a classic hit with Scruggs-style banjo players as well as bluegrass fans, and you would be hard-pressed to find many people claiming one track is better than another. Several professional banjoists point to *Foggy Mountain Banjo* as being one of the first albums that motivated them to play. Greg Cahill, founder of the bluegrass band Special Consensus (aka Special C), elaborates on how the LP became a game changer for him to pursue Scruggs style. "When I was in this folk group, and the guy that I played with in this group came over one Saturday afternoon, and I was still living in a dorm at that time, and he said, 'You're not going to believe this,' and he put the *Foggy Mountain Banjo* album on my record player. It was stunning, just jaw dropping, and that was it for me—that did it."

The appeal of that early concept album transcends musical genres, even decades after its release. The proof of its insightful reach beyond the boundaries of bluegrass, folk, and Americana can be found in the declaration of avant-garde musician/composer Colonel Bruce Hampton:

> Jeff Mosier [former bandmate in the Aquarium Rescue Unit] played *Foggy Mountain Banjo* for me in '87 or '88, and I just sat there on the floor dumbfounded. I've studied every form of music there is for thirty years and I couldn't believe that Earl escaped me. I thought, this is impossible, no one else could do this on earth, you know, nobody can do this. There are probably ten albums that are the greatest of all time and *Foggy Mountain Banjo* is certainly one of them. It's a masterpiece. Earl is the king of kings as far as I'm concerned.

According to the International Bluegrass Music Museum, Earl Scruggs wrote or co-wrote over 150 songs and instrumentals during his professional career. Most people are unaware of the plethora of compositions he made popular in the world of country and bluegrass music. His instrumentals are considered bluegrass classics and are some of the most copied tunes heard in jam sessions and bluegrass festivals worldwide to this day. Not to mention that many of the vocal songs he recorded with Lester Flatt, the Earl Scruggs Revue, guest artists, and his Family & Friends band have become either standards or fan favorites.

In addition to chronicling his musical history, depictions of the banjo man's quiet and humble demeanor are a recurring theme throughout this book. Comedic actor and professional banjoist Steve Martin recalls: "His sweet nature, his kindness. . . . Earl was very polite." As Doyle Lawson recollects, "Earl was a funny guy, he had a dry sense of humor, and it just came natural. He was a smart man too and had a good head for business." Many of Scruggs's personal attributes are revealed, as well as a few bumps in the road that he encountered while traveling through his eighty-eight-year journey of life. He was well respected and appreciated for his gracious treatment of people with whom he had contact. Generosity with his time, talent, and possessions came naturally without strings attached. No doubt, the most treasured commodity Scruggs acquired was his prized prewar Gibson RB-Granada Mastertone banjo. Regardless of the instrument's monetary or sentimental value, Earl was very trusting in letting others touch it, play it, and even borrow it. Steve Dilling shares such an account from an event at the International Bluegrass Music Association convention:

> We were at the IBMA in the fall of 1996, and my wife and I went up to Earl and Louise's room to visit some with them. Out of the blue, Earl asked me if I wanted to play his banjo. He knew we were doing the Flatt and Scruggs tribute album and wanted to know if I wanted to play his Granada on the album. I said, "Well sure, I'd be honored to." So that was earlier in the day and he told us to come back later, and I could pick up the banjo, and take it back to my room, and change strings if I wanted, and whatever. So we went back up to Earl's room and hung out with them a few minutes, and then I took his banjo. So we got back to our room, [and] I couldn't wait to get it out of the case. I started taking the resonator off and my wife is like, "What are you doing?" I said, "I just want to take some pictures." I told her, "Just think of all the licks that have been played on this banjo. Think of the licks that all us banjo players play, that were born on that banjo," you know, when you think about it that deeply, because that was his main axe. Licks that [we] have grown accustom to playing, that are just standard banjo licks, were probably born on that banjo.

The following chapters are a testament from the collective memories of numerous musicians and entertainment professionals who were influenced or inspired by Earl Scruggs. Together, with members of the Scruggs family, their stories provide a personalized account of the life and legacy of the banjo man. "Earl's contribution to the world of music is very important," notes Steve Martin. "Bill Monroe might've invented bluegrass, but it was Earl who gave it the sound that lives on today. And there's very few musicians who actually have changed the nature of their instrument—one of them is Earl." Despite his passing in 2012, Earl's legend continues with every new generation of banjo players; no matter how progressive the style gets, Scruggs can be heard in every roll.

1

HUMBLE BEGINNINGS

Earl was humble. He was a man of the people. He was a man who respected working men. He was a man who did not ever put himself above other people. This is a guy who could have been, at any point along the way, changed by the enormous success he had due to the fact that he was very precisely great in his art form.
—David Hoffman, documentary filmmaker

There was a sound. Though silent to the world, it was loud and clear in the southern Appalachian Mountains and the rural farmlands of southwest Virginia, West Virginia, Kentucky, Tennessee, North Carolina, and South Carolina. It happened at a time when the country was dry from Prohibition and *Runnin' Wild* on Broadway spawned the most popular dance craze of the decade, the Charleston. While many in America's big cities were swinging to the beat of jazz during the Roaring Twenties, another form of music was resonating without the echoes of horns, woodwinds, and percussion instruments. Instead, its repertoire was made up entirely from the soft sounds of stringed instruments: fiddles, guitars, mandolins, bass fiddles, autoharps, and five-string banjos.

Old-time "string music," as it was commonly known, featured acoustic arrangements set behind an almost piercingly high-pitched singular voice bearing a lonesome quality in its raw delivery of gospel tunes or songs about events from life: love, family, and hardships. But unlike the grandness of the professional jazz ensembles that were then thriving, these smaller string bands were scarce, as the rural populace lacked the mobility of those in cities. Hence, most of the old-time string music was played within neighboring family circles.[1] Documentary filmmaker David Hoffman, whose first production, *Bluegrass Roots: On the Road with Bluegrass Musicians*, took him from New York City to Madison County, North Carolina, in 1964, characterizes the region's seemingly unchanged musical heritage:

> This was a time when America didn't yet know bluegrass and really didn't know country either. [Americans had] no understanding of it, and here I was, like other Northerners, coming down there and finding this was the most unbelievable music I have ever heard—but to them, it was just picking together. And the reason so many musicians came out of that culture was because the older people supported the younger people. They didn't put them down; they didn't send them to music school. You didn't go see their performance in grammar school choruses. It was all inside these families. It's unique—a wonderful, unique culture. There isn't a culture I've ever seen in the world or read about as beautifully musical, dance-, or poetic-oriented as these people. In that family, everybody danced, everybody played something, just like all the other families.

In the small farming community of Flint Hill, North Carolina, in the Piedmont region, just outside of Shelby and Boiling Springs in Cleveland County, was one such musical family that bred a prodigy who ultimately became a pioneer of bluegrass music as well as the most transformative five-string banjo virtuoso of the twentieth century—Earl Scruggs.

THE SCRUGGS FAMILY

With only a general store, a two-room grade school, and a church, Flint Hill was made up of farms where down-to-earth country folks made their living from the rich soil that God gave them. They were a community of Baptist Christians who believed in exercising respect and humility toward their family and fellow man.[2] George Elam Scruggs, son of David and Sarah (Green) Scruggs, was born on January 10, 1876, and grew up to become a farmer and bookkeeper. He also earned credentials in education that elevated him to the chairmanship of the Flint Hill community school board, where he occasionally lent assistance in teaching mathematics at the schoolhouse. By the age of thirty, he married Lula Georgia Ruppe on November 4, 1906. As the daughter of John David Ruppe, Lula was born on April 15, 1892 (d. October 26, 1955), and was only fourteen years old at the time of her marriage to George Elam. A year later, she gave birth to their first child, Bessie, on December 18, 1907, who sadly died in her infancy three months later on March 27, 1908.

In the subsequent years, George Elam and Lula would have more children: first a son named Junie Emmett, born on September 9, 1911 (d. December 15, 1995), followed by a daughter, Eula Mae, on December 4, 1912 (d. January 6, 1994), and another daughter, Ruby Genette, seven years later on August 4, 1919 (d. September 2, 1990). Then came two more sons, James "Horace" on March 10, 1922 (d. July 19, 2007), and Earl Eugene on January 6, 1924 (d. March 28, 2012).

Planting and picking cotton became the family's primary source of income. While it's not known when George Elam and Lula began farming in Flint Hill, Junie's son, James Thamer "J. T." Scruggs, highlights his grandparents' acquisition of their forty-acre homestead:

> Well, my great-grandfather [David Scruggs], as I understand it, owned quite a bit of land. My grandfather [George Elam Scruggs] was farming some property and had a home on the property before my great-grandfather died. My grandfather [actually] died first and then, when my great-grandfather died, my grandmother inherited some property, and that's how they acquired the farm.

When Earl was just four years of age, his father George Elam, at the age of fifty-two, passed away after an eight-month bout of tuberculosis on October 10, 1928. With the eldest children, Junie and Eula Mae, in their mid- to upper teens, Lula was now a widowed mother of three children below the age of ten. But her status soon changed, if only for a brief period. "She remarried after Grandfather passed away, and Venie Mae was born with the other husband," admits J. T. "And I don't think they really stayed together very long."

Raised among multiple siblings, Earl's strongest bond was with his brother Horace, who was a year and ten months his senior. "Horace and Earl remained close their entire lives," says Horace's son, Elam Scruggs. "They were six and four when their father died. The other children were older. Eula Mae got married the year their father died."

Yet, despite the age gap, Earl also formed a close relationship with his sister Ruby, who often helped the two boys in their daily household chores. And during this period of Earl's childhood, older brother Junie became less present, according to J. T. Scruggs:

> Dad was real close to both girls, and he was close to Horace and Earl too, but not as close as Earl and Horace [were]. They grew up together, and they were very close. Dad moved away not long after Grandfather died. He got married and moved out. And so Dad, he was home for a while after Grandfather died and did help raise the crops. But then Dad went to work at Public Work and moved away.

Without a father figure in their formative years, Earl and Horace became the men of the house. Their shared responsibilities served, in part, as a catalyst for the ties that bound them permanently together, as explained by Elam Scruggs:

> They grew up in extreme poverty, and many of the chores were assigned to them at a very young age. I remember Dad talking about how he and Earl would cut stove and firewood and plant corn, cotton, and a garden. They also had fishing lines, "throw lines," as they called them, in Broad River, which was near their house.
>
> Dad and Earl often told this story: One day after the morning chores were completed they came into the house, and their mother had baked an apple pie. She had to leave for a couple of hours, and she told them they could have one piece of pie each. They waited for her to leave and they cut the pie down the center. Each of them ate half of the pie, but it was one piece each!
>
> They remained very close, visiting each other two and three times a year. Our family normally went to Nashville at Christmas, and they would come to see us in the summer. They shared a compassionate love for each other. If one of them had a medical issue, the other one was burning down the roads to get to them. They were always there for each other.

When it came to faith, the Scruggs family attended Flint Hill Baptist Church, where all of Lula's children were baptized in the Broad River (Earl was eight years old at the time of his baptism). And even though the family was unified in their church attendance, their public schooling levels varied due to differentiating circumstances, affording Earl the honor of being the only high school graduate in his family. Scruggs's eldest son, Gary, briefly sketches his father's formal education:

> His early school years were at the little two-room Flint Hill community school. Both rooms were sectored off relative to the age and/or grade level of the students. When a teacher addressed one group, the other students would be kept busy studying another topic relative to their grade level. He attended high school in Boiling Springs, which is a couple of miles or so from the Flint Hill community. I think it was in his senior year that he helped lay the sidewalk in front of the school.

THE BANJO MAN EMERGES

Though the Scruggs family consisted of farmers, many were also amateur musicians who saw music as a means of escape from the labor and economic hardships of farming. Everyone in the family was blessed with the gift of music according to Gary Scruggs:

> Father George Elam mostly played an open-back five-string banjo and fiddle. He also knew chords on the guitar. Mother Lula played a pump organ. All the siblings played guitar and banjo. Brother Junie gravitated toward banjo, and brother Horace gravitated toward guitar. The sisters, Eula Mae and Ruby, played mainly guitar and frailing-style banjo, but not to the degree that the brothers played. Dad, of course, took up banjo and guitar as well as learning to play fiddle. The family also had an old autoharp that I think everyone would pick up and strum on now and then.

With all of this talent flowing through the Scruggs household, Earl fondly recalled, in a 1979 interview with Tim Timberlake in Lanexa, Virginia (printed with permission), the everlasting impression music made upon his childhood:

> I was raised up at the tail end of the depression days, and I know the banjo and the family get-togethers, and the music and singing, played a big part in making us forget about the hard times and that with music and family reunions got us right through. I remember, in addition to the music, they used to have what they call "all-day sing-

ing and dinner on the ground" at some rural church. And I like good
gospel singing, and you know it's so relaxing and you can just forget
all of the worldly things. It's just good.

   And [also] quite frequently, like Sunday afternoon is referred to
or a certain time of the year when we could all get together, [and] we
would all find ourselves having a little family session and usually wind
up using our instruments, picking and singing, and that was kind of a
typical afternoon for us. If we all got together before the day was
over with, we'd be all picking together.

Earl's son Gary touches on his dad's recollection with further insight:

   I think most people are exposed to music in one way or the other,
   and some simply are inspired to learn to play an instrument and
   some aren't. As in Dad's case, I suppose being the youngest of several siblings, with all the older ones playing music to some degree,
   might have had something to do with how he became interested in
   the five-string. His father also had an old fiddle that Dad was somewhat interested in and practiced on from time to time, but not anywhere near the degree in which he played banjo and guitar.

Around the time of Earl's discovery of the five-string banjo at the age of
four when his father passed away, there were two main styles of playing
the instrument: one was a method commonly known as frailing or clawhammer (where, by definition, a banjoist uses a downward stroke motion with the back of the fingers/nails to strum the strings, then strikes
the top string with the thumb); the other was two-finger picking with
the thumb and index finger. The three-finger roll (thumb, index finger,
and middle finger) was virtually nonexistent, with the exception of a few
banjoists in the Carolina Piedmont region where the Scruggs family
resided. It's difficult to pinpoint exactly where and when this style of
banjo playing originated, but there has been speculation among banjo
historians that three-finger style may go back as far as the early 1800s.
Exactly why there was a concentrated number of three-finger stylists in
this one particular region is not really known; however, some of them
had a profound impact on young Earl. The primary players who laid the
foundation on which he built are designated by Gary Scruggs:

   Smith Hammett was a local banjo picker married to a woman named
   Ola, who was a cousin of Dad's mother. The Hammetts and the

Scruggs family members often visited one another in the 1920s and
'30s. Smith played a primitive three-finger style on his five-string
banjo that Dad was drawn to. Smith died when Dad was six, but
Dad's memory of him stuck with him forever. Smith was the first
banjo player that Dad knew of who picked with three fingers. Smith
also had a small-scaled banjo that he would let Dad play on during
visits. At an early age, he also had heard another three-finger banjo
player, a blind man named Mack Woolbright who had recorded with
an old-time musician and singer named Charlie Parker for Columbia
Records in the late 1920s. Dad absorbed those banjo influences and
pretty much lived and breathed playing the banjo.

Earl's dedication to the banjo at such a young age and his small size
meant practicing in an awkward position, as he could only play it while
sitting on the floor with the round body along his right side, sliding it
around to accommodate his left hand's position on the banjo's neck.[3] At
the same time, Scruggs was also learning the guitar, as he recounted to
Doug Hutchens in a 1989 radio interview for *Bluegrass Today* (printed
with permission):

> Actually, I don't remember which instrument I started trying to play
> first. My father died when I was four, so I don't remember his play-
> ing, but we had in the house a banjo, a guitar, autoharp, fiddle, and
> instruments like that. But my older brother [Junie] picked banjo, and
> my brother that's almost two years older than me [Horace], he
> played guitar. I believe I started playing the banjo some. But when I
> played with my older brother [Junie], he wanted me to play the
> guitar with him because he wanted to play the banjo. So anyway, I
> started playing guitar back as far as I can remember, and my idol, at
> the time—the main person that I ever loved most—was Mama May-
> belle Carter, and so that's who I copied.

By the time Earl reached ten years of age in 1934, his love for the banjo
had grown to the point where he was picking either his father's old-
fashioned open-back banjo (circa 1900) or his brother Junie's modernized resonator banjo (purchased for approximately seventeen dollars)
with two fingers.[4] Yet it was that three-finger rolling style he heard from
Smith Hammett, Mack Woolbright, and his brother Junie that fascinated him most. Even though he won first or second prize for his rendition
of "Cripple Creek" in a banjo contest at a local fiddlers' convention a

few years earlier, he wasn't going to be satisfied with his playing until he learned the three-finger method.[5] Oddly, his incorporation of the middle finger into his technique evolved somewhat serendipitously as the result of his "pouting and picking" after an argument he had with Horace.[6] "Dad told this story many times," recalls Elam Scruggs. "Earl went in the front room picking alone for quite some time. Finally he came out excited saying, '*I've got it!*' I think he had finally found the sound and note progressions he was searching for to make the sound he wanted to make." "The first tune he played with three fingers at the age of ten was 'Reuben,' also known as 'Reuben's Train' and later 'Lonesome Ruben,'" adds Gary Scruggs. "He played it in D tuning."

Excited about his newfound ability to roll with three fingers, young Earl left the banjo in D tuning for a week while he practiced nothing but "Reuben" to improve the coordination of his middle finger. Standard G tuning for the five-string banjo from the fifth string to the first is G, D, G, B, D (the short fifth-string G is an octave higher than the third-string G), whereas D tuning is F#, D, F#, A, D (the fifth-string F# is an octave higher than the third-string F#). In D tuning the banjo has a more bluesy, sad, and dark sound, which is what gave the tune "Reuben" that lonesome feel (hence "Lonesome Ruben"). "Reuben" also has an old-steam-engine feel, and the way Earl eventually picked it, you could almost imagine a big locomotive "balling the jack" (railroad slang for "going at full speed") down a stretch of track. This particular tune became one of his favorites throughout his life.

Soon after learning "Reuben," his brother Junie dropped by and asked him if that was the only song he knew. Stunned by the question, Earl changed his banjo back to the standard G tuning and began practicing other songs while developing different right-hand rolls, which he understood as being critical to the flow of melody lines. However, his determination to pick melodies correctly didn't come until his mother redirected his concentration from youthful showboating with hot licks on the banjo to playing a song so it could be recognized.[7] "He practiced and played for many, many hours," notes Gary Scruggs. "I would say thousands and thousands of hours—a lot of time alone and a lot of time picking with his brother Horace. He also picked 'for fun' with other players in the area."

To ensure he was always in sync, Earl adopted an unusual approach with Horace. "To work on timing they would start playing a tune and walk in opposite directions around the outside of the house," Elam Scruggs describes. "When they met they would know if they kept time. 'Reuben' and 'Cripple Creek' were two of their early favorite songs." Much of what Earl heard throughout his youth in songs and favorite artists contributed significantly to his skillful progression with the five-string banjo, as Gary Scruggs outlines in specificity:

> Dad greatly refined and redefined the three-finger method of picking he had heard. He developed different syncopated roll patterns of the picking hand that added additional speed and clarity to a song's melody that the more primitive method could not [do].
>
> From hearing recordings, he was a big fan of the "original" Carter Family, which consisted of Alvin Pleasant "A. P." Carter, A. P.'s wife, Sara Dougherty Carter, and Maybelle Addington Carter, who married A. P.'s brother, Ezra. Sara and Maybelle were also cousins. Dad also enjoyed the recordings of Jimmie Rodgers, the "Father of Country Music." Dad especially liked Jimmie's song "T for Texas," also known as "Blue Yodel No. 1," and that song became an early fixture in our Earl Scruggs Revue concerts.
>
> It was in 1937 when he bought a "mail-order" banjo from the Montgomery Ward company. It cost ten dollars and ninety-five cents [and was the first one he ever owned]. When Dad was around fifteen or sixteen years old, his family got a battery-powered [Sears Roebuck] radio. He listened to it when he could, and one artist he was especially drawn to was Jesse "Blind Boy" Fuller, who was also a product of the Piedmont region of North Carolina. Blind Boy Fuller recorded a song titled "Step It Up and Go" that had a jazzy, early "boogie-woogie" beat that Dad really loved, and which he adapted for playing on the five-string banjo. "Step It Up and Go" became a fixture in the set lists of the Earl Scruggs Revue, and later, the Earl Scruggs with Family & Friends band. With the radio, Dad was also able to listen to a three-finger banjo picker named DeWitt "Snuffy" Jenkins, who sometimes played on a radio station [WIS] in Columbia, South Carolina.
>
> He began "playing for money" very early on in his life. But I would deem those times as "semiprofessional"—playing at local dances, parties, and local radio shows, et cetera. Many times those types of gigs would pay only two or three dollars, but it was a good experience for a young player. When he was fifteen years old, he began playing in a local band called the Carolina Wildcats. The band played for fun and also locally for parties, dances, et cetera, and was

together for several months. They also made some Saturday morning
radio appearances on a radio station in Gastonia, North Carolina.

At fifteen years of age, Earl was not only playing in his first band; he
also spent Saturday nights performing at house parties with an old-time
fiddler, Dennis Butler, who was a World War I veteran and had been
slightly gassed during the war. The scarcity of pickers in the rural areas,
due to a lack of transportation in those days, brought the young banjoist
to Butler as an accompaniment for the fiddle.[8] The harmonious sound
of the banjo and fiddle playing together brought Scruggs a level of joy
that stayed with him for the rest of his life. The pleasurable experience
gave him the idea to include banjo and fiddle duets in the repertoires of
his subsequent bands.

Another impressionable moment came in that same year, 1939,
when Earl connected with the Morris Brothers—Zeke, Wiley, and
George—a professional band that appeared on WSPA radio in Spartanburg, South Carolina, whom he greatly admired. After becoming acquainted with them personally, Scruggs eagerly accepted their invitation to pick with them on their early morning program for several weeks
that winter.[9] Zeke and Wiley's adaptation and rearrangement of the old
song "Salty Dog Blues," also known as "Old Salty Dog Blues," would
become a mainstay in the Flatt and Scruggs catalog. And while Earl
satisfied his need to play semiprofessionally through the winter months,
he was still grounded to the farm during the crop season for the remainder of his adolescence.

In 1941, the year he graduated from high school, Scruggs upgraded
his banjo from Montgomery Ward to a Gibson RB-11 he saw hanging in
a pawnshop. This was a highly decorative, fancy looking banjo with a
resonator back that had a veneer made of celluloid and a silkscreened
flower design on the peghead and fingerboard. Following in his older
brothers' footsteps, Earl sought to leave the dawn-to-dusk drudgery of
farming for hourly employment in a factory. "I think he began working
in the mill in 1942, which was around the time he and his mother
moved from the farm to Shelby," says Gary Scruggs about his father's
first steady job. "It was in the Lily Mills thread mill in Shelby. His job
was to take care of the machinery and repair any problems that might
arise with the equipment. He worked there until World War II ended
in 1945."

As a machine mechanic working seventy-two hours a week, Earl's wages helped to support his mother and younger half-sister, Venie Mae. While the lengthy hours prevented him from playing in the types of venues he had grown accustomed to, Scruggs made the most of his spare time.[10] His niece Grace Constant mentions, "When Uncle Earl worked at Lily Mills, he was always playing on breaks, during his lunch break, and any chance that he could."

It was during those break times that a fellow mill worker and friend, Grady Wilkie, who helped Scruggs acquire his employment there, joined in with his guitar to jam in the backseat of Earl's '36 Chevy. Their informal sessions quickly drew the attention of the other employees, one of whom threw his hat on the ground and excitedly shouted, "Hot damn!"[11] The unsuspecting crowds at the mill became another added ingredient toward Earl's decision to play professionally as he realized folks were showing an interest in his talent. When World War II ended, he terminated his employment at Lily Mills to pursue music full-time.

With none of the children born to George Elam and Lula Scruggs left to work the family farm, the property was eventually sold. And despite the musical talent the family had developed over the years, twenty-one-year-old Earl would be the sole Scruggs to become a career musician. Junie's son, J. T., explains why his musically accomplished father never traveled the same path as his youngest brother:

> My mother did not want Dad to pursue music, and so he did not. My understanding is that when Mother and Dad was first married and for a few years after that, Dad played a lot of weekend music at different places. He done some fiddlers conventions, he done a lot of square dances on the weekends, and then he didn't play for a while. So I remember when he picked it back up, he played banjo and he played guitar and he did do, actually, one recording, which had several different people on it. A guy came around and spent two days at the house, and Dad done two numbers on that piece ["Sally Goodin"/"Sally Ann" medley and "Cripple Creek"[12]].
>
> Dad was a very friendly person, had a good personality. He never liked farming, and so he went to work at Public Work, and he worked construction work for a number of years. When he was in Virginia working, he had meningitis and almost died. In fact, the nurse who was his nurse did die; she caught it from Dad and did die. But he

pulled through it and came back home, and he went to work for Duke Power for the rest of his career, which was thirty-some-odd years before he retired. For a long time he was a control technician at the plant and then ten years maybe, before he retired, they made him a supervisor. So when he retired he was a shift supervisor.

Earl's talented sister Ruby also chose a life apart from music according to her daughter Grace Constant:

> My mother Ruby was a stay-at-home mom while my dad worked on the railroad. In later years they divorced and she went to work as a nurse's aide at Royster Memorial Hospital in Boiling Springs, North Carolina. She worked very hard to make ends meet and see that her children got a good education. My mother was a Christian lady and always saw to it that we attended church at Boiling Springs Baptist. She later went to work at the Cleveland Sandwich Company in Boiling Springs, where she retired. In 1988 she married my stepdad, Coleman Vinesett. They both enjoyed music, dancing, and, most of all, spending time with family. Her hobbies were working in her flowers.

And what of Earl's closest sibling and main practicing partner, Horace? Elam Scruggs discusses the circumstances that prevented his father from playing professionally and how he never lost his affinity for music:

> Dad never played professionally. He married and then he was drafted, so providing for his family became his priority. For several years after he left home, he did not own a guitar. After serving our country in the army, Dad worked as the maintenance supervisor for Gardner-Webb College and Crawley Memorial Hospital. He enjoyed picking with everyone, and he spent a lot of time practicing and playing for benefits, fund-raisers, et cetera. He remained true to the string music that he grew up on, and his timing was always perfect. He also had a gift to tune instruments to near perfect pitch very quickly.

"My uncle Horace was an excellent rhythm guitarist," echoes Gary Scruggs. "When it came to playing bluegrass and old-time music, he was as good as any rhythm guitar player I've ever heard."

THE ROAD TO NASHVILLE

By the time Earl Scruggs was ready to embark on a musical career, old-time string music had already undergone a few stylistic changes: vocal harmonies ranging from duets to quartets and alternating instrumental breaks within a tune, similar to jazz, were implemented.[13] The music also included comedy bits in between song sets, usually by the banjo player. Though Scruggs himself wasn't a comedian onstage, his mastery of the three-finger roll secured him a paid position with a country band in September 1945, as referenced by Gary Scruggs:

> His first salaried music job began when John "Lost John" Miller hired him to join his band, "Lost" John and His Allied Kentuckians, in 1945 after World War II had ended. Lost John's band was based in Knoxville, Tennessee, and Dad's salary was fifty dollars a week. He first came to Nashville as a member of Lost John's band to do a live Saturday morning radio show. The band came in from Knoxville to do the show and would then go back to Knoxville soon after the show was over.

While Scruggs was commuting back and forth between Knoxville and Nashville in the autumn of 1945, one of the *Grand Ole Opry*'s headliners, Bill Monroe, was given notice by his comedic banjoist, Dave "Stringbean" Akeman, that he wanted to leave the Blue Grass Boys (named in honor of Monroe's home state of Kentucky) in order to team up with the *Opry*'s one-man band vaudevillian Lew Childre. Monroe founded his famous musical act after the breakup with his brother Charlie (the Monroe Brothers) in early 1938. Over a year later in October 1939, Monroe and the Blue Grass Boys impressed the *Opry*'s founder and announcer, George D. Hay (known as the "Solemn Old Judge"), and his associate, David Stone, so much with their renditions of "Mule Skinner Blues" and "Fire on the Mountain" that they immediately became part of the show's featured acts.

At the time of his inclusion in the Grand Ole Opry, Monroe didn't have a five-string banjo player in his group. By 1942, Stringbean (Akeman had a tall, lanky physique) joined the ensemble as their first banjoist. However, unlike Scruggs, Akeman wasn't a three-finger picker; he primarily frailed the ole five-string. That same year, Bill's fiddler, Howard "Howdy" Forrester, was drafted into the navy and replaced by

Robert Russell "Chubby" Wise (on a trial basis initially) until March 1943, when he became a full-fledged member. Jim Shumate took over upon Wise's exit in 1944. After Stringbean's resignation, comedic tenor banjoist Jim Andrews filled in briefly, and by late November Monroe asked Shumate if he knew of a banjo player who could assume the vacancy.[14] Shumate recommended Earl Scruggs, with the disclosure that he didn't play banjo at all like Stringbean.

In the years prior to his joining the Blue Grass Boys, Jim Shumate had his own Saturday evening program on WHKY radio in his hometown of Hickory, North Carolina. It was during that period when he first met Earl Scruggs, who came to see his show with Grady Wilkie. Both Scruggs and Wilkie performed a tune on Shumate's program that very evening. As Shumate recalled decades later, he thought Earl was the best banjo player he had ever heard. When he learned that Scruggs was part of Lost John Miller's band, he approached him to audition for Bill Monroe. Scruggs declined at first, as he was satisfied with his spot in Miller's group. However, an unforeseen circumstance prompted him to call Shumate back for a second chance.[15] "On December 1, 1945, a Saturday, Lost John told the band that he was quitting the road," says Gary Scruggs. "At that point, Dad asked for an audition with Monroe, and he auditioned on that very day."

Knowing his style was radically different from Stringbean's, Earl chose to play a couple of tunes he thought likely to be unfamiliar to Monroe.[16] Gary Scruggs recalls Earl's induction into the Blue Grass Boys:

> He auditioned at the late Tulane Hotel in Nashville and played two tunes, "Sally Goodin" and "Dear Old Dixie." I think maybe Monroe wasn't sure what to think, because he asked Dad to come to the Grand Ole Opry that night so that he could play along backstage with his band, the Blue Grass Boys. Lester Flatt, who was a member of the band [hired earlier that spring], was not happy when Monroe told him a banjo player was going to be at the Ryman that night because Lester thought a banjo hurt the sound of the band. Previously, David "Stringbean" Akeman had played five-string banjo in the band, and Lester had thought Stringbean couldn't keep up on the more up-tempo songs. After hearing Dad pick with the band, Lester heartily encouraged Monroe to hire Dad. Monroe did so, and Dad's first appearance with Bill Monroe and his Blue Grass Boys was

on the following Saturday night, December 8, 1945. He received the same salary that other band members received, which was sixty dollars a week.

Within days of Earl's audition, fiddle player Howdy Forrester returned to Nashville after his discharge from the navy. In accordance with a government statute, drafted servicemen were guaranteed their previously held civilian jobs upon their release from military duty. The fiddler, Jim Shumate, who served as the conduit linking Scruggs to Monroe, was now on his way back to Hickory as Forrester went onstage at the Ryman Auditorium the following Saturday when Scruggs made his historic debut.

A NIGHT TO REMEMBER

Just about the time Earl Scruggs was ready to enter the doors of the Ryman in early December, the country was ripe for entertainment, which played a pivotal role in launching the success Scruggs was about to achieve. Professional banjo player and Scruggs historian Jim Mills paints a picture of the atmosphere:

> If you think of the timeline of Earl Scruggs, it's amazing. He joined Bill Monroe in December 1945. World War II had ended just a few months before, and this was the beginning of a huge boom for the music industry as a whole, simply because for the preceding three or four years these boys had been away from home, [most] of the population in America was women, and everything was being rationed. Gas was being rationed, tires were being rationed—I mean, everything was being rationed. Entertainment in general was rationed. I mean, nobody could even go to barn dances since the husbands and boyfriends were off to war. At the exact moment that Earl Scruggs joined Bill Monroe's band, all these boys were returning home. They're starved to death for entertainment. America was starved to death for entertainment.

On Saturday night, the skinny twenty-one-year-old from Flint Hill, North Carolina, who was unsure if his style of banjo picking would even be accepted by the crowd in the auditorium as well as the massive audience tuning in to WSM radio's 50,000-watt clear-channel signal

crossing multiple state lines, unwittingly triggered a response that forever changed the course of the five-string banjo. Bluegrass banjoist
Butch Robins depicts the vibe of this unforgettable moment in time:

> Nobody had ever made that sound before. It's like Jimi Hendrix
> walking out onstage at the Grand Ole Opry for hillbillies back in
> those days, the way Earl did, because, pretty much, the way he
> played the banjo hadn't been heard before. Most of the folks were
> out frailing banjos. All of a sudden here comes some guy, and I mean
> he's dynamic, and he had a certain poker-faced charisma about him-
> self.

While the audience was fortunate enough to witness this musical revelation, thousands heard it over the radio and buzzed about it for days on
end, as North Carolinian banjo picker Jay Adams recalls:

> I have friends who lived around the area that I live [Spray, North
> Carolina], and they can remember back to the first time that Earl
> Scruggs performed on the Grand Ole Opry as a part of Bill Monroe's
> Blue Grass Boys. They heard him on the radio back on December 8,
> 1945, and after hearing him, that's all people talked about for like a
> week. "Did you hear that guy playing banjo on the *Opry*?" They had
> never heard anything like it.

And as Hurricane Earl ripped through the airwaves on that wintery
night to remember, the man caught up in the eye of the storm could not
have predicted the revolutionary transformation of his beloved five-
string banjo that followed in the wake of his evening's program. Gary
Scruggs confirms his father's energetic performance and the lifeblood it
pumped into a seemingly dying instrument:

> Dad was excited by the audience's reaction. The Ryman Auditorium
> was by far the largest room in which he had ever played at that time.
> I've heard him say the first tune he played as a soloist was "Dear Old
> Dixie." I'm sure the audience's reaction to his playing during his
> debut on the Opry and soon after must have thrilled him. I've heard
> that the applause was thunderous whenever he took a break at that
> time. On that debut night, I'm sure George D. Hay was as surprised
> and stunned as anyone in the Ryman audience to hear Dad play his
> three-finger style. I've heard several radio transcriptions where
> George D. Hay [later] introduced the band as "Bill Monroe and Earl

Scruggs and his fancy five-string banjo," but no mention of other band members other than Bill Monroe and Earl Scruggs.

Before his Opry debut, five-string banjos had become widely thought of as mere stage props used only by country comedians playing rowdy old-time banjo styles. The manufacturing of new five-string banjos had all but ended. Dad's refined musicianship electrified audiences and banjo sales soon skyrocketed. His way of picking became known around the world as "Scruggs style."

One of the many banjoists seriously impacted by the arrival of Scruggs on the Opry was Ralph Stanley. Hailing from the mountains of southwest Virginia with his older brother Carter, Ralph learned the clawhammer technique of banjo playing from his mother. In retrospect, Stanley revisits the awakening he felt that altered his method of picking. "I believe it was on the Grand Ole Opry around 1945. Well, I liked what I heard. Nobody in the music world was playing the banjo like Earl was. Earl had a unique drive when he played the banjo. It was something that caught people's attention when they heard it. He brought something new to everybody."

That same night, when Earl Scruggs "stole the show" on the *Opry* with his spitfire three-finger rolls, another phenomenon ensued as a consequence of the band's epic performance—the Birth of Bluegrass, although it would be many years before the name *bluegrass* took root in the music industry and general public.[17] What was planted in 1939 by Bill Monroe in his effort to create a new brand of music was now harvested by Earl Scruggs in 1945. His endless hours of practicing and perfecting three-finger rolls on the five-string banjo that he loved so much paid enormous dividends when he blended it with Monroe's mandolin, Flatt's guitar, and Forrester's fiddle as a new musical sound was created.

By March 1946, Howdy Forrester headed for Texas and, in the interim, Chubby Wise returned along with Howard "Cedric Rainwater" Watts on the upright bass, who had previously been in and out of the group. Together with Bill Monroe, Earl Scruggs, and Lester Flatt, these five men, all of whom came from different regions—Kentucky (Monroe), Tennessee (Flatt), North Carolina (Scruggs), and Florida (Wise and Watts)—would become the original bluegrass ensemble in the genre bearing the name of the band given to them by their "founding father," Bill Monroe. And for the next two years, the humble banjo man from the cotton farm in Flint Hill would experience a whirlwind of highs and lows that forced him to contemplate his stamina in showbiz.

2

FROM BLUE GRASS TO FOGGY MOUNTAIN

It was a time of musical change and innovation. I say that especially in country music. Most of it, or a lot of it, was attributed to Bill Monroe and his Blue Grass Boys, which is where the name [blue-grass] came from. And part of that band that Bill put together had Lester Flatt and Earl Scruggs in it. And one of the most significant parts of that was Earl Scruggs's banjo work.
—Pete Kuykendall, banjoist and editor, *Bluegrass Unlimited*

THE BLUE GRASS BOYS

Stepping onstage, sometimes in jodhpur trousers, riding boots, and a Stetson homburg hat, Earl Scruggs became a gigantic presence in the Blue Grass Boys from his historic debut on December 8, 1945. And unlike other banjoists, such as Uncle Dave Macon, whose talents were more defined by their clownish antics, Scruggs changed the rules of the game for future banjo players with a different philosophy. He expounded his position on National Public Radio's (NPR) *Fresh Air* with Terry Gross in 2003 (printed with permission):

I used to try and see if [there] was some kind of routine I wanted to do as being a comedian 'cause [every] player, and there were very few, but they were all comedians and kind of used the banjo as a prop to get into their comedy routine. But all my interest was just in

picking, not only tunes but songs behind the singers, not only in the
lead part but doing a backup—playing an alto or something to support the singer. So that's where my interest was as a lead picker with
the banjo but also a supporter with a banjo.

"What made Earl great is that inside Earl there was a perfectionist with
an intensely precise precision," states documentary filmmaker David
Hoffman, who chronicled the banjo man in *Earl Scruggs: His Family
and Friends*. "So he's like the culture he came from, but when he heard
something that wasn't exactly right, he knew it. He also knew who the
great ones were. He knew that Flatt was great, he knew Bill Monroe
was great, they knew he was great." Bluegrass guitarist Peter Rowan (a
subsequent member of Monroe's band) also affirms how Earl's strategy
seriously improved the sound of the Blue Grass Boys and strengthened
their camaraderie:

> Earl's genius was because of his syncopated timing. He let all this
> other stuff blossom. He let Bill blossom. Bill had it all in him, but he
> needed people around him to bring out every aspect. If you were
> Earl Scruggs, you could build a blossom, and all kinds of stuff would
> come out because of Earl, and whatever Earl took away from there
> was a life lesson.

Though Lester Flatt's mellowed voice complemented Bill Monroe's
lonesome-sounding high-pitched vocals, it was still Scruggs who received the attention, with his greased-lightning three-finger roll that
spawned an unfathomable following of banjo pickers who wanted to
copy him. Though many of the well-known banjoists labeled as Earl's
disciples heard him after 1948 during his Flatt and Scruggs period,
there were two noted followers whose first exposure came during his
stint with Monroe. Country music star Roy Clark was just an adolescent
when he first heard the buzz about Scruggs:

> It was incredible. I was born down in the rural part of Virginia. When
> I think back on the first time I heard Earl play, naturally [it] was on
> the radio, and word-of-mouth was just getting around about this
> banjo player that was playing with Bill Monroe. You could hear him
> Saturday night on the Opry. So my cousin and my uncle and I, we
> were playing with a little Sears and Roebuck radio that we put high
> on the mantelpiece and waited standing there like Eagle Scouts try-

ing to just imagine what this night was going to be—and when he started playing, that audience just came unglued, not any more than I did or my cousin because we both played [guitar] a little bit, and I was trying to envision what this was all about because I never heard anything like this five-string banjo and what was later known as Scruggs style. I figured it was just somebody that had seven fingers on one hand and ten on the other. It was just hard to imagine how unique this sound was coming from that one banjo.

The other follower was string musician Curtis McPeake, who later became Earl's substitute in 1955 following a car crash in which Earl was seriously injured. As a young member of the Rhodes Brothers, his ear tuned in to Earl's fancy five-sting banjo. He summed up the infectious effect that Scruggs had upon him:

> I was playing steel guitar and mandolin and some regular guitar when I first heard Earl with Monroe. I could [also] play banjo then, but I didn't play three-finger style. I played my dad's old banjo. He was a two-finger player, and I could play two-fingered similar to what he played. But I never took the banjo seriously until I heard Earl with Monroe. And I said to myself, "That's what I want to learn—I want to do that."

During 1946 and 1947, Earl recorded twenty-eight songs as a member of the Blue Grass Boys, both secular and gospel (the latter featured him as part of Bill's famous Blue Grass Quartet). In addition to the volume of songs recorded for 78-rpm releases, the group maintained an extensive performance schedule, as highlighted by Gary Scruggs:

> "Heavy Traffic Ahead" [taken from a contradictory signpost in Flatt's hometown of Sparta, Tennessee, where there was no traffic to be found[1]] was the first song Dad recorded with the Blue Grass Boys. Other titles among those twenty-eight songs include "Molly and Tenbrooks," "Blue Moon of Kentucky," "Toy Heart," "Wicked Path of Sin," and "Blue Grass Breakdown." The band played primarily rural areas at venues such as schoolhouses, fairgrounds, and on top of concession stands at drive-in movie theaters.

"When Lester Flatt, Earl Scruggs, Bill Monroe, Chubby Wise, and Howard Watts were a band, they said they could play six nights a week, and pack them out twice a day," adds professional banjo player and Scruggs historian Jim Mills. "It was just unbelievable how they could go anywhere they wanted to and fill up an auditorium."

In 1979, Earl reflected on the good ole days with the Blue Grass Boys to Tim Timberlake in a radio interview, ironically on Monroe's tour bus in Lanexa, Virginia (printed with permission). He also expressed how Bill Monroe helped him grow as a musician:

> We had some great times together. Bill has always been a strong, happy-type guy, and we really had some good times. We worked awful hard. Bill used to work seven days a week; of course Lester and I did too—six and seven days a week; that's including travel. We used to work Monday through Saturday and a lot of time, I believe, on Sunday. Back in those days we was all younger and the more picking was the merrier. We really had some good times.
>
> Bill has his standards, which I appreciate. I like to know how a feller stands, and he has his dos and don'ts and I do the same thing with my group [the Earl Scruggs Revue]. And it's something that I don't ask somebody to do that I don't do myself. We go out, we have fun, but we still take our music very seriously, and when it comes time to go onstage, everybody's straight and goes out and tries to do what the people expect us to do, and that's basically what Bill did.

During his travels across the southeastern United States, Earl never forgot his family and took time to visit them despite the band's busy schedule. Horace Scruggs's son, Elam, points out one such incident when his uncle used the company car to make an unexpected visit in 1946:

> When Dad was drafted, he was stationed in [Crestview] Florida for a while. He and my mother went to a movie theater once a week, if possible. Dad had conveyed that to Earl. Earl was traveling with Bill Monroe at that time. One evening at the theater, Dad and Mother were surprised by Earl's voice behind them saying, "I thought I would find you here." Earl had borrowed Monroe's show bus, really a stretched station wagon, and went to find them.

By the winter of 1948, the grueling schedule in a cramped, non-air-conditioned vehicle with meager pay began to take its toll on Scruggs.

He was quickly becoming discouraged with showbiz and contemplating quitting, as he revealed to Terry Gross on NPR in 2003:

> It was terrible. If I hadn't have been twenty-one years old and full of energy, had just came off of a farm and a thread mill where I could— you know, I thought to do an hour show on the road was a pushover compared to eight hours in the mill or, from sun up to sundown, on the farm. And music was my love, so to get into a group that had good singing and playing, and Bill had that, especially good singing, and had a good fiddle player, so I went in, and it just seemed to make a full band, especially for that style of music. That was long before anybody had tagged it as bluegrass, it was just country music. But, it really made an outstanding group for that day and time especially.
>
> Why did I hate it? It was because we did it twenty-four hours a day, practically. Back then there was only two-lane highways, and [we] traveled in a '41 Chevrolet car and we'd leave after the Opry on Saturday night and maybe work down south. Georgia was about as far as you could get for a Sunday afternoon show. And on down to Miami someplace for Monday or Tuesday and worked till about Thursday and started working back to Nashville. So it was just— you'd only be in Nashville long enough to do the Grand Ole Opry and to get a change of clothes and pack your suitcase and head out again. I was single at the time, so I was living in a hotel and had one suitcase and so it—I had to really work on it to keep clean clothes for every night doing a show on the road.

Burned out from the road in February of 1948, Scruggs was ready to return to a more stable life back home in Shelby, North Carolina. He turned in his two weeks' notice to Bill Monroe, who didn't take the news very well. After failing to convince Scruggs to reconsider, Monroe told him that the name "Earl Scruggs" would never be heard from again. During those final weeks, Bill refused to speak to or look at Earl, even though Scruggs agreed to stay an extra two weeks beyond his notice.[2] However, just prior to exiting Nashville, Earl played a show with Roy Acuff, who offered him an opportunity at a much higher wage than Monroe.[3] Scruggs turned him down, as his decision was final. Gary Scruggs elaborates on his father's disillusionment with the entertainment business:

When he left Monroe's band, he was planning to quit showbiz permanently. He was exhausted from all the extensive and constant travel involved with going from town to town to play show dates. Sometimes the band would go for days without even seeing a bed, just sleeping in the car as they traveled from one town to another. Monroe paid no per diem, not even paying for a hotel room when the band would stay over in a town for a night. Dad never got a pay raise from the initial salary of sixty dollars per week. He was helping support his mother, sending her money to help with weekly expenses, and he was barely making ends meet.

After returning home to live with his mother, Earl resumed work at Lily Mills when he received a proposition from one of his now-former bandmates. "When my father left Monroe's band, Lester Flatt told Dad that he too was going to quit Monroe's band, and a short time after Dad returned to Shelby, Lester called and said he wanted to team up with Dad to form a new band," explains Gary Scruggs. "Lester told him he didn't think either would be happy going back to mill work—Lester had also been employed in a mill before getting into show business. Dad thought about it and decided to give it a shot with Lester." Earl specified his reasons for accepting Lester's offer in his 2003 NPR interview:

> Well, I liked his singing, and his playing fit in good with that style of music. And we palled around together. You know, in a group you, kind of, find one or two guys that you like better than the other part of the group, or the other may be interested in things that you don't care for. So, anyway, Lester and I got along with each other and roomed together [on the road], and so we did that for [over] two years. That's when, we really never talked about starting a show ourselves, but I had made up my mind that I was just going to get off the road. So I worked two weeks' notice, and when I started to leave that night, Lester turned in his notice. And while he was working his notice, he gave me a call over in North Carolina and said, "Why don't we get on a radio station over close to your home and try it as a group ourselves."

Of course, when their former boss received word that the duo formed a new band, he was less than pleased; in fact, he was outraged. "Monroe pouted around for years," states bluegrass music entertainer Mac Wiseman. "He dropped the ball. He could've maintained his status and just have one good band. There was a lot of friction between Monroe and Flatt and Scruggs." One of Monroe's many subsequent banjo players, Bobby Atkins, further echoes the begrudging sentiment toward Lester and Earl by the father of bluegrass music:

> When they left Bill, they hurt Bill big because he could never find nobody else that could do what they done with him. They were just as good of singers and pickers as Bill was, and so when they left him, it hurt him. Then he took a grudge to them. He claimed that was *his* music. It started with him, but Lester and Earl was with him. It was not bluegrass music until they was with him. He didn't have that same sound that he had when Lester and Earl was with him, and he never had it again.

CHANGE YOUR NAME TO MRS. EARL SCRUGGS

As the only child of Ewing and Mamie Certain, Anne "Louise" was born on February 17, 1927, and raised on a farm in Grant, Tennessee, just outside of Lebanon, east of Nashville. Growing up, Louise dreamed of the world she heard through her grandparents' battery-powered radio. Believing that a better life was awaiting her, she left the farm after graduating from high school to work as an accountant at a company office in Nashville while taking up residence in her grandfather's house.

On Saturday nights, Louise occasionally visited the Grand Ole Opry at the Ryman Auditorium for an entertaining evening of country music. One particular night, on December 14, 1946, would change her life forever. Seated in the front row with her cousin, Louise was captivated by Bill Monroe's young banjoist who picked his instrument with machine-gun precision to the thunderous cheers of the crowd. Their eyes met as Earl gave her a "fleeting smile," and soon they would meet after the show through a friend of her grandfather, Opry member Kirk McGee of the McGee Brothers, in the Ryman's back alley.[4] From that moment, Earl and Louise began a courtship for the next sixteen months, seeing each other on weekends when the Blue Grass Boys came home to play at the Opry after weeklong road trips. It was soon after Earl ended his tenure with Bill Monroe that he made up his mind to tie the knot with Louise. Gary Scruggs describes the circumstances that led to his father's decision about matrimony and the unsettled life his parents endured in the early days of their marriage:

> They got married pretty soon after he and Lester Flatt formed their band in 1948. The band was received well by audiences, and Dad became confident they were going to make a good enough living that he could afford to marry and support a wife. Mom and Dad married on April 18, 1948, in Gaffney, South Carolina, which is around twenty miles south of Shelby, North Carolina.
>
> I think then they first lived together in Bristol, Tennessee. Flatt and Scruggs originally started out in Danville, Virginia, and soon moved to Hickory, North Carolina, and later to Bristol, Virginia, and then Knoxville, Tennessee. Flatt and Scruggs were also based in Tampa, Florida, and Raleigh, North Carolina, for a while. They first moved to Nashville in 1953, where they had an early morning live radio show on WSM. They then moved to Virginia a year or so later. They moved back to Nashville in 1955, becoming members of the Grand Ole Opry. There were a few other moves prior to the final 1955 move to Nashville.

Exactly thirteen months after taking the name Mrs. Earl Scruggs, Louise gave birth to the couple's first child, Gary Eugene, on May 18, 1949, in Knoxville, Tennessee. Two more sons were born to the Scruggs family: Randy Lynn on August 3, 1953, and Steven Earl on February 8, 1958, both in Nashville. Surrounded by the music and fame of their father, each one of Earl's sons expressed a desire to follow in his footsteps by learning and mastering musical instruments on their own. Spending some of their school breaks on the road with Flatt and Scruggs, the boys were quickly gaining exposure to a life they ultimately chose to live with their dad years later as the Earl Scruggs Revue under the management of their mother, Louise.

THE FOGGY MOUNTAIN BOYS

Like all bands, Earl and Lester needed a name for their newly formed ensemble. Both men were fans of the A. P. Carter song "Foggy Mountain Top," which they enjoyed playing in their repertoire. According to Earl in his 2000 interview on WSM, he chose the name Foggy Mountain Boys as a tie-in to the song they would use as a theme and nothing more. Flatt, in particular, really liked the name, leaving no others to be considered. However, what did come under consideration was that the band would be fronted by Lester and Earl, thus placing their names at the top of the bill: "Lester Flatt, Earl Scruggs, and the Foggy Mountain Boys," which eventually led to them being known simply as Flatt and Scruggs.

With upright bassist/comedian Howard "Cedric Rainwater" Watts also resigning from Monroe's Blue Grass Boys, Lester and Earl enlisted him along with guitarist Jim Eanes as the Foggy Mountain Boys landed on WDVA radio in Danville, Virginia, for their debut in March 1948. Their stay in Danville lasted no more than a couple of weeks when they decided to relocate to Hickory, North Carolina, for the next month in order to recruit their choice fiddle player. It was around this time that Eanes suddenly left the group and moved to Nashville after being hired by Bill Monroe. The void from his departure was quickly filled by guitarist and tenor singer Mac Wiseman, who outlines his induction to the Foggy Mountain Boys and the purpose of their brief stay in Hickory:

> They wanted [fiddler] Jim Shumate in their band because he had worked with Monroe and he was in Hickory, North Carolina, where he had a furniture store; he had family: a wife and three little girls. He wanted to be sure that the Foggy Mountain Boys was going to work or fly before he would quit his job. So they went to Hickory, North Carolina, to a little radio station—that's where I joined them—and after we worked together there, things weren't working out [as] it was just a 500-watt station and it wasn't getting off the rooftops, so to speak. We were working to some very small houses [for] twenty dollars, and stuff like that was our percentage. So I suggested that we go to Bristol where I had been and use the territory. We went over there [to WCYB] and auditioned and they hired us immediately. We started on a Monday because I already had Friday, Saturday, and Sunday booked that week. I knew the territory from having been there the year before.

Lester, Earl, and the Foggy Mountain Boys were now part of the popular noontime show *Fun and Farm Time*. One of the many listeners of that program was a man named Cleo Lemons, who was preparing to organize a country music concert in Sandy Ridge, North Carolina. On March 19, 2011, Lemons stood before a crowd in Sandy Ridge delivering a monologue on the origin of what became a traditional venue for all subsequent bluegrass bands to this day (recorded by Doug Hutchens and printed with permission):

> Lester Flatt and Earl Scruggs left the Bill Monroe show back in '48. Well, I just happened to pick up the Lester Flatt and Earl Scruggs program on Bristol, Tennessee, radio one day in my car. And they said they were [the] Foggy Mountain Boys now, so I got to thinking a little bit about it. I wondered if they'd come to Sandy Ridge and put on a show sometime. I said, "Since I'm a member of the Ruralton Club, I'm going to write and ask them if they'll come." So I did and asked them if they'd put on a show in Sandy Ridge. So it wasn't but a few days before I got an answer. They were ready to come. They sent me a date and the percentages they'd work on. So the day that date was, I rushed up to the school here that day. I wanted to see 'em when they'd come in. Well, when they did come in, it was a show. They were in an old beat-up '37 model Ford two-door sedan, so you can imagine how much room they had. There were five men: there was Lester Flatt, Earl Scruggs, Howard Watts, Jim Shumate, and Mac Wiseman all in that car with a bass fiddle tied on top. It was one more thing to see, how they all got in that car!

"It was a very good date," claims Wiseman about that historic event. "I remember distinctly we worked on a 70–30 percentage basis—the band got 70 percent, the sponsor would get 30—but [at] Sandy Ridge, which was a very good date, would only go 60–40. So we would bite the bullet and go ahead working for 60 percent and still make good money." Earl Scruggs, from his 1989 interview with Doug Hutchens on *Bluegrass Today* (printed with permission), also revisited the popular schoolhouse locality he helped launch:

> When Lester and I started in 1948, we went to WCYB in Bristol and we started working around that area and worked Sandy Ridge—went over there and had a packed schoolhouse full of people. We played Sandy Ridge, I guess, better than twenty times—always had a full house, part of the time two shows. It turned out to be one of—I guess, we played that place more than any other place, single place, that we ever worked.

Soon afterward, the band headed to a Kentucky courthouse, in the months following Earl's April marriage to Louise, where the dividends of the boys' hard work began to literally pay off, as Scruggs recollected in 1989:

> I should, if I get enough chips together, should build a monument there because that was the first place—Well, I start a little bit preceding that. We had been married probably two or three months, and we [weren't] making anything. We worked a little while in Hickory, North Carolina, and my wife was staying with my mother in Shelby, so we moved up to Bristol and I think about the second week, we played Hindman, Kentucky. And it doesn't sound like a lot of money, but we did, I guess, close to four hundred dollars up there, and we were on a five-way split, and back then—of course I'd been used to working here with Bill Monroe for sixty dollars a week, so my split [eighty dollars] really looked good, and I think I took most [of] my part in one dollar bills. Anyway, I called Louise, down in Shelby, and I said, "Come up. I've struck it rich!" She came up and I showed her that bundle of money, and most of it was ones, but it looked as big as a limousine Cadillac as far as I was concerned. That is how we got started off, and from then on it seemed like everything fell into place. [We] really had a lot of listeners.

And while bookings and popularity were now beginning to take off for the band, Mac Wiseman remembers one particular show where they employed primitive technology to find their way home:

> When I was working with them in Bristol, I booked us a schoolhouse over in the mountains out of Bristol there over beyond Damascus, Virginia. We went up there and played the shows. It's just a dirt road up there, and on the way back in Lester's old station wagon, the generator went out and the lights went out of course. The motor would run but the generator wasn't working, and we were going to have to stay there till daylight to get out of the mountains. But we had stopped in Abingdon and picked up fifty or a hundred posters where we had our posters printed on the way up to that school. So after sitting there for a while realizing we couldn't do anything else, we saw lights up on the side of the mountain in different houses, but we weren't about to go up there at that time of night and wake anybody up. So I got those posters out, rolled them up one at a time sitting on the fender of that station wagon, and burned those posters

till we got out of the mountains. We burned them so we could see! I'd roll the poster up and light it, Earl would drive, and we'd go a little ways till the poster burned down, then light another one.

After Wiseman's departure from the Foggy Mountain Boys, his replacement in March of 1949, oddly enough, was a tenor-voiced mandolin player whom Lester and Earl knew from his time with Charlie Monroe prior to joining Mac's band in 1947—John Ray "Curly" Seckler (originally spelled Sechler). The early exits of Wiseman and Eanes were just the beginning of a revolving door within the band that didn't stabilize until the mid-1950s. Gary Scruggs illustrates much of the group's transiency from the late 1940s to the early 1950s:

> There was quite a bit of turnover in the early years. I suspect it had something to do with all the relocations that went on. Most if not all of the musicians and their families lived in mobile homes, and I'm sure there just came a time when they simply wanted to stop the moving from one location to another or perhaps just a case of not wanting to move to a particular area. And there was quite a bit of movement from one band to another back in those days.
>
> Flatt and Scruggs always had a strong fiddle player, including, in no particular order, Jim Shumate, Benny Sims, Chubby Wise, Benny Martin, Howard "Howdy" Forrester, and Paul Warren. Ex–Blue Grass Boy Howard "Cedric Rainwater" Watts was the original Foggy Mountain Boys bass player. When Cedric left the band in the early years, bass player Charles "Little Jody Rainwater" Johnson joined the band, as did mandolin player Everett Lilly around that time.
>
> In the early years, Flatt and Scruggs would have a live morning radio show in whatever town they lived in. It was a way to promote the band, and they would book themselves out to towns in that region that were in the radio station's broadcast range. They would also supplement income by selling "song books" on the road and over the radio airwaves. The venues in which they performed were similar to what they had known while traveling with Monroe.

In addition to playing many of the same outlets they had learned from Monroe, they also sometimes donned similar apparel with regard to hats, ties, and the occasional jodhpurs with riding boots. During their stay in the Bluegrass State, Lester and Earl mesmerized two young Kentuckians who were so inspired by their music and stage presence that both grew up to become musical masters in their own rights as well as personal friends of Earl Scruggs. Veteran bluegrass banjo player J. D. Crowe reminisces about his first impression of Flatt and Scruggs:

> I met Lester and Earl when I was just a kid, and I've known them since about 1950 or '51, and they lived here in Lexington for about a year. Flatt and Scruggs had their radio show here, and that's how I got to be around them a lot. It was a fifteen-minute radio show every Saturday morning in a little town called Versailles, Kentucky, and the radio station was in the library at the time, and my dad would take me down there, and we'd get to watch them rehearse in the studio before the show. Flatt and Scruggs were so aggressive when they played. When they kicked off songs, their breaks, and in their back-up, I mean, they didn't quit.

Storytelling singer-songwriter Tom T. Hall tells the tale of how his introduction to Flatt and Scruggs in a Kentucky courthouse became the subject of a song years later:

> The first time I saw Earl Scruggs, I think my father and I went. My father was a Baptist preacher, and he was a closet clawhammer banjo player. He took me to a show and I remember it was in a courthouse, and since the courthouse was a public building, they used to have shows, I guess, in where they held trials—that sort of thing, the chambers or whatever. Anyway, we walked in the door and my father had given me some money, which I assumed was to pay my way into the show. We walked into the auditorium and I remember dropping my money into a King Edward cigar box, and there was a young man sitting there watching the box, and he's seeing what you dropped in and waving you on down for a seat. We sat there for a while and then Earl and Lester and the Foggy Mountain Boys walked onstage, and I looked at the banjo player and told my father, I said, "Wow, Earl Scruggs is the guy I gave my money to when I came in the door." I said, "I could have stopped and talked to him and asked some questions," but my father shushed me down and we listened to the music.
>
> I remember thinking at the time it was the shortest show I'd ever seen because I was so enthralled with the music that I guess that the time just—*vroom*—went away, and it seemed to me like a fifteen-minute show, but I'm sure it was about an hour and a half, but I remember how brief that show sounded to me. Later, my wife, Miss Dixie, and I wrote a song called "The Boys in Hats and Ties." I don't

know, at this moment, all the words to the song, but the story of me going to see Lester and Earl for the first time is in that song.

TRADING BANJOS

When Earl Scruggs joined Bill Monroe's Blue Grass Boys, he brought with him a Gibson RB-11 (RB is the Gibson acronym for Regular Banjo) that he purchased from a pawnshop, the very same make and model used by his predecessor, Dave "Stringbean" Akeman. By July 1946, Earl was in the market for a new banjo as his RB-11 had become weather-worn with the veneer loosened up. The opportunity came for him to acquire a Gibson RB-75 when he crossed paths with another banjo player who had one for sale.[5] In an interview from 2011 by Doug Hutchens, Haze Hall disclosed the transaction between himself and Earl Scruggs (reprinted with permission):

> I went up here to Rocky Mount [North Carolina] one day. He [Earl] and Bill Monroe was supposed to be [driving] up there to play with Tommy Magness and the Hall Twins. They got in up there that evening about dark. I had done played there all day. I'd done give[n] out. I told Earl I had me a Mastertone banjo, and I reckoned that Saford [Hall] and Clayton [Hall] told him so too. He come down here that night about 10:30 to buy it. I sold it to him. My wife begged and cried for me not to sell it, but I'm an old hard head and sold it anyway.

Earl's ownership of the instrument didn't last more than two years, as a bigger prize in his eyes laid in wait. One of Scruggs's early influences, DeWitt "Snuffy" Jenkins, had a Gibson Granada that carried a tone that always intrigued Earl. Bluegrass banjoist Curtis McPeake provides a brief history on Jenkins's acquisition of the Granada:

> He got it in a pawnshop. Snuffy was a barber, and [when] he'd go back and forth to work, every now and then, he'd stop in there and look at this banjo. It was for sale for a good while; of course banjos back then weren't very popular. Snuffy offered a lower price and [the shopkeeper] wouldn't take it. Snuffy kept stopping in and aggravating him about it until he got it for [$37.50[6]].

Years later, Jenkins sold that Granada to another notable three-finger picker from North Carolina, Don Reno. By the time Reno reported for army duty at Fort Riley, Kansas, in 1944, the shipment of the Granada back to his hometown took an unconventional turn. "What had happened is that he shipped his banjo back home by bus," cites Doug Hutchens. "They slid it under the bed upside down, and of course with the hot summers in Spartanburg, South Carolina—there was fiddle rosin in the case, and it melted and ran around the tension hub."

By the time Scruggs and Lester Flatt formed their new band, Earl was poised to make a trade with Don Reno in the late 1940s. As fate would have it, Reno very much liked Earl's RB-75 and was willing to make an exchange when they met up at WCYB in Bristol. Considering the damage that had been sustained to the instrument from the melted fiddle rosin four years earlier, Don felt he was getting the better end of the deal, and to make it fair, he threw in a Martin D-18 guitar as part of the swap. Scruggs acknowledged the trade during his interview with Doug Hutchens in 1989 and recalled how he went to great lengths to refurbish what he referred to then as his "working banjo":

Well, first off, back in [1949], Don Reno had the banjo that I have. And I had a good banjo, [an RB-75] I believe it was, and he came through Bristol, and he was wanting my banjo and his banjo that I have now was in bad shape. I mean, it was a Granada gold-plated, but it had looked like a penny would look after it had been laying out for ten years on the soil or something; it looked terrible. And part of—the metal part of it was broken on the thing, but I could hear a tone in it that I liked. And I didn't like the neck on it because it was an extra-large neck, but anyway, I traded with him. I gave him my banjo for his banjo and a D-18 Martin guitar. Well, in a little while, I contacted the Gibson people up at Kalamazoo [Michigan]—that's where they were at that time—and I asked them about cutting the neck down, and they wrote me back and said that they could do it but the neck would warp if they did it. Well, I was stubborn enough to believe that that older piece of wood might not warp, and I just didn't want it the way it was. So I sent it back, and they cut it down and made it a nice-size neck, but it did warp and I had to have another neck put in it. But now, it's all restored back the way it came from the factory back in [1930 when] it was made.

My problem with gold has been that it would tarnish and once it starts looking bad, it just looked pretty bad, and too, it went through a period of time when it was hard to get any repair work done on a banjo at all, much less gold plating. They didn't understand what you needed, and to just solve the problem I just went to chrome metal, all except the tone ring. Now the basic part of the banjo, the tone ring and the resonator and the finish on the outside part of the resonator, has never been touched, and I wouldn't touch that for nothing in the world. Because that's where the sound is when the neck is—you got a good neck mounted in there good. But anyway, the tone's still there.

Satisfied with their exchange in early 1949, Earl played his restored Granada for the remainder of his life, as did Don Reno with the RB-75 he nicknamed "Nellie." In his 2003 appearance on NPR's *Fresh Air*, Earl spoke candidly about the instrument he picked up from Reno without any regrets:

It produces the sound that my ear's looking for. Maybe I've just gotten used to it, but I like the sound that I get out of that particular banjo. I feel at home with it when I take it out of the case and start—you know, when you start with another instrument, they all have their feel, and playing the same instrument, you know what it's going to feel like when you take it out of the case and start to perform.

CUTTING VINYL

As Flatt and Scruggs and the Foggy Mountain Boys began to make strides in 1948 on WCYB's *Fun and Farm Time* program along with their road shows, the next step was to start making records. However, 1948 was not the best of years in which to sign a recording contract. Mac Wiseman summarized the political condition of the music industry at the time, and how they finally got to cut their first record:

The union, the AFM—the American Federation of Musicians—was on strike during that time, and nobody could record because they were negotiating the different contracts and such as that. And King Records, who was very popular at that time, approached us about recording, [but] they only wanted to pay, like, one half of one percent. And not long [afterward], Murray Nash, who was the A&R man for Mercury Records, called us and wanted to bootleg a session. So we sneaked into Knoxville, Tennessee, and recorded in the radio station, WROL, in their studio. We did four songs: "My Cabin in Caroline," "We'll Meet Again Sweetheart," "God Loves His Children," and "I'm Going to Make Heaven My Home."

With only a two-microphone operation, one for the bass and the other for the rest of the band, two of the four songs recorded in November 1948 were released on a 78-rpm vinyl disc on January 15, 1949, following the December end of the AFM strike. Oddly, it was the two gospel tracks where Earl's banjo was noticeably absent, "God Loves His Children" and "I'm Going to Make Heaven My Home," that Mercury chose to issue first. Scruggs played Wiseman's Gibson guitar on both songs, which flushed out his aptitude for the occasional use of a lead guitar in their repertoire. Interestingly, those banjoless songs were the very first two songs the band recorded. "Earl was a fine guitar player," says Curtis McPeake. "He had his own style, which not a whole lot of people play, his style today, on the guitar. It's what we call kind of a thumb style, but it was a very good method." Gary Scruggs reiterates his father's six-stringed talent. "He enjoyed playing guitar on several different songs because it gave him a chance to adapt his picking style to the sounds of a couple of guitarists who had inspired him in earlier years, namely, Maybelle Carter and Merle Travis."

Having never played guitar as a Blue Grass Boy, Scruggs now added a unique dimension to his new band that helped differentiate them from their competitive forerunner. Earl's lead guitar work began to evolve more as the years went on. Some of his best guitar picking is heard in their later recordings of "Jimmie Brown, the Newsboy," "You Are My Flower," "Georgia Buck," and eight out of the twelve songs from their 1961 *Songs of the Famous Carter Family* album, which includes the instrumentals "False-Hearted Lover," "Pickin' in the Wildwood," and "Gathering Flowers from the Hillside."

Another component in Flatt and Scruggs's quest to establish their own musical identity, apart from Monroe, was original material. "Lester was the [initial] songwriter," asserts Wiseman. "So he was constantly writing songs for us to sing on the radio as well as record when we had the time to do it." However, it didn't take long for Scruggs to become a partner in the compositions with Flatt, as the four songs from their first recording session were jointly credited.

While the goodbye ballad "We'll Meet Again Sweetheart" and the wishful, cheery "My Cabin in Caroline" projected contrasting messages of optimism through their lyrics, their next original, "Down the Road" (recorded in May 1949), became a prime example of Earl's ability to paint pictures through the notes of his banjo. His breaks on this recording give the impression of a leisurely walk down the road to see a girl named Pearly Blue. The way he played slide notes on the third string created a bouncy feel that was achieved often by bending the string slightly to give it a slurry, lazy, let's-not-be-in-a-hurry sound that complements the song's storyline (complete with old man "Flatt" who owned the farm). "I love the way Earl did 'Down the Road,'" praises bluegrass guitarist Tim Stafford. "I love the way Earl could wrap his ideas around just about any tune and still state the melody."

"FOGGY MOUNTAIN BREAKDOWN"

By the end of 1949, none of Flatt and Scruggs's recorded songs had been an instrumental. Their third recording session at a radio station in Cincinnati on December 11 of that year produced the magnum opus from the sole creativity of Earl Scruggs. With plenty of ammo in his fingertips, Earl blazed the strings of his newly acquired (and cleaned up) Gibson Granada on that wintry day with a composition that would become the quintessential standard for the five-string banjo. Gary Scruggs depicts the evolution of his father's iconic song "Foggy Mountain Breakdown":

> Dad has said that he actually wrote the instrumental "Blue Grass Breakdown." I'm not sure if Bill Monroe contributed anything to the composing or arrangement of the instrumental, but Dad did not get any writer credit for it at all. Monroe was the only listed writer on the Blue Grass Boys recording. The opening lick of "Foggy Mountain Breakdown" is very similar to the opening notes in the banjo breaks of "Blue Grass Breakdown." It's played with a unique roll that a lot of banjo pickers refer to as the "Foggy Mountain roll."
>
> He composed "Foggy Mountain Breakdown" in 1949, the year Flatt and Scruggs recorded it. I don't know how long it took to write, but I imagine it might have evolved over the time it was first written and then recorded because there are several banjo breaks, and al-

most all of them differ in some way, sometimes with significant variations. It's truly an inspired and amazing work.

The deviation between "Foggy Mountain Breakdown" and its predecessor is the replacement of the F chord with an E minor. The chords in
"Blue Grass Breakdown" are G, F, and D, whereas those in "Foggy
Mountain Breakdown" are G, E minor, and D. That simple second
chord substitution, as well as the change in arrangement (Earl's banjo is
secondary to Monroe's mandolin in "Blue Grass Breakdown"), made a
world of difference. Not only did "Foggy Mountain Breakdown" sur-
pass "Blue Grass Breakdown" in popularity; it also showcased the very
best in Scruggs's musical agility as touted by Jim Mills:

> The timing on Earl's 1949 recording of "Foggy Mountain Break-
> down" to this day makes me stop in my tracks, and I don't care if it's
> three o'clock in the morning in a truck stop and I'm listening to an
> eight-inch speaker, I'll stop and listen to it all the way through. If you
> listen to that recording to this day, his right hand is like a jackham-
> mer. I mean, every note is perfectly in time, a perfect separation of
> notes.
>
> I told Earl one time in his house that that recording is almost
> anointed. It's just one of those things that couldn't be any better to
> me, and I've tried to play with that intensity that he played with on
> that song, but I've never been able to do it. If you listen to that
> recording now, the December 11, 1949, recording of "Foggy Moun-
> tain Breakdown," he never lets up; his right hand is absolutely rock
> solid from beginning to end. When he backs away from the mic while
> the fiddle takes a break, he's still digging in. He never loses that
> power and intensity. I never heard him play it like that again. I've
> heard so many great banjo players say that it was that same recording
> that made them want to play the banjo.

The imagery used to describe Earl's performance is testimony to the
significance of his creative abilities. Terms like *machine gun* and *metro-
nomic* are but a few adjectives that have been used by musicians and
critics. Earl Scruggs re-recorded this tune multiple times over the
course of his career, yet all subsequent versions seemed to take a backseat to the original in the ears of his biggest fans. "The old original 1949
version of 'Foggy Mountain Breakdown,' the old Mercury version: it
burned, it warped the grooves right off the record," notes bluegrass

banjoist Vic Jordan. "It was straightforward, and I guess *forceful* might be a good word for his playing in some instances." Dr. Banjo, Pete Wernick, mirrors that very sentiment in saying that it was "an immaculate, powerful cut, recorded when he was just twenty-five. No one can deliver like that."

In his NPR interview from 2003, Earl recapped the significance of his most recognized instrumental. "I've written several other tunes and had some pretty big hits, but nothing like 'Foggy Mountain Breakdown.' You'll have a 'ringer' as I call it, one that might make a hit with just about everybody, and so 'Foggy Mountain Breakdown' was one of them. I will say that the one, I guess, that really launched the banjo further, as far as a tune that I had written, was 'Foggy Mountain Breakdown.'"

In 1999, the prestigious National Academy of Recording Arts and Sciences, also known as the Recording Academy, inducted Flatt and Scruggs's 1949 recording of "Foggy Mountain Breakdown" into its Grammy Hall of Fame.

MOVING ON

With sixteen tracks recorded for Mercury by the summertime, along with the departures of fiddler Jim Shumate (replaced by Art Wooten and then Benny Sims) and comedic bassist Howard "Cedric Rainwater" Watts (replaced by Charles "Jody Rainwater" Johnson), Lester and Earl received an offer to upgrade their recordings that was too good to pass up. Gary Scruggs details their contractual transition:

> Columbia Records, a much larger recording company than Mercury Records in those days, offered Flatt and Scruggs a recording contract in the summer of 1950. Flatt and Scruggs wanted to accept the offer, and Mercury agreed to release them from their contract, provided Flatt and Scruggs record twelve more songs for Mercury. They did so in Tampa, Florida, in October of 1950, recording all twelve sides in one day.

And that twentieth day of October at Tampa's WDAE, affectionately referred to as the "Hurricane Sessions" (named after Hurricane King, which was threatening to blow through the area while they recorded), not only completed the balance of their twenty-eight-song contract for Mercury, but it produced some of the duo's more classic tenor harmonies. The result included such catchy songs as Lester's "My Little Girl in Tennessee," the Morris Brothers' "Old Salty Dog Blues," featuring fiddle player Benny Sims's lead vocal, and the Monroe Brothers' "Roll in My Sweet Baby's Arms."

On the flipside to these lively lyrical numbers is the duo's cover of Jimmie Skinner's morose prison tune "Doin' My Time," the story of a man who gets thrown in the big house and sings a song of lament about "doing his time" pounding rocks on a chain gang and about the girl waiting for him after he's freed. In Skinner's original recording, the frailing banjo lacks the pain Earl's three-finger style adds to the song. Scruggs presents a sense of weariness, or even exhaustion, one can imagine, for the guy doing his time. There's also several places in the song where Earl plants a boogie-woogie lick, one in his second banjo break and the other during Lester's vocals in the third verse. Another creative use of Scruggs's backup comes out in the same third verse, where Lester sings, "You can hear my hammer, you can hear my song," as he plays harmonic chimes on the twelfth fret picking the fourth, third, second, and first strings.

Additionally, their final Mercury session included two instrumentals: a countrified cover of the 1920s jazz tune "Farewell Blues," along with "Pike County Breakdown." Composed by Rupert Jones, "Pike County Breakdown" is a tune that Lester and Earl played with Bill Monroe during their time as Blue Grass Boys. Interestingly, the duo's version was cut and released before Monroe attempted his own recording, which further agitated their former boss. The melody of "Pike County Breakdown" has sometimes been referred to as a fast, instrumental take on the old song "Sweet Betsy from Pike," as it bears a striking similarity. Another prominent feature is a series of single-string notes picked on the first string of the banjo. Scruggs used his thumb and index finger to pick the notes, yet he did not, as a rule, play single-string banjo as did Don Reno. At the end of Earl's second and third banjo breaks, he plays a sequence of hammer-ons and pull-offs, left-hand techniques that weren't used by other banjoists in that day, which made him sound years ahead of his contemporaries.

It was also during this period that Scruggs was without his Gibson Granada. Over a year earlier, when he and Lester decided to move to

Knoxville to work at WROL, Scruggs knew he needed to find himself another banjo since he was planning to send the Granada back to the Gibson factory for repairs. After utilizing their media access to freely advertise on air about Earl's hunt for a Gibson banjo, a local woman called to announce that her late husband left behind a Gibson banjo that she was willing to sell. Upon inspection, Scruggs noticed that it was a Mastertone model RB-3 in pretty good condition. He then purchased the banjo to use as a temporary replacement for his Granada from early 1950 until March 1951.[7]

When Flatt and Scruggs stepped into their new Nashville-based re-cording facility in November 1950, they were no longer subject to radio station makeshift setups with limited technical resources at multiple locations. They now had the luxury of state-of-the-art equipment in a central location where they dropped anchor for the next nineteen years (although Earl continued with Columbia for another fifteen years while Lester signed with RCA Victor after one solo album, *Flatt Out*, on the Columbia label, following their breakup in 1969). Some of the earliest releases on their new label included "Come Back Darling," "I'm Head Over Heels in Love," and "Jimmie Brown, the Newsboy," backed with "Somehow Tonight," which was the first vocal song credited solely to Scruggs. It wouldn't be long into their new contract before Earl found a way to stretch the boundaries of the five-string banjo with an old idea that propelled a roster of new signature songs.

DETUNING THE STRINGS

Earl Scruggs was more than just the grand master of the three-finger roll for the five-string banjo; he was also a true inventor and innovator. His ingenuity dates back to his childhood when he experimented with simpler ways to capo the banjo's fifth string as opposed to retuning it to a higher pitch, which only stressed the string to the brink of breaking. Gary Scruggs describes the process:

> As a child around ten or eleven years old, it was Dad's idea to use "spikes," also known as "hooks," to change the pitch of the fifth string, which served the same function as a fifth-string capo would do. His first hook, or spike, was fashioned out of one of his mother's hairpins and placed at the seventh fret in order to raise the fifth-

string G note to A. The top of the spike was shaped at a right angle so that the string could be hooked beneath it. Today, HO-scale toy train railroad spikes are often used for that function. Dad used two spikes during his professional career, one at the seventh fret and one at the ninth fret. He also designed and built a banjo capo for the five-string banjo's four long strings when he worked at the Lily Mills thread mill in the early to mid-1940s.

Earl's understanding of the instrument's mechanics in conjunction with his desire to create new sounds sparked a revolutionary device for detuning called a Scruggs Tuner, which enabled him to accurately change the pitch of a note while playing at full speed. As a boy, Earl and his brother Horace toyed with an idea of retuning the banjo from G tuning to D tuning as part of the melody for a song.[8] "Memories of those childhood musical experimentations stayed with him and indirectly led to his creation of Scruggs Tuners," notes Gary Scruggs. "By 1951, he had thought of the design for a cam-type tuner that would accurately detune a string and then retune it back to pitch, but he hesitated in making it because installing it would involve drilling holes in the peghead of his banjo."

Meanwhile, he recorded his first detuning composition, "Earl's Breakdown," on October 24, 1951, having to manually detune the second string B note down to A and then back up to B by ear while using the standard tuning peg. In 1989, Earl discussed the recording of his premiere detuning number with Doug Hutchens on *Bluegrass Today* (printed with permission):

> I recorded that thing without a tuner at all, and my banjo at the time had bone buttons on it. And we went in the studio and we were using Howard Forrester as a fiddle player for the show, and Howard is a tremendous fiddle player, but he never plays a tune twice the same way. So we went into that tune. I had written [the] tune and I just about halfway knew it myself; I knew the tuning part had to go in there. We cut that thing, and I did real good; the tuner worked fine. I mean, I used the standard peg as opposed to a tuner that has stops on it. The tune went great up until the very end of the thing, and I goofed it. And Howard Forrester, he just outdid himself, I thought, with the fiddle break. And Don Law was the A&R man, and back in those days, we didn't have twelve or twenty-four tracks; it was monaural. So I said, "Hold that. Let's put a 'shave and a haircut' on it or

let me 'doop-de-doop' it again and do that." And I messed around
and let Don Law—he said, "Well, Earl"—he was from England—he
said, "Earl, it won't take but three minutes to do it over." And I said,
"You can't do things over like that," and he said, "You can do it
again." I said, "Hold that one and let's do it again and see which one
turned out the best." And I didn't know it, but he ran the tape back
to the very start and we had to do it a second time—I mean, do it
again—but we erased over the first cut and that's always been a sore
spot every time I think about that because neither Howard Forrester
[nor] I, either one, did it like we did that one take.

And not only was the second take of the tune played differently than the
"lost" first track; the difficulty of manually retuning by ear at such a fast
pace became evident as observed by bluegrass melodic-style banjo
player and builder Bill Keith. "If you listen very carefully, you'll hear
that it doesn't always go down to the right pitch—and at one point he
doesn't get it back up to the right pitch, so he finishes his break by
completely staying off the second string. And then during the fiddle
break after his break, you can hear him tuning the second string back
up."

Although slightly flawed to the "tuned" ear, "Earl's Breakdown" be-
came a huge hit and a frequently requested song for Flatt and Scruggs.
This was all the inspiration Earl needed to create his new tuning device.
Keith analyzes Earl's installation process:

> "Earl's Breakdown" only involved [tuning] the second string. So Earl
> drilled a hole near the middle of the headstock and used an addition-
> al tuning peg and threaded the hole, where the string goes through,
> and put a slotted screw in it so he could adjust the offset by popping
> a string out of that groove and screwing the screw further in or
> further out from the tuning peg. So it was basically a cam operation.
> Then he had to drill another hole or two to put pins in to stop the
> cam from going past dead center. If you turn one way or raise it—
> continue to turn that direction—the string would go down in pitch
> because it would pass the high point of the cam. He decided [later]
> to move the tuner for the second string over near the edge so he'd
> have room for another tuner for the third string. He said it made a
> mess of his headstock, so as he told me, he took the cover off the
> little lamp on his wife's floor polisher—a little rectangular box, and
> he attached it over the mechanism that he made. You can see it easily

on a lot of those early [publicity] photos, especially [on] the *Foggy Mountain Jamboree* album. People thought he was hiding what was going on there, but he said, "No," it was really to cover up a messy situation 'cause it disrupted some pearl, and it just wasn't a pretty sight.

Realizing just how much he could expand his catalog of songs with the tuners, Earl's second detuning composition involved a more complex arrangement of detuning and retuning both the second and third strings, which kicks off the tune "Flint Hill Special," named in honor of his birthplace and recorded in November 1952. Though the instrumental features left-handed acrobatic-like finger work in the C chord, it was the rhythmic detuning that became the main focal point.

Noted singer-songwriters and musicians Leon Russell and Norman Blake collectively remember the impression Earl's inventive ditty left on them, as it was also their introduction to the man himself. "I was fascinated with him—I mean, James Burton told me about him," Russell comments. "James one day played 'Flint Hill Special' on his guitar by bending the strings up above the little bridge that goes in front of the tuning keys. He said that Earl had actually invented some tuners for the banjo that go on there to actually play that song. I was pretty fascinated by that, really."

"The first time I ever heard Earl, we were boys, and this was back in the '50s," recalls Blake. "We were driving along in a car down here, close to where I live, and we had the radio on in the car and 'Flint Hill Special' came on the radio, you know, the record 'Flint Hill Special,' and we just had to stop and park the car. Man, we couldn't believe what we were hearing."

The fascination of bending the strings produced two more instrumental classics written by Scruggs: "Foggy Mountain Chimes" in 1953 and "Randy Lynn Rag" in 1955. Earl is also heard doing a little bit of tuning in between vocal breaks on "Till the End of the World Rolls Round" from 1954, "Joy Bells" in 1956, "Bound to Ride" from Flatt and Scruggs's 1963 album *Hard Travelin'*, and their 1969 covers of Johnny Cash's "I Walk the Line" and Bob Dylan's "Honey, Just Allow Me One More Chance," featured on the Flatt and Scruggs LP *Final Fling—One Last Time (Just for Kicks)*. The addition of the Scruggs Tuners necessary for playing these new signature songs for bluegrass banjoists required serious alterations to their instruments' headstocks. In 1964, Bill

Keith and his friend Dan Bump discovered a way to improve upon Earl's invention without drilling new holes into the banjo pegheads to accommodate an extra set of tuners. Keith defines the mechanical innovation that has become the standard D tuners for banjos and guitars to this day:

> In my military [reserve] unit was a college friend [Bump] who was also interested in the banjo, and he suggested that we start a company making banjos. His ideas were to make banjos with fiberglass necks and aluminum rims. I thought the current bunch of banjo players that I knew would not be so receptive to that kind of construction. So I suggested, why don't we make something that people that already own a banjo could use—and we focused right on the D tuners. So one of the times I was up in Boston, I spent more time in my reserve meetings with him, planning the making of what became known as the Keith Tuners. I finished a second prototype set before really going down and spending any time in Nashville, so [Dan] worked with a machinist I knew who had done some work for me in the past, and he finished off the D tuners and sent them to me. I showed them to Earl, and he was very impressed, and he said that if there was any way he could help then he would be happy to do that. Well, as it turns out, we wanted to use his name. So he said the way we'd be able to use his name was if he were part of the company. We incorporated and sold [Earl] some shares—and we went into production in early '64. We started to use Earl's name, and they were called Scruggs-Keith Tuners until about 1970.

3

FLATT AND SCRUGGS

They were the only [country] band, when Elvis Presley come on the scene, [where] it didn't hurt 'em. They still got their crowds like they always did, and that's saying a lot. I can just hear the names Lester Flatt and Earl Scruggs and the Foggy Mountain Boys, and it just runs chills over me.

—Bobby Atkins, bluegrass banjoist

MARTHA WHITE MILLS

Shortly after the departure of their comedic bassist Charles "Little Jody Rainwater" Johnson in the summer of 1952, Lester Flatt and Earl Scruggs were on the cusp of receiving a major shot in the arm from one of Nashville's biggest sponsors of the Grand Ole Opry, Martha White Mills. During their performances outside of Knoxville, Tennessee, in the fall of that year, Flatt and Scruggs, along with their current lineup of Curly Seckler on mandolin, Benny Martin on fiddle, and Bob Moore replacing Rainwater on bass, caught the attention of Efford Burke, a salesman for Martha White Mills.[1] Upon Burke's recommendation for a possible sponsorship, Martha White's president, Cohen T. Williams (the man who coined the company's famous slogan "Goodness gracious, it's good!"), decided to witness the chemistry of Flatt and Scruggs himself, as touted by professional banjo player and Scruggs historian Jim Mills:

The president of Martha White Mills, outside of Nashville, Cohen Williams, gets word that this band might be a good band to promote his flour company. He goes out and sees a show and signs them to a WSM radio job, fifteen minutes a day basically. They're not members of the Grand Ole Opry, but they are affiliated with WSM, they get to play this show and be heard by WSM's listeners. Well, a lot of those listeners remember them from playing with Bill Monroe to start with, and man, they have a tight band; they've got Benny Martin in there on the fiddle, Earl on the banjo—I mean, the best band ever. My dad even saw that band live.

In June 1953, Earl, along with a very pregnant Louise (she was two months shy of giving birth to their second son, Randy, in August) and their four-year-old son, Gary, relocated to Nashville as the Flatt and Scruggs radio show premiered on WSM at 5:45 am for fifteen minutes Monday through Friday with an all-hymn show on Sundays. During his appearance on National Public Radio's (NPR) *Fresh Air* with Terry Gross in 2003, Earl recalled how those tiresome early morning hours, after late-night performances, eventually led to better bookings:

> We'd come in [at] two o'clock and go to bed and get up at four to try to get awake enough to do a live radio program. But that was your bread and butter in those days. By that, I mean we made our real— really our living by the road work that we did. We'd go out and do shows and charge admission and get a percentage of that and also some flat rates too. But that just put us to working in better and bigger auditoriums and bigger crowds.

By September 1954, after fiddler Paul Warren was hired to replace Benny Martin, and English P. "Cousin Jake" Tullock stepped in on bass and comedy bits, Lester and Earl accepted an offer away from Nashville that prohibited them from appearing live on WSM. In a 1979 interview with Tim Timberlake in Lanexa, Virginia, Scruggs recounted how his band stayed on WSM while temporarily stationed in Virginia:

> Well, Lester and I was on the *Old Dominion Barn Dance* for about three months, I guess, in 1954. We had gone to WSM for the Martha White people and we decided to leave, and they didn't want us to leave the program, so we'd tape the programs and would send them back, and that worked for Sunshine Sue at WRVA in Richmond. I

think Wilma Lee and Stoney Cooper was there and Mac Wiseman was there, and I don't remember all of the people that was there, but it was in the year of 1954 in the latter days of the old original *Barn Dance*.

Prior to their temporary move to Virginia was the crediting of Gladys Stacey and Louise Certain on Flatt and Scruggs tunes in May 1954. As a means of publishing songs outside of their contract with Peer International, the duo implemented a common practice from that era of using pen names for their choice compositions—Gladys Stacey refers to Lester Flatt's wife, Gladys, in her maiden name. The same held true for Scruggs employing Louise's maiden name of Certain.[2] The earliest example of these assumed identities is found on Earl's snappy boogie-woogie instrumental "Foggy Mountain Special"—a rework of their 1951 original song (under Peer) "Don't Get above Your Raising."

That pre-rock-n-roll backbeat Scruggs loved so much from his youth in the song "Step It Up and Go" was instituted in a number of his early works, including Bill Monroe's "Heavy Traffic Ahead." However, all of his previous efforts were restricted to vocal songs. "Foggy Mountain Special" presented a new aspect to Scruggs style. It demonstrated Earl's willingness to experiment with contemporary rhythmic styles that fit some of bluegrass music's southern blues influences. Essentially, the tune features Earl Scruggs and his band playing a bluegrass version of the twelve-bar blues around which blues and rock-n-roll are built. It was recorded in the key of G and follows that simple G, C, and D chord progression with a rhythmic bounce. All of the Foggy Mountain Boys take a break on this track, including Lester Flatt, with his famous G-run lead break, and Curly Seckler, with a bluesy mandolin break (Curly and Lester seldom played lead breaks). And to give the song an even greater rock-n-roll feel, bassist Jake Tullock takes a hand-slapping solo on the upright as the other instruments play stops on the chords before joining back in all together.

Other Stacey–Certain compositions soon followed, such as "Blue Ridge Cabin Home" in 1955. An interesting side note about this song is the way Earl plays his backup banjo, as he seems to use the same patterns throughout the entire song, especially the choruses. The chord progression of the song (with a capo at the third fret to B-flat) during the choruses, is G, C, D, and G, and Earl does a series of forward rolls on the fifth, second, and first strings as he plays the C and D chords, ending back on the G chord with fill-in licks that take him back down to the lower end of the neck. Home and family are deep-rooted themes in bluegrass music, and this song tells the story of one man's love to go back there. "When [Earl] took a break on 'Blue Ridge Cabin Home,' the banjo was singing it," says bluegrass banjoist Kenny Ingram. "You know, he just had that clear language. You could understand it."

The Stacey–Certain credits also entailed collaborative numbers like "Shuckin' the Corn" from 1957, with Burkett Graves (Uncle Josh), which became the opening and closing for their *Flatt and Scruggs Grand Ole Opry* television show. The lightning-fast tune is one of the earliest recorded representations of Earl's mastery at choking notes up the neck as well as a series of double notes that are prominently featured in the song. The Graves–Stacey–Certain acknowledgment also appears on their 1959 Dobro-based composition "Foggy Mountain Rock." Another song bearing the wives' names from 1959 is "Crying My Heart Out over You" with Carl Butler and Marijohn Wilkin, for which, oddly, Lester's "Stacey" is listed as either Gladys Stacey Flatt, G. Flatt, or G. Stacey, depending on the record label.

THE GRAND OLE OPRY

In January 1955, Lester and Earl trekked back to Nashville, where they remained anchored for the rest of their careers. It was at that moment that the president of Martha White Mills presented them with an offer they couldn't refuse. "Cohen Williams and Flatt and Scruggs were a wonderful team," professes Jim Mills. "They sold millions of dollars' worth of flour for him, and he did wonderful things for them in return. He believed in them so much, he gave them a television show, and during this time, nobody in country music had a television show. This was early, early television. I mean, televisions were only just starting to come into people's homes." Gary Scruggs gives more details:

> Flatt and Scruggs started hosting their live Martha White–sponsored television show that was shown at six o'clock on Saturday evenings in Nashville. The shows were also produced in five other cities in the southeast and aired in each of those cities once a week. At first the shows in all six cities were live, and they were traveling around twenty-five hundred miles a week doing the TV circuit and also perform-

ing show dates in places relatively near the TV stations. When they later started taping the shows in Nashville, tape copies would be sent to other cities' television stations for airing.

Jim Mills deduces the impact of their increased exposure:

> So, now, that's a boon for them, they're on radio, that all goes good. Now the biggest thing that ever happened to Flatt and Scruggs was a new industry coming into America—television! Man, television cannot be understated at the time. Man, we take things for granted today. My gosh, we've got the Internet and seven thousand channels to choose from, but back then TV was a new thing. It was new as new could be. It was monumental in their career. Folks watched Flatt and Scruggs every week, religiously.

"Many, many people, probably millions, in the southeastern United States viewed their shows in the latter half of the 1950s and throughout the 1960s," asserts Gary Scruggs. And among those millions of viewers spread throughout forty cities in the southeast was Earl's family back in North Carolina. "I remember the first time we saw Earl on TV," notes Elam Scruggs about the thrill his father, Horace, felt upon seeing his brother on television. "Dad was very excited and kept saying, 'He's made it! He's finally got there!'"

Fans who only heard the banjo man on the radio now had an opportunity to see his talents up close and personal in their living room, courtesy of the *Flatt and Scruggs Grand Ole Opry*. Sporting new Stetson hats with Kentucky Colonel ties in place of their homburgs and standard neckties, Lester and Earl were given a fresh makeover for the television audience—one that stayed with them for the next fourteen years. Opry announcer T. Tommy Cutrer, whom the duo previously met in Jackson, Mississippi, opened and closed the episodes along with hosting the live commercials.[3] Martha White's special self-rising ingredient trademarked as "Hot Rize" gave way to a catchy jingle that became synonymous with Flatt and Scruggs—"You Bake Right with Martha White (Martha White Theme)," as featured in their animated cartoon spots.

Their half-hour weekly program showcased every aspect of the band's talents, including close-ups of Earl's rare thumb-style picking on the acoustic guitar, as in his and Lester's originally composed instrumental "Georgia Buck." The entire show was devoted to the band's repertoire of songs, accented by some of their instrumentals and at least one gospel number in each episode. Guest artists would occasionally drop in, such as Mother Maybelle Carter and a very young Ricky Skaggs, who played Earl's "Foggy Mountain Special" on the mandolin before belting out the notes to "Ruby" at seven years old in 1961. It wasn't very long before Flatt and Scruggs became fixtures in other syndicated programs as Gary Scruggs points out. "They also taped a few TV shows for the United States Armed Forces syndicated show called *Country Style USA* that featured different country music acts and aired on many stations."

The success of Flatt and Scruggs on their WSM radio and television programs paved the way for them to become actual members of WSM's Grand Ole Opry itself. However, their membership request in 1955 was greeted with hostility from their former employer, Bill Monroe, who was still a well-known act on the Opry. "Cohen Williams's sponsorship of Flatt and Scruggs had proven to be beneficial to both the Martha White Flour Company and Flatt and Scruggs," states Gary Scruggs. "Williams lobbied the Grand Ole Opry to induct Flatt and Scruggs as Opry members in order to make them the regular hosts of the Martha White–sponsored portions of the Opry." Jim Mills also contends, "Bill Monroe had petitions signed to keep them off the Opry because he felt like they were infringing on his music, and he was the only one there doing bluegrass music at the time. Well, Cohen Williams marched into the Opry offices and said, 'Either make Flatt and Scruggs members of the Grand Ole Opry or I'm pulling my sponsorship.' They were made members immediately."

Despite Bill Monroe's failed attempt to ban his former subordinates from joining the Grand Ole Opry, it didn't stop him from many years' worth of cold shoulders and resentment toward Lester and Earl when they arrived to play at the Ryman Auditorium. Bluegrass guitarist Peter Rowan attests to Monroe's longstanding rudeness: "I would see [them] at the Grand Ole Opry because I was a Blue Grass Boy from 1965 to 1967. When I was in the Blue Grass Boys there was this whole rivalry between Bill Monroe and Flatt and Scruggs. As Blue Grass Boys, it was unheard of in those days [for us] to show up at the enemy's show." Bluegrass fiddler Byron Berline, who also played with Monroe in 1967, adds:

Bill didn't want us hanging around Flatt and Scruggs because they had a little feud going at that time. The Blue Grass Boys didn't want to be associated with Flatt and Scruggs, and they would warm up by the Coke machine backstage at the Opry. Before they'd go on, they'd tune up and go over the songs they were going to do on the Opry by the Coke machine. Bill didn't really tell me directly, but the other Blue Grass Boys said, "Now don't be patronizing with Flatt and Scruggs whatever you do. It will upset Bill." I would say, "Yeah, okay," but I would go and stand over by the Coke machine, kind of looking the other way, but all the time listening to them [laughter].

Another former Blue Grass Boy, banjoist Bobby Atkins, specifies a guiding principle that contributed to Flatt and Scruggs's momentum versus that of Bill Monroe, which was taking shape in 1955. "One of the things that kept them going was Flatt and Scruggs kept the same band. Monroe changed bands every six months, and that didn't help him. Bill didn't have no management at all about him. But Flatt and Scruggs did. You would hear Flatt and Scruggs ten times more than you did Bill. They stayed with the times more."

The newest addition to the Foggy Mountain Boys helped to define the distinctive sound of Flatt and Scruggs: Burkett "Uncle Josh" Graves. Gary Scruggs clarifies the reasoning behind the hiring of his father's new musician, who doubled as a comedic artist:

Keeping the sound and image of Flatt and Scruggs unique and distinct from other similar country artists of that era was important. I think one reason mandolin solos were a rarity in Flatt and Scruggs recordings and shows is because lead mandolin was such a big part of Monroe's sound and they wanted to distance themselves from Monroe. In [May] 1955 they hired Josh Graves, who added the sound of his Dobro guitar, which made a big difference in the sound of Flatt and Scruggs. To my knowledge, no other bluegrass group at that time had a Dobro or resonator guitar player.

Josh was initially hired to play upright bass, but Dad and Lester, particularly Dad, was impressed with Josh's Dobro playing. Josh was greatly influenced by Dad and was thankful for Dad's advice and tutelage regarding three-finger picking. Josh adapted that three-finger style and incorporated those adaptations to the Dobro. Josh switched from bass to Dobro after a month or so in the band.

Graves's "Uncle Josh" persona later paired with Tullock's "Cousin Jake" (who returned permanently by 1956 after a brief absence) and gave the band's ensemble its comedy bits that were sometimes part of their stage shows in between musical sets. Jake and Josh also provided short comedy routines for the *Flatt and Scruggs Grand Ole Opry* television shows. Flatt and Scruggs remained stabilized with Warren, Graves, and Tullock until their breakup in 1969. Only Seckler's spot would be subject to rotating membership.

A TWIST OF FATE

On Sunday, October 2, 1955, Earl and Louise Scruggs packed up the car for a road trip to Charlotte, North Carolina, in response to a family crisis. They never made it out of Tennessee as an unforeseen incident stopped them from reaching their destination—one that carried lifelong consequences for Earl. In his 1989 interview with Doug Hutchens on *Bluegrass Today*, Scruggs detailed his life-changing close encounter:

> One Sunday afternoon, pretty late in the day, my brother [Horace] called me and he didn't want to excite me too much, afraid that I might try to drive too fast. Anyway, he said there's something wrong with our mother. What had happened: she had had a stroke. Back in those days, the only way you could [fly] from here [Nashville] to Charlotte, and Charlotte is about forty miles east of Shelby, you would have to catch a plane out of here, I believe you would have to go through Atlanta and change [planes], and go to Columbia, South Carolina, and change and [then] go to Charlotte. That would take all day, and of course this being late Sunday afternoon, we decided we'd just drive over 'cause we could be there by early breakfast next morning by taking our time.
>
> So we started driving and we had gotten about fifteen miles east of Knoxville, I guess at the time—that was during the two-lane highway days. We was on [Highway 70] and we was on the straightest road, I guess, between here and Shelby about three o'clock. Well, my watch had broken at five minutes to three in the morning. There was a car [that] came out of a side road [with a] boozed up man and woman in it, and that's where it happened. Luckily—we had two boys at the time, Gary and Randy, they were two and six, and they were asleep—one was in that pallet on the floor and one laying in the

back seat. This was before seatbelts—and when I hit that car, and I wasn't driving—well, everybody said I was driving about fifty-five [miles per hour], but when I hit that car, that seat stripped on the carriage in a yaw position. Louise knocked a hole in the windshield. She messed up her face real bad for several years, had a lot of plastic surgery done, but it dislocated my hips and broke us up real—real bad. But we was young enough until after a few months—seven or eight months came out of it—well, about three months, I guess, went by, then one of my hips broke and had to have a metal hip put in—and later had to have another metal hip put in. But everything, I thought, came out real well mainly because our two boys were not injured that much and after enough years went by, we got to where we could get along all right even though we still have pain with it.

The ramifications of this unfortunate event cost Earl his last chance to say goodbye to his beloved mother as Lula Ruppe Scruggs passed away on October 26, 1955. The long months in the hospital also threw a wrench into Earl's busy touring schedule, not to mention that the accident occurred less than a year after the Flatt and Scruggs television show premiered. For the first time in his professional career, an "understudy" was needed to fill Earl's shoes as the commitments were too vast to cancel. The man requested to play the part of Earl Scruggs was Don Bryant (known as "Donnie" at the time), who picked for Mac Wiseman. Bryant spoke openly about his initial reluctance to accept the job:

> I got a call from Lester Flatt one time in early October of '55, and he'd told me about Earl being in an accident. He was very shaken and asked me would I come and fill in. I knew that Josh [Graves] had recommended me, but [Lester] seemed to want me really bad, and I tell you what, I turned him down. I said to him, "I am not qualified to do this. There are other banjo players better than me." He was adamant, but I turned him down. A couple hours later a disc jockey named Don Owens showed up at my house, and I walked in and saw him in the kitchen talking to my parents. Lester Flatt had called him to help him get me to fill in for Earl. He told me that this would be something that you'll never regret, and something you'll always remember, and that it will be a wonderful experience, and it didn't matter that I was nowhere near as good as Scruggs, because neither is anybody else. I guess that did it.

Well, Lester called me back, or maybe I called him back, anyway, and I told him I would come, and that was on a weekend, and I think I met him the following Tuesday. They were playing a TV show in Huntington, West Virginia, on Tuesday one week and the next week they would play on Tuesday in Atlanta, and then they'd work the surrounding areas, sometimes significant distances away from where the TV shows broadcasted. Anyway, I caught a Greyhound bus to Huntington. I went out with my banjo, my suitcase, and met Lester—it was, like, October [or] November.

In the meantime Earl was recovering from his accident. Anyway, I worked that week, and then we went on back to Nashville and did the fifteen-minute radio shows and then back on the road again. There really wasn't much time to do anything but just the travel and the music, but after Earl got better, just a month or six weeks or so, I saw him early on. I remember he talked to me and he offered me his Granada. He asked me if I wanted to take his banjo on the road. I told him that I'd really better stick to the one I have, but I had an old archtop banjo, which was loud. Mac Wiseman loved that banjo. It was an older archtop Gibson. It sounded good. It didn't sound anywhere as good as Earl's, but at the time I probably thought it did.

Earl came back in early January of 1956. I don't think he played more than a week or two when he had a relapse. I think he had to go back in the hospital. He was hurt pretty bad. I played about every night with Lester, and I was with him for almost three months solid.

Bryant's time as Earl's substitute came to a halt at the end of 1955, when he received his draft notice for military service. With Scruggs back in the hospital for the next several months, Curtis McPeake, the front man of a band called the Rocky Valley Boys, became Flatt's next choice to cover for Earl. McPeake had become friends with Flatt and Scruggs in the early fifties and shares his story about the beginning months of 1956, when he was awarded that coveted gig:

Lester told me one time—I just thought it was showbiz talk. They all called me "Red" back then—he said, "Red, if I ever get a chance to help you, I'm going to," and I thought, well, that's kind of showbiz talk, I guess, but he kept his word. It wasn't too long after that until Earl had the wreck and had surgery in the hospital. I was working the radio station there in Lexington [Kentucky], and I came in one day [on a Friday] and a mutual friend called me and said, "Lester Flatt is trying to get in touch with you." He had called the radio station. So I called Lester, and he said, "Can you be up here on Monday morning to go to work?" I had another job that I was doing, and I said, "Yeah, I will." So I called my boss of the other job and I said, "I'm gone!" We left Nashville on Monday morning early, and we went to Columbus, Georgia. We worked a TV show there and then a booking, if there was one after that. Then the next night we were on WSB [TV] in Atlanta on Tuesday. We always worked a gig out of there; it was a real good station. From there, we went to Florence, South Carolina, on Wednesday. Same deal there, a TV show and then a gig after that. Thursday night we were in WSAZ-TV in Huntington, West Virginia. Always a booking there. That was a good area too. Then the next night was [nearby] my hometown: Jackson, Tennessee—and then the Opry on Saturday night, and then it was off Sunday and it all started again on Monday morning. That was the circuit. I did that for ten weeks straight the first time I ever worked with them.

Unsure how the audience would react to his presence, McPeake, who would continue to substitute for Scruggs (when available) until the group's breakup in 1969, recalls, "They accepted me much more than I [thought] they would. I walked out on that stage, or before the camera, every time feeling like I was a disappointment—'cause nobody [could be] Earl Scruggs. I tried hard to do my job, and it worked out fine." Even though fate kept Earl Scruggs away from the spotlight temporarily, it didn't hinder him from the thing he loved most. "Earl was in St. Thomas Hospital," McPeake adds. "I went up to the hospital to see him, and he was sitting on his bed playing on his banjo."

Before his return in the spring of 1956, Earl phoned Haskel McCormick, who was on the cusp of high school graduation, to cover some of the band's travel dates after McPeake's commitment ended. Though his travel was limited during this brief period due to frequent back pain, Scruggs did resume his position next to Lester Flatt, seated on a stool or chair, for local performances, as observed in their televised appearance on *Purina's Grand Ole Opry* from April 28, where they performed their latest single, "On My Mind" (the flipside to "Randy Lynn Rag"). Fatefully, that particular show guest starred a man with whom Flatt and Scruggs would be closely associated in the coming decade, Buddy Ebsen, aka Jed Clampett. Much of the second half-hour of the program featured Ebsen tap dancing, singing, and participating in comedy sketches. Hence, his debut on the Opry, in a roundabout sort of way, gave authenticity to the shtick of Lester and Earl being old friends of Jed's in their subsequent appearances on *The Beverly Hillbillies*.

Earl Scruggs continued to battle with lifelong hip and lower-back problems and surgeries stemming from his untimely car accident, in addition to walking with a permanent limp. One of the remedies instituted to accommodate Earl's physical condition was a change in his ground transportation. Gary Scruggs describes the acquisition and amenities of the Flatt and Scruggs bus:

> Following the car crash, to make traveling a more viable possibility for Dad, he and Lester bought a bus to replace the automobile they had been traveling in. It was a used bus, which they renovated by having the seats stripped out of the back two-thirds or so of the bus and replacing them with bunk beds. A small lounge area was included behind the bunks in the rear of the bus. There was plenty of room for the band, and Dad could sit or stand up or lie down whenever he wanted, but travel could still be a struggle for him when long trips were involved.

Heeding warnings from his doctor to avoid long road trips, Scruggs acquired a pilot's license to fly small planes (first becoming single-engine rated, then twin-engine rated, and instrument rated).[4] However, his doctor's advice wasn't the determining factor in Earl's decision to take to the air, as he told Doug Hutchens in 1989:

> I started flying in [1958], so I started flying really for [a] couple reasons: one was I got to thinking if I was able to fly, I could be home with my family more, and the other thing, of course it's too late, my mother died—I didn't get to go to the funeral, of course. She died two weeks after we had the car wreck, but I thought, if I had been flying all this time, I could've gone over and visited with her and got to seen her a lot of weekends where, as it was, we could only see her about once a year—once or twice a year.

Flying not only became a more convenient means of travel for Scruggs; it also became a passionate hobby of his that he enjoyed up until the last several years of his life. "I liked when he talked about aviation, which was a major hobby of his for a long time, and how he'd deliver emergency blood to remote places," comments Hot Rize's banjoist Pete Wernick. "That was a whole other life for him, pretty separate from the music world, and he loved it."

NEW MANAGEMENT

Before his life-altering automobile collision, Earl Scruggs had managed the band's business affairs for a number of years. After the departure of Mac Wiseman in 1949, who originally handled all of the bookings for the Foggy Mountain Boys since its formation in 1948, Jody Rainwater occasionally booked dates during his tenure with the group. Showing no interest at all in the business side of the act, Lester Flatt was comfortable with Earl spearheading their enterprise. As the popularity of Flatt and Scruggs increased, so did their transit times. The dual role became overwhelming for Earl, who was looking for a centralized home base to channel all of their business activities through. Gary Scruggs recalls how the baton was passed from Earl to Louise in 1955, thus making her country music's first female manager and booking agent:

> It was difficult to book the band while being on the road traveling to and from other show dates. There were, of course, no cell phones, emails, answering machines, or fax machines back then—when on the road, a booking agent would have to find a pay phone, or use a hotel phone if lucky enough to be checked in for a night. Dad was leaving to go on the road one day, and he handed Mom a piece of paper with a promoter's name and phone number on it and asked her to later try calling him and booking a show date. She did so. It was something she enjoyed doing, and she was good at it. She was soon doing it full-time.
>
> The music business was strictly "a man's world" back then—Dad simply advised her to be strong and not be intimidated by those with much more experience than she had at that early point. Mom loved the challenge, and she gradually took on other duties, such as writing press releases, bookkeeping, and music publishing that expanded her role from just being a booking agent to what would become known as "artist management."

Scruggs family friend and former member of Earl's post–Flatt and Scruggs band, the Earl Scruggs Revue, Jody Maphis confirms Louise's clout in the music industry. "Louise was an incredible businesswoman.

She knew what she was doing. She wasn't taken lightly back in those days in the music business. Everybody respected her."

One of the most notable changes under Louise's administration was the emergence of full-length record albums (an album was also known as an "LP," an acronym for "long play" or "long playing"), soon to be followed by "concept" albums. In the summer of 1957, Columbia released the duo's first long-playing record, *Foggy Mountain Jamboree*, along with a few EPs (extended plays—typically four songs per disc). The twelve-inch vinyl revolver was a well-showcased compilation of their previously issued 78-rpm "singles," as noted by Gary Scruggs:

> *Foggy Mountain Jamboree* was in several ways a landmark album and somewhat of a historical sampler of the Flatt and Scruggs years with Columbia Records up to that time. The LP consisted of twelve tracks, six being instrumentals. The instrumentals alternated with the vocal songs throughout the album, starting with Dad's "Flint Hill Special" on side A, followed by the vocal duet "Some Old Day." All of the then-current Foggy Mountain Boys were involved in the LP, having done recent recordings, as were several former members of the band who had played on the early Columbia recordings. In 2012, the National Academy of Recording Arts and Sciences (also known as the Recording Academy) inducted *Foggy Mountain Jamboree* into its Grammy Hall of Fame.

In 1958, Mercury took its turn at consolidating a few selections from their catalog of the group's material with *Country Music by Lester Flatt and Earl Scruggs and the Foggy Mountain Boys*. Three other collection-oriented records followed between 1959 and 1960 from Columbia, Harmony (a division of Columbia), and Mercury: *Songs of Glory* and two self-titled *Lester Flatt and Earl Scruggs with the Foggy Mountain Boys* (one from Harmony, the other from Mercury).

It wasn't until early 1961 that Louise's efforts to overhaul the production of the duo's albums (in both concept and packaging) became public. First in line was their groundbreaking album *Foggy Mountain Banjo*, which demonstrated the power of Scruggs style better than any of their past or future recordings. Still regarded as one of the finest instrumental records showcasing the five-string banjo ever pressed, the Scruggs masterpiece contains his arrangements of traditional fiddle tunes like "Sally Ann" and "Sally Goodin" (on the record, *Goodin* is spelled as *Goodwin*), in addition to old banjo standards such as "Cumberland Gap" and "Cripple Creek" (where Earl's backups to the fiddle are just as impressive as his lead breaks from the driving forward roll he plays, coming off the slides on the fourth string from the second to the fifth fret). Earl's signature chokes up the neck are well demonstrated in "Lonesome Road Blues," "John Henry," and his cherished "Reuben." The LP also features cover versions of such ditties as A. P. Carter's "Little Darlin', Pal of Mine," the chuga-chuga locomotive-sounding "Fireball Mail," big band jazz classic "Bugle Call Rag" (where he plays harmonic chimes), and the only Scruggs original, "Ground Speed," which jumpstarts the album. The songs were recorded with an echo effect that really brings out the rich tone of Earl's Gibson Granada as the notes are crisp, distinct, and evenly spaced, which makes this particular project, produced in the fall of 1960, one of the best in sound quality among Flatt and Scruggs records.

Yet, unlike all of the other Granada-based songs on this album, "Ground Speed" is the only tune Scruggs played using a Gibson RB-4 and was recorded over a year earlier in January 1959. He acquired this particular banjo in the 1950s for backup purposes in the event his Granada needed servicing. According to Jim Mills, Earl "reluctantly" sold the RB-4 banjo to Mike Longworth (future C. F. Martin historian) sometime during the summer of 1958. By the beginning of the new year, Scruggs's Granada was in the repair shop again, so he contacted Longworth to loan him the RB-4 banjo for an upcoming studio session later that month. Longworth agreed and has since verified that only the RB-4 Scruggs borrowed back from him could have been used to record "Ground Speed" in light of the dates the banjo was in his possession.

Banjo players have often referred to "Ground Speed" as one of the more challenging of Earl's instrumentals due to its fast tempo and combination of backward and forward roll patterns. It's not your typical bluegrass banjo instrumental, which more often than not kicks off in the range between the first and third frets. Earl starts the tune off with two backward rolls up the neck starting at the twelfth fret of the first and second strings, moving down to the tenth fret of the first and second strings. Backward roll patterns are often more challenging to learn, given that it sometimes feels less natural to pick the strings in an opposite pattern than one is used to with forward rolls. It's almost like walking backward or trying to write with the opposite hand.

As difficult as "Ground Speed" is to play, it continues to be a favorite among banjoists. Bluegrass mandolin player Sam Bush, who also picks the banjo but doesn't really consider himself a banjoist, references the challenge of playing this tune: "'Ground Speed' was the perfect tune, one that sounded fun and was fun to play for other people in the band as well, but it was technically really challenging with the right hand and how you do that, and making that melody. So I've always loved 'Ground Speed.'"

The backup Earl plays on "Ground Speed" showcases his technical creativity, as he slides from one chord pattern to another on the third and fourth strings, which makes the banjo sound like it is pronouncing words.

Another noteworthy song from *Foggy Mountain Banjo*, one that's widely popular with Scruggs fans and disciples, is "Home Sweet Home," which immediately follows "Ground Speed." This particular rendition bears the marks of blind banjoist Mack Woolbright, one of Earl's childhood influences. When Scruggs was six years old, he visited an uncle's house where he heard Woolbright play "Home Sweet Home" in C tuning as he rocked back and forth in a rocking chair. He was amazed at how a blind person was able to play a banjo so "beautifully" and was especially attentive to the G7 chord.[5] Earl's arrangement of "Home Sweet Home," in comparison to Woolbright's playing on a Columbia Records recording of "The Man Who Wrote 'Home Sweet Home' Never Was a Married Man" with old-time music artist Charlie Parker (circa 1927), is strikingly similar, especially when he plays the portion of the melody where the G7 chord comes in (lyrically it would be where you sing, "There's no place like home").

Scruggs recorded the song in the key of C while in C tuning, which meant that he tuned the fourth string of his banjo down to a C note. The fourth string is tuned to a D note when playing in G tuning, the standard tuning for the five-string banjo. Earl's backup in this tune is haunting in the way he plays up the neck but in particular in the way he moves from a lower F chord up to a higher C chord on the fingerboard while playing with his right hand closer to the neck of the banjo. This gives the tune a more mellow tone that, again, sounds almost like the banjo is speaking words.

Not only did *Foggy Mountain Banjo* convey a theme, as all of the songs were banjo-laced instrumentals highlighting Earl; the cover art set a precedent for nearly all future Flatt and Scruggs albums. Gary Scruggs explains how a photograph of an oil painting that accompanied an article written by Alan Lomax, called "Bluegrass Background: Folk Music with Overdrive," in *Esquire* magazine landed on the cover of the Flatt and Scruggs LP:

> Mom came up with the idea of using artwork on the Flatt and Scruggs album covers. Artist Thomas B. Allen did the artwork for an article on country music that appeared in *Esquire* magazine. There was an Allen painting she loved of Flatt and Scruggs included in the article. She got in touch with Allen and requested permission to use that painting for the cover of the *Foggy Mountain Banjo* album. Allen agreed, and he subsequently did artwork for many Flatt and Scruggs covers. The album covers were strikingly different and unique when compared to most of the country music album covers of that era. Allen, who was born and raised in Nashville, Tennessee, was a fan of Flatt and Scruggs, and was particularly drawn to Dad, having learned to play Scruggs-style five-string banjo. His family and our family became friends. He visited regularly until he moved to upstate New York and then later to Florida.

That landmark banjo album became a huge inspiration to generations of pickers identified as Earl's disciples. Gary Scruggs characterizes the impact of the *Foggy Mountain Banjo* album and his mother's contribution to his father's recordings:

> It was a very popular album, and a country music rarity in that it was an all-instrumental album. It was released in 1961, when the folk boom was still exploding, and it appealed to many folk music fans. *Foggy Mountain Banjo* was Mom's idea, and it was destined to be inducted into the Recording Academy's Grammy Hall of Fame in 2013. She suggested themes or concepts for several Flatt and Scruggs albums such as *Songs of the Famous Carter Family* in 1961, an album of all Carter Family songs. It was also her idea to record the live albums at Carnegie Hall and Vanderbilt University in Nashville.

VEGA BANJOS

Another brainchild of the Scruggs home office was the endorsement of an Earl Scruggs line of banjos for retail sales. Gibson USA retiree Doug Hutchens, host of *Bluegrass Today*, tells how the Earl Scruggs brand for the Vega Company was developed:

> Earl had contacted Gibson back in the late '50s about us doing an Earl Scruggs banjo. I think it probably was more Louise than Earl, because she was the business manager. At that point in time, Gibson was really far removed from what was going on in country music. Their endorsing artists were people like Wayne Newton on the banjo. They dealt with the cream of the crop, the Everly Brothers, and people like that, could put high-dollar names on stuff, but as far as country artists, there were very few new Gibson instruments being played in Nashville. The Vega [endorsement] came after he met Mr. [Bill] Nelson, one of the guys who actually owned the company, and they worked out a deal of doing the Earl Scruggs banjo. They did a super fancy model. It basically was like a thin resonator vox, highly ornate like the super-high-priced tenors and plectrums they did with the thick resonator, but they did a thin-resonator model of it [that] had basically plastic [wrapped around] on the side with floral designs, and then they did a plainer model. They did different series models: there was the Earl Scruggs, the first one, and then there was an Earl Scruggs Professional, then there was an Earl Scruggs Mark II, and there was an Earl Scruggs SR-5.

Beginning in 1959, Scruggs participated in Vega's campaign to market their new line of banjos bearing his name. One of the most notable promos came courtesy of NBC's *The Price Is Right* hosted by Bill Cullen. As part of a prize package giveaway, Earl appeared live playing an SR-5 model, complete with Scruggs Tuners and a hard-shell case. A photo from the broadcast, along with two other publicity shots of Earl posed with his Vega product, were printed in the 1961 issue of the Flatt and Scruggs *Picture Album—Song Book*. Though all of the Vega catalogs and advertisements marketed the banjos as being constructed to Earl's design specifications, the manufacturing fell short of his standards as a musician. "I remember seeing Earl play that Vega some," Curtis McPeake recounts. "He never cared much for it. He kept that banjo for a while and they sold several Earl Scruggs model Vegas. They were good banjos. They just wasn't what Earl wanted to play."

Despite his personal preference for his Gibson Granada, with which he continued to perform and record, Earl's endorsement with Vega lasted until 1970, when the organization was purchased by C. F. Martin & Company, who changed the terms of Scruggs's agreement, which led to its dissolution.[6] His name would not appear on another brand of banjos for more than a decade, when his wish for an Earl Scruggs Gibson banjo was finally achieved.

HOOTENANNY

The end of the 1950s brought about the organization of a major plat-form in Newport, Rhode Island, that proved to be vital in the launching of what became known as the folk boom. Newport Jazz Festival founder George Wein, with the full support of his board members Theodore Bikel, Pete Seeger, Albert Grossman, and Oscar Brand, established the first-ever Newport Folk Festival.[7] The fest would become a venue for introducing new artists along with featured veteran performers. And among the list of invites to the historic premiere were Lester Flatt and Earl Scruggs. However, this was one performance Earl attended solo, without his partner and band, as he mentioned in his 1989 *Bluegrass Today* interview: "In 1959, I went up to Newport, Rhode Island, and played the folk festival up there—met a lot of people up there that put us into the hootenanny days. I said I went up; I did go by myself because I had to fly and at that time Lester wouldn't fly."

Backed by Hylo Brown and the Timberliners, Earl demonstrated his riveting Scruggs style to a whole new audience, which became critical in keeping his band alive during a period of change in the bluegrass scene. Jim Mills discusses the transformation that was beginning to take shape as a new decade dawned:

> In the early '60s we get into the era where the terms *bluegrass* and *country* were being used separately. The Nashville sound had changed from the older, more straight-ahead, traditional sound to more progressive sounds, using orchestras and so on. At this time you saw the growth in musicians like Del Reeves and Patsy Cline; the banjo had a skull and cross bones on it, and the disc jockeys didn't

want to hear it. That was just too hillbilly, and they did not want to represent it. Almost overnight, bluegrass and country music were segregated, but Flatt and Scruggs were pretty much the only band, I think, still being played some in country music, and the Dobro was starting to get a little more leads and that kind of thing, and they were changing their format a little bit.

[In] 1962 they played some dates out on the West Coast, and they were playing at the Ash Grove, which was a popular folk kind of thing out there. The 1960s brought in the folk boom; folk music is starting to pick up now, and some of the folkies are combining blue-grass into their music. They liked some of the same stuff. They had the Kingston Trio, which had a banjo in the band, and said let's check out this Earl Scruggs guy. So a lot of the people who didn't care for the new orchestral sound in the new country music picked up on the folk stuff, and there was another boon for Flatt and Scruggs. They just fell into the folk scene, and people started calling them "folk music with overdrive." They started playing coffeehouses and other places of that nature that other bands hadn't done too much of.

Newport not only opened the doors for Scruggs to align himself with a new audience and venues; he was inducted into a talent pool of performers who would remain influential to him for the rest of his life, one of them being Joan Baez. In the made-for-TV documentary *Earl Scruggs: His Family and Friends*, Scruggs and Baez reminisce about their meeting at Newport in 1959. Joan candidly expressed how shy Earl was before he confessed that his shyness was driven by his admiration for her singing. Their friendship led to Baez appearing with Flatt and Scruggs onstage and in several recordings with Earl in his post–Flatt and Scruggs years.

Another performer who attended that famed event as part of the Greenbriar Boys was a young banjoist by the name of Eric Weissberg. Though he was just beginning his journey as a professional musician, he would gain worldwide fame in 1972 for his arrangement of "Dueling Banjos" featured in John Boorman's acclaimed motion picture *Deliverance*. Weissberg reveals a treasured piece of memorabilia he discovered at the festival completely by accident:

> I was playing at the very first Newport festival. It was an amazing event, and so I was standing backstage, and I decided I was going to

go down, off the backstage, to this area that was like a big contained lawn to listen to the music. So as I'm walking around in that area, I look down and see something lying on the ground, so I bent down to pick it up and looked at it and saw it was a performer's pass that you pin onto your clothing. So I look at it, and lo and behold, its Earl Scruggs's pass. Of all the people on the planet, I pick up *his* pass. I still have it, by the way, and it's hanging in the little building where I keep my motorcycles, and I see it every day.

As a result of Newport, Earl Scruggs and Lester Flatt (who participated in two of the subsequent Newport Folk Festivals in 1960 and 1966) were now fully vested in the growing folk scene. One of the side effects to come out of this movement was their experimentation with a snare drum. Given the acoustic-strings-only rule for bluegrass favored by Bill Monroe and other traditionalists, Flatt and Scruggs continued to push the envelope by adding new sounds to their recordings. Their cardinal sin of including percussion instruments on such tracks as "The Great Historical Bum" and "Polka on a Banjo" started in April 1960. Even though the snare drum played with brushes helped to enhance their backbeat, the duo never hired a drummer as a member of their Foggy Mountain ensemble to accompany them onstage. The inclusion of a full drum kit in their recordings wouldn't surface until 1967, when they began work with their new Columbia producer, Bob Johnston, who also added another "no-no" to bluegrass—electric instruments.

The incorporation of a snare drum was just a foreshadow to an epiphany that hit Earl Scruggs right between the eyes that same year, when they were booked on the *Revlon Revue—Folk Sound USA* on CBS, their first national television program. Also billed on that show was jazz saxophonist King Curtis. During a rehearsal break for the live broadcast, Curtis asked Scruggs to pick with him. Their jam session became an inspirational moment for Earl, who realized the banjo's potential to blend well with other instruments in genres outside of bluegrass.[8] The harmony heard in his ear that day stayed with him for the remainder of his life. However, the implementation of such progressive musical arrangements in his repertoire took years to fulfill.

As an insurance policy to keep Flatt and Scruggs identified with the folk music craze that was sweeping the nation, Louise Scruggs made a bold decision that paid off in spades. Gary Scruggs summarizes his mother's strategy:

With my mother's focus trained on expanding their audience, Flatt and Scruggs began touring the college circuit in 1961. The folk boom had hit, and it appealed to many younger people, and thanks to Mom's PR work Flatt and Scruggs were, on a national level, considered to be a part of that folk music genre, perhaps even more so than the bluegrass/country genre. By keying in on the folk boom, she expanded their popularity out of primarily the southeastern states into all the states of the USA. A Flatt and Scruggs album that was released in 1962 was titled *Folk Songs of Our Land*.

In the midst of Flatt and Scruggs's popularity escalation, senior bandmate Curly Seckler was dismissed from the group. Since joining the Foggy Mountain Boys in the spring of 1949, Seckler had been one of its most solid members, until a dispute with Lester Flatt forced his resignation in 1958. After a year's absence, he was hired back, but by March 1962 Scruggs told him they were reducing the personnel in their band. The mandolin was becoming less relevant for their arrangements, and Curly's wife had become mentally ill (stemming from a struggle with diphtheria in the winter of 1952–1953) during this period, which took its toll on him personally. Frequent appearances by Hylo Brown had also given Seckler the impression that he was being replaced. After his release from the Foggy Mountain Boys, Curly quit the music business as his primary occupation until 1973, when he returned as part of Lester Flatt's Nashville Grass. Drawing upon his experience as one of the main bus drivers for the ensemble, Seckler took to the highways as a truck driver, pulling mobile homes.[9] Ironically, it wouldn't be long after Curly's departure that Lester and Earl would be loading up their own truck to move to Beverly—Hills, that is!

The Scruggs family in Flint Hill, North Carolina, circa 1913. Earl's parents, George Elam and Lula Georgia Ruppe, with their eldest children Junie (left) and Eula Mae. Courtesy of the Horace Scruggs family.

Young Earl (with banjo) and his brother Horace. Courtesy of the Horace Scruggs family.

Earl (far right) and Lester Flatt (center right) helped Bill Monroe (center) give birth to bluegrass music as members of the Blue Grass Boys. Here they are performing with fiddler Robert Russell "Chubby" Wise (center left). Courtesy of the Jim Mills Collection.

Earl borrowed Bill Monroe's station wagon in 1946 to pay his brother Horace (left) a surprise visit in Crestview, Florida. Courtesy of the Horace Scruggs family.

Earl and his future bride, Louise Certain, strolling the streets of Nashville in 1947. Courtesy of the Junie Scruggs family.

After leaving Bill Monroe's Blue Grass Boys, Earl and Lester launched their new act at Danville, Virginia's WDVA in March 1948. Courtesy of the Jim Mills Collection.

A poster from 1950 for an upcoming Flatt and Scruggs show in Hillsville, Virginia. Courtesy of the Jim Mills Collection.

An early 1950s publicity shot showcasing the products of the band's new sponsor, Martha White Mills: (left to right) Bob Moore, Benny Martin, Curly Seckler, Lester Flatt, and Earl. Courtesy of the Country Music Hall of Fame and Museum.

Earl and Lester in front of their tour bus at the G Bar B Ranch on June 16, 1957, in Collamer, Indiana. Courtesy of the Jim Mills Collection.

The Flatt and Scruggs Grand Ole Opry TV show, circa 1960: (left to right) Burkett "Uncle Josh" Graves, Frank "Hylo" Brown, Earl, Curly Seckler, and Lester Flatt. Courtesy of the Gordon Gillingham Collection, copyright the Grand Ole Opry, LLC.

Appearing with the cast and music director of *The Beverly Hillbillies* in early 1963: (top to bottom, left to right) Max Baer Jr., Earl, Lester Flatt, Buddy Ebsen, Irene Ryan, Perry Botkin, and Donna Douglas. Courtesy of the Country Music Hall of Fame and Museum.

A mid-1960s performance in front of a local hardware store. Courtesy of the Jim Mills Collection.

The Scruggs boys watch their parents conduct business in the family's home office, circa 1965. Courtesy of the Nashville Public Library, Special Collections.

Flatt and Scruggs's final appearance on *The Beverly Hillbillies* in 1968. In the episode's final scene, Milburn Drysdale (Raymond Bailey), dressed as Super Banker, is thrown through the bank's glass door in front of Lester and Earl. Courtesy of Stephen Cox/Paul Henning Collection.

Earl and his sons, Randy and Steve, with Doc Watson and his son, Merle, under the direction of David Hoffman in the NET documentary *Earl Scruggs: His Family and Friends*. Courtesy of David Hoffman.

An early glimpse of the Earl Scruggs Revue coming together at the Scruggs home, circa 1970: (left to right) Randy Scruggs, Leon Silby (aka Quincy Snodgrass), R. Stevie Moore (son of Bob Moore, former upright bassist for the Foggy Mountain Boys), Louise Scruggs, Lea Jane Berinati, Gary Scruggs, Earl, and Steve Scruggs, with Jody Maphis (not pictured) on the twelve-string guitar. Photo by Al Clayton, courtesy of Mary Ann Clayton.

The Earl Scruggs Revue in a 1975 photo shoot for their upcoming *Anniversary Special* album: (clockwise) Jody Maphis, Steve Scruggs, Earl, Randy Scruggs, and Gary Scruggs. Photo by Slick Lawson, courtesy of Scott Lawson.

Earl picks a Kay banjo with his brothers Junie (left) and Horace (center) outside Junie's home in Boiling Springs, North Carolina, in the early 1970s. Photo by Joe DePriest.

Earl talks on the phone while recuperating from his plane crash in late September 1975. Courtesy of the Nashville Public Library, Special Collections.

Paul Henning and Earl in 1993 on the set of CBS's *The Legend of the Beverly Hillbillies.* Photo by Stephen Cox.

Earl and Roy Clark play "The Ballad of Jed Clampett" for the 1993 *Hillbillies* special. Photo by Stephen Cox.

Earl's Hollywood Walk of Fame ceremony on February 13, 2003, with Max Baer Jr. and Donna Douglas. Photo by Rex Features via AP Images.

Béla Fleck and Earl perform together at Benaroya Hall on July 14, 2008, in Seattle, Washington. Photo by Santosh Tawde.

The banjo man plays his final show at UCLA's Royce Hall on November 5, 2011. Photo by Barbara Davidson; copyright *Los Angeles Times*, 2011, reprinted with permission.

Charlie Daniels eulogizes Earl during his funeral at the Ryman Auditorium on April 1, 2012. Photo by AP Images.

4

THE BEVERLY HILLBILLIES

When I think of Earl, I think of "Foggy Mountain Breakdown" rather than "The Ballad of Jed Clampett" because the first time I ever heard that was on the set of *The Beverly Hillbillies*, and it was immediately catchy. It was just great and I loved it!
—Max Baer Jr., actor, *The Beverly Hillbillies*

On the night of Wednesday, September 26, 1962, America was introduced to a man named Jed Clampett, a poor mountaineer who unexpectedly became a millionaire while "shootin' at some food." The oil-rich country bumpkin and his clan from the southern backwoods would soon load up their truck and move into a mansion waiting for them in Beverly Hills, California. And not only did Jed and all his kin strike it rich with "black gold" and "Texas tea," so did Lester Flatt and Earl Scruggs with a brand-new hit song that chronicled the complete back-story of *The Beverly Hillbillies*. The overnight success of this television phenomenon would elevate Flatt and Scruggs to new heights that were unimaginable, particularly for musicians rooted in bluegrass.

For the next nine years, Earl's banjo would become a weekly prime-time fixture in millions of living rooms across the United States, and later, around the world. The series piqued the interest of the mainstream populous to the clear, crisp sound of the five-string banjo and the awesome syncopated three-finger roll of Scruggs style. It wouldn't be long before the end of season one, when audiences would get their first glimpse of the banjo man and his partner as they sang about their undying love for Jed's cousin Pearl on an airplane bound for Los Angeles. This would be the first of seven guest appearances made by the duo as old friends of the Clampetts from back home.

The success of the rural-based sitcom, along with its infectious theme song, cannot be underrated, as Earl Scruggs recounted in a 1993 interview with the authorized *Beverly Hillbillies* biographer Stephen Cox: "No doubt about it, the *Beverly Hillbillies* theme was one of our biggest pushes Lester and I had in our career. A great boost to us. I cannot measure the help that it did for us." So "set" a spell, take your shoes off, and discover the tale of how this iconic TV series married up with Flatt and Scruggs without firing a single shot.

PAUL HENNING AND THE PILOT

After becoming a part of the hootenanny circuit in 1959, Flatt and Scruggs received a booking in the summer of 1962 for multiple performances at one of Los Angeles's premier folk music coffeehouses, the Ash Grove. Having completed his pilot episode for *The Beverly Hillbillies*, the show's creator, producer, and head writer, Paul Henning, stepped into the famed club on Melrose Avenue during Flatt and Scruggs's run and quickly became a huge fan—so much so that he went back a few more times. It's not known at this point if he had already composed the ditty that would become "The Ballad of Jed Clampett," but upon his visits to the coffeehouse, he was convinced that Lester and Earl were the perfect musicians to play the theme music for his new series. "Paul always just said that he loved their music and so he decided to go with them," says Cox. "Paul never mentioned any other considerations as far as having someone else do it. He really, really enjoyed Flatt and Scruggs. He loved banjo music and felt that it was the type of music that just went back to rural America. It was the type of music he enjoyed all the way through his life."

It wasn't too long after Flatt and Scruggs's appearances at the Ash Grove that Henning contacted their manager, Louise Scruggs, about the boys recording the program's theme. Surprisingly, Mrs. Scruggs rejected Henning's offer without hesitation. In 2003, Louise recollected her phone conversation with Paul Henning on NPR's *Fresh Air* with Terry Gross (printed with permission) and described the elements that changed her mind:

I turned it down at first because of the word[s] "Beverly Hillbillies." I didn't know what connotation that was going to take with country people and didn't want to offend them. So he said, "Well, the premise of this show is that the Beverly Hillbillies are going to always be outsmarting the city slickers." So, anyway, we talked about that two or three times, and he ended up sending the pilot to Nashville for us to see. And after we looked at it, we thought, "Okay, that looks all right."

"THE BALLAD OF JED CLAMPETT"

Dissatisfied with executive producer Al Simon's handpicked songwriting team's compositions, Paul Henning was in dire need of a theme song. Out of sheer necessity, he penned his own lyrics to a simple melody that he heard in his head.[1] The result was the first television theme to illustrate a backstory. Who knew that his storied ditty would inevitably be copied by other shows, such as *Gilligan's Island*, *F-Troop*, and *The Brady Bunch*. With the aid of a friend who played the piano, Henning's "Ballad of Jed Clampett" was polished up and ready to record.[2] However, just prior to music director Perry Botkin's trip to Nashville, there would be one change that Paul would make before Flatt and Scruggs could pick a note—enter Jerry Scoggins.

As a former backup singer for Gene Autry and Bing Crosby, Scoggins had become a Los Angeles–based stockbroker who continued his singing act on weekends. The richness of his smooth-sounding voice not only fit the show's title track very well; it had a resonating bass tone common among television announcers of that era. With Flatt and Scruggs headquartered in Nashville and constantly touring, Scoggins became a convenient luxury for Henning as Earl Scruggs explained in 1993:

That didn't bother Lester or me. Paul had told us he preferred Jerry Scoggins to do it because he said that, from time to time, they'd have to redo the theme for commercials and add new words. Jerry was out there in California and they wouldn't have to fly us out there every time they wanted to change the words for the Winston commercials or the Kellogg's Corn Flakes commercials. That's the way it should've been.

At Columbia Records in Nashville, Lester, Earl, and the Foggy Mountain Boys met with Botkin to record "The Ballad of Jed Clampett" instrumentally. Scruggs provided the details of that session from his interview with Stephen Cox:

> The way we did it was really hard. The way it was recorded the first time we had to figure it out. See, when I play a tune, I try to put the syllables and the words into my picking if I can. And boy, that song was full of syllables. The up-tempo, the faster part, is the easy part, but the slower part was a booger, and I rassled with it, but I finally nailed it down. I arranged it mostly, and Lester just played the chords along with it. That was no problem for him. The banjo's really up front in the song. And as I remember, Paul Henning loved what we did with it.

Louise Scruggs instantly recognized the theme's potential to be a hit single, not to mention the added publicity for her husband and his partner. She shared her account of it on NPR in 2003:

> While they were doing the theme music, I said to Perry Botkin, who was the music director at the time, "I think that would make a great single." And so I called Mr. Henning and I said, "What do you think about them recording that for a single for Columbia Records?" And he said, "I think it's a great idea." So I spoke to [Columbia's] A&R director Mr. Don Law, who was doing their records at the time, and so they recorded it three weeks later.

On October 10, 1962, the very day Columbia released Flatt and Scruggs's new single "The Ballad of Jed Clampett," showcasing Lester's voice over Earl's up-tempo banjo licks, the third installment of *The Beverly Hillbillies* aired, which had amazingly shot to the top slot on the A. C. Nielson ratings list. Earl and Lester were now on the fast track toward commercial fame. "After the show started airing," Louise Scruggs remembered in 2003, "I started getting calls for them for dates and concerts, and within about a month, I had them booked up for a year in advance, so it was tremendous." *Beverly Hillbillies* biographer Stephen Cox further elaborates:

> Paul was the type of person that told the cast, and I'm sure Flatt and Scruggs as well, that if you hang in here with me, everyone's going to

get some exposure on this. And as the show hit number one, which was like the [third] week—it shot to number one so quick—it made all of their heads spin. Paul knew that everyone could benefit from it, including Flatt and Scruggs, and they did by releasing their own single.

Just two months later, on December 8, the same day they performed their historic concert at Carnegie Hall, Flatt and Scruggs's recording of "Jed Clampett" hit number one on *Billboard*'s country music chart—the first time for any bluegrass band. And if that wasn't enough, the single crossed over to *Billboard*'s pop music Hot 100 list, where it peaked at number 44 that same month.[3]

OLD FRIENDS FROM BACK HOME

By the end of 1962, *The Beverly Hillbillies* had solidified itself as the highest-rated series in America, while "The Ballad of Jed Clampett" was topping the music charts. Flatt and Scruggs were now poised to be in a league of their own. But for Paul Henning, who was a big fan of theirs, just hearing the duo wasn't enough. He thought all of America should see them on the show as guest stars.

The ongoing shtick in all of their appearances was that Lester and Earl were old friends of the Clampetts, from back home, who had hit the big time as musical entertainers. In each of the episodes, they couldn't wait to eat Granny's "vittles" and would often have to pick a tune for their meals. If their spouses, Gladys (played by Joi Lansing) and Louise (portrayed by Midge Ware), came with them, one of the gags was that the wives knew best. However, on a more serious note, audiences were treated to the musical talents of Flatt and Scruggs, particularly Earl's banjo and his signature songs.

Their first appearance was on February 6, 1963, in an episode called "Jed Throws a Wingding."[4] In keeping with the story of Lester and Earl yearning to see their long-lost love, Pearl Bodine (Jed's cousin and Jethro's ma, played by actress Bea Benaderet), Henning composed another number that also became a Flatt and Scruggs single, "Pearl, Pearl, Pearl." This comedic novelty song of the duo taking friendly jabs at each other was the very first recording to feature Earl Scruggs singing two solos, in one of which he claims that Lester Flatt "slicks his hair with possum fat."

In March 1964, Earl and Lester came back in the episode "A Bride for Jed," which featured a rendition of "Foggy Mountain Breakdown" that was beautifully transitioned from an old Flatt and Scruggs album jacket next to Miss Jane Hathaway's turntable in Milburn Drysdale's office to a live performance of the duo in the Clampett mansion's foyer. Their next visit to Beverly Hills, on March 31, 1965, in "Flatt, Clampett and Scruggs," brought the boys to Jed's old cabin, now situated on the estate grounds where Granny has secluded herself, longing to return to the simple country life she cherished back home. Attempting to cheer up Granny, Elly May assembles a band of critters outside to play cheerful music that includes her chimpanzee, Bessie, with a toy banjo. Unbeknownst to Granny, Lester and Earl are also outside with Jed. They commence with Scruggs's "Flint Hill Special," which Granny thinks is coming from the chimp. When Jed calls out to Granny asking her to see who was making the music, she responds, "I've seen 'em, especially that little goomer with the banjo!" Earl responds with a comedic look of shock as he pivots to Lester.

Other episodes included "Flatt and Scruggs Return" on March 16, 1966, which features them singing "Little Brown Jug" in Jane Hathaway's car as well as picking "Earl's Breakdown" in the fancy eatin' room. We see Earl playing the guitar for the first time on the show while he and Lester accompany Gladys Flatt (Lansing) singing "You're Nobody Till Somebody Loves You" as she comes down the foyer staircase. Later, Scruggs retrieves his banjo for a sing-along of "The Wreck of the Old 97" at the program's conclusion. "Foggy Mountain Soap" on December 14, 1966, reprised another performance of "Flint Hill Special" as the boys awaited the filming of a laundry detergent spot. On March 29, 1967, they were back in "DeLovely and Scruggs." This particular episode was more centered on Lester Flatt, as he tries to foil Gladys's acting ambition with a second honeymoon in the Clampetts' cabin. After Gladys shrinks Lester's suit before a publicity photographer arrives, both he and Earl borrow Jethro's and Elly May's tattered clothes for the shoot, where they entertain with Scruggs's classic instrumental "Reuben."

Riding the wave of popularity from the 1967 motion picture *Bonnie and Clyde*, which incorporated Earl's 1949 recording of "Foggy Moun-

tain Breakdown," Flatt and Scruggs visited Jed and his kin for the last
time on November 20, 1968, in an episode appropriately titled "Bonnie
and Flatt and Scruggs." At the outset, audiences saw Lester and Earl
arrive at the Clampett mansion in a 1930s automobile dressed in gangster suits with prop machine guns, similar to the duds they donned on
the cover of their latest album for Columbia, *The Story of Bonnie &
Clyde.* In fact, they tell the Clampetts that they just came from a photo
session for their latest record.

However, the quick one-liner to promote their recent album paled
in comparison to the enormous promotion Earl received for his new
instructional book *Earl Scruggs and the 5-String Banjo* in the same
episode. *Hillbillies* cast member Max Baer Jr. (Jethro Bodine) surmises
how the publication wound up in the script: "I think Paul Henning just
did it because he was the writer and creator of the show and Earl
might've said something to him or Earl's wife might've said something
to him. So I think probably it was just Paul Henning that Earl mentioned something to, and Paul said, 'Yeah, I'll just write that in.' It was
not a big deal."

Oddly enough, one of the funniest gags in that episode was based on
Earl's book. Shortly after Flatt and Scruggs sing a spoof of the *Hillbillies*
theme in honor of Commerce Bank president Milburn Drysdale in the
Clampett kitchen, Earl plugs his instruction book to Jane Hathaway.
Just then, Jethro enters with a line to Miss Jane and then grabs the book
from Earl. This exchange follows:

JETHRO: (reads aloud) Earl Scruggs and the 5-String Banjo—
(looks at Earl). Hey, you learnin' how to play the banjo, Mr.
Scruggs?

LESTER: (interjects) Answer the boy, Earl.

EARL: (grinning) Yeah, Jethro, I'm learning.

Just like in the movie *Bonnie and Clyde*, "Foggy Mountain Breakdown"
is peppered throughout the program, though it's an updated version
from the one used in the film. In addition to Earl and Lester's performance of it in the drawing room with Jed blowing on the jug, in their
final scene the duo plays the melody of "Jed Clampett" outside the
Commerce Bank as the musical act for Drysdale's hokey "Super Bank-

er" TV commercial, which they were suckered into participating in by the money-loving bank president.

Though *The Beverly Hillbillies'* "first run" continued for another three years, it did so without any further guest appearances by Flatt and Scruggs, as they broke up just three months after "Bonnie and Flatt and Scruggs" aired. However, all was not lost as the Hillbillies and their old friends from back home would live forever in the world of syndicated reruns.

BEHIND THE SCENES

Through the years that Earl Scruggs appeared on *The Beverly Hillbillies*, his personal demeanor never changed. He didn't think any more of himself than he did before his association with the network series began. Max Baer Jr. characterizes Earl's amiable shyness on the production set:

> He had that funny little smile on his face all the time. When you'd sit on the set waiting for the shots, you could talk to him, and he'd answer your questions, and anything you'd want to talk about he'd talk about it. But he'd never initiate it, you know. I guess he didn't want to infringe on your space. That's the way it appeared to me. I don't know how comfortable he felt about talking about a variety of things. He really didn't talk very much, and so we were always cordial, and we would laugh together, and people would tell jokes, but he wasn't a person that would tell a joke or tell a story. He seemed very relaxed on the set, and the only time he got uptight was when he had to talk. But [as] soon as you put that banjo in his hands, he was right at home. That was his baby.

Unlike most sitcoms of today, and even some from yesterday, the *Hillbillies* wasn't shot using multiple cameras; rather, it was produced with a single camera à la film. In 1993, Scruggs discussed some of the more technical aspects of the production along with his feelings at the time:

> I was nervous up until I got on the set. We'd only do a few minutes at a time, and once we got on the set it was so well organized with stand-ins and all, they didn't wear us out. They used one camera and they'd have to measure off the lights and reset. Some of the tunes we

did on the show were prerecorded, and we'd play along with the tune. It looked like we were playing. Curt Massey [the music director after Perry Botkin] had a studio at his house and we'd record them there, but some of the songs we did on the set were live. They made us look great on every episode we did. Lester and I looked forward to doing the shows.

And one of the ways that Henning ensured Flatt and Scruggs were shown in the best possible light was to limit their dialog. Knowing up front that the boys were not actors, he kept their lines to a minimum, especially for Earl, who seemed to have less to say than his musical partner. Max Baer Jr. recalls Earl's nervousness and how the banjo eased his fears:

Earl was not an actor, and Earl was very self-conscious, in my opinion, except when he had the banjo. When he had that in his hands, he had no problems at all. He was totally in command. He was so good at what he did that he let the banjo speak for him. He was nervous, as far as stage fright was concerned, of speaking, but he was totally comfortable with the banjo in his hands. Take the banjo out of his hands, then he became nervous because he didn't feel protected and safe. That's why on the show Lester did most of the talking.

Ironically, though, it was Earl Scruggs that Paul Henning thought of when it came time for him to cast his next television series, *Petticoat Junction*. Earl spoke freely about the opportunity that "could've been" in 1993:

Paul thought I'd be good as a banjo-playing train engineer on *Petticoat Junction*, but that never worked out. With all the good things about Flatt, he had a little bit of jealousy and if he thought I was getting too much recognition, it'd grind on him a little bit. Certain things I'd have to back off a little bit. If I'd taken that part, it might have broken us up then, I don't know. I rassled with the idea, but I thought, well, I'm more known for my picking than my acting, so I'd better stay with the picking. I know Paul would have made me look good. I know that. I've often wondered how life would've been if I'd done that.

Even though he declined the role of Charlie Pratt, which ultimately went to comedic singing cowboy Smiley Burnette, Scruggs did record, with Lester Flatt, a powerfully banjo-driven version of the theme song to *Petticoat Junction* as a single in 1964 and, later, the theme for another one of Henning's programs, *Green Acres*, in 1966 with June Carter. Ten years after the cancellation of *The Beverly Hillbillies*, CBS made a poor attempt to resurrect the Clampetts in a 1981 TV movie called *The Return of the Beverly Hillbillies*. Not only was the script bad and the budget small, but Earl's participation was reduced to a single scene. "There's a wingding, which is a big party, and Earl is one of the musicians there and that's pretty much it," notes Stephen Cox. "Paul just wanted to add some authenticity and bring in some people from the series."

Twelve more years would pass before Earl Scruggs would fly to Hollywood again to be part of a *Beverly Hillbillies* production once more. The 1993 *Legend of the Beverly Hillbillies* paired Earl with Jerry Scoggins and Roy Clark (filling in for Lester Flatt, who passed away in 1979) to re-create the unforgettable recording of "The Ballad of Jed Clampett." Cox, who served as a consultant on the project, opens a window into the production:

> It was supposed to be a "mockumentary" for CBS as a TV special. It didn't turn out the way the writers really wanted it. There [were] three main writers, and they were all three very hip—I mean, just great writers that came from, like, *Saturday Night Live* and that type of show and humor. By the time they wrote their treatment and it got to CBS, CBS just mutilated it, and they didn't quite get the humor and were asking questions with these memos like, "Do we have to have Jethro play so dumb?" In the offices, we were just laughing because there was great stuff in the script, but the people at CBS didn't get it. They weren't even fans of the *Hillbillies*, but they just knew there would be some sort of ratings involved. So the documentary or mockumentary didn't turn out as well as we would've liked.
>
> I didn't even realize that Jerry Scoggins was still alive, and they found him. Scoggins sounded exactly the same; he had these incredible pipes. So when they told me that they were going to fly in Earl Scruggs and partner him with Roy Clark and have Jerry retool the song a little bit, I couldn't believe it. I thought, oh my god, this is historic! This is incredible! And I went to the studio and watched these guys get together, and it was phenomenal. It just gave me chills watching these three legends.

And so goes the tale of a man named Jed whose story gave Earl Scruggs and his five-string a "heapin' helpin' of hospitality" that he had never known before, as recapped by Louise Scruggs in 2003: "It eventually ended up being shown in seventy-six countries around the world. So what it did actually insofar as spreading country music, it helped country music and it helped, well, the banjo in particular, because Earl gets mail from people all over the world."

5

CHANGIN' TIMES

I always loved Lester Flatt and Earl Scruggs, and I just went after 'em and saw that they didn't have anybody to produce 'em, so I went and asked 'em if I could produce 'em, and they said, "Yeah," and they loved it. So I was doing Dylan, and Simon and Garfunkel, and Cohen, and Cash, and all those people, and I figured, hell, I might as well do them too.

—Bob Johnston, retired producer, Columbia Records

SOARING HEIGHTS

Immediately following the success of *The Beverly Hillbillies*, Flatt and Scruggs were well on their way to soaring heights. The first major milestone to emerge was Carnegie Hall on December 8, 1962. Even though Earl Taylor and the Stoney Mountain Boys predated Flatt and Scruggs at Carnegie, their appearance was part of Alan Lomax's musical production *Folksong '59* and not as a headline attraction under their own name.[1] Thus Flatt and Scruggs hold the distinguished honor of becoming the first bluegrass band to headline at the prestigious concert hall in New York City. According to liner notes written by Earl Scruggs for *The Essential Earl Scruggs* album, Louise Scruggs telephoned Columbia producer Don Law several days before the group's date to make arrangements for the concert to be recorded. With the aid of the record company's New York office, the thirty-two-song recital was successfully taped. However, when the vinyl release of *At Carnegie Hall!* landed in stores nearly a year later in October 1963, only thirteen tracks made the grooves as there were no plans to press a three-record set for the event.

Regardless of the number of songs left off the album, the product did contain material by the band that had not been previously recorded in studio for consumer release, such as their famous "Martha White Theme" jingle and Earl's long-running novelty "Mama Blues." The latter interestingly dispelled an allegation once made by Uncle Dave Macon that Earl Scruggs wasn't funny. He wrote "Mama Blues" several years earlier as a short, humorous little tune where he talks to his banjo and chokes the second string in a way that mimics a little boy conversing with his daddy. Years after the initial *At Carnegie Hall!* release, Columbia Records issued a CD containing the entire thirty-two-song set list, subtitled "The Complete Concert."

Even though another studio recording, *Hard Travelin'*, was issued before *At Carnegie Hall!*, the live album was the first Flatt and Scruggs record to feature their newest addition to the Foggy Mountain Boys, rhythm guitarist Billy Powers, who remained with the group until a serious motorcycle accident put him out of commission in 1964 and he was replaced by Johnny Johnson. Mandolinists Monroe Fields, Everett Lilly, and Earl Taylor also took brief turns in the band during the 1960s.

Carnegie Hall would soon be followed up by another historic feat in May 1963—a Flatt and Scruggs concert at Vanderbilt University. Regardless of the fact that its campus is located in Nashville, the school was typically hostile toward acts associated with the Grand Ole Opry.[2] Nonetheless, its negative attitude didn't deter Louise from orchestrating another live album. Vanderbilt captured the mood of the youth of America in full swing with the growing folk boom. Though Flatt and Scruggs had been touring the college/university circuit since 1961, none of their campus performances had ever been recorded. Distributed in 1964, *Recorded Live at Vanderbilt University* was not only the duo's second concert album (stamped with thirteen tracks); it would also be their last concert recorded by Columbia.

Soon after Vanderbilt, Flatt and Scruggs traveled to George Washington University in Washington, DC, for the taping of ABC's short-lived Saturday night series *Hootenanny*, a folk music variety show that broadcasted from a different college each week. Their videotaped appearance would air on the program's season finale on June 15, 1963.[3] In an interview on WLOE radio in late May of that year, Scruggs commented to disc jockey Ernie Knight that he and Lester were already booked out for the next twenty-eight weeks, with scattered dates as far as two years in advance. All of this on top of their ongoing tapings for their daily radio show and their weekly television program. In midsummer on July 14, they played to an estimated crowd of more than twenty thousand at Nashville's Centennial Park.[4]

In the midst of all this activity, Earl embarked on an idea that he had for an instruction book to teach beginners how to play the banjo. Ever so generous to show aspiring banjoists his tricks of the trade, Earl's idea sprang from his previous "Suggestions for Banjo Beginners," a page that first appeared in the Flatt and Scruggs Picture Album Song Books in the midfifties. Since Scruggs didn't read music or tablature, he would need assistance in executing this ambitious task. His help arrived most unexpectedly from a "Yankee" five-string picker who was in sheer awe of Earl's full utilization of the banjo's resources. Noted developer of the melodic style of banjo playing Bill Keith illustrates the evolution of the tablature for *Earl Scruggs and the 5-String Banjo*:

> I started transcribing Earl's material and putting it in tablature form. I learned the tablature system through Pete Seeger, who was the author of the first book I had on how to play the five-string banjo, and he was using tablature as well as music notation. So I picked up the tablature system, which I find is an excellent way to represent the music. I had basically written out all of Earl Scruggs's instrumentals and a few vocals during the latter part of 1962. I was living in Washington, DC, and apprenticing [for] a banjo builder named Tom Morgan and also playing with Red Allen and Frank Wakefield. During the day, I would be transcribing and annotating the recordings that I had available.
>
> Then, in December of '62, Tom Morgan and I noticed that Earl and his band [the Foggy Mountain Boys] would be appearing in Baltimore, which was a short hop from Washington, DC. That event was organized, or promoted, by a fellow named Manny Greenhill, who was from the Boston area. Tom and I decided to drive up to Baltimore to see the show, and Manny was producing it, so I took along my book of transcriptions and after the show I asked Manny if we could get into the greenroom to visit with Earl—Louise was there too—and he said, "Sure," so we went in there.
>
> I also had brought a book published by Peer International that had representations of Earl's instrumentals, some of them, in music

notation. But they weren't anything like what Earl was doing—they weren't correct at all. So when we got into talking about Earl's music, I made the remark that these were not accurate at all. And [Earl] said he couldn't read music, so he couldn't ever really tell if it was right or wrong. And I said, "Well, here's what they have written," and I played [on Earl's banjo] one of the transcriptions. Then I pulled out my book [of tablature] and opened it up to the same tune and played it, and [Earl] said, "Yes, that's correct."

So he tested me by choosing a tune in the book and opening up to that page and had me play it. While his head was turned toward the book, his eyes were shifted over to watch my right hand. I think that tune was "Home Sweet Home." I played it just like it was on the record—and he said, "Yes, that was right." And then he opened up to "Sally Goodin" and asked me to play that, and I did. He said that was largely correct also. He said there was one mistake I was making and that was holding down the E at the ninth fret constantly instead of just fretting when the note should be heard. That was easy enough to correct. He checked me on one or two other things, and he then consulted [with] Louise and they asked me to come down to Nashville to work on Earl's book—and yes, I agreed.

In early '63, I flew to Nashville and was staying at Earl's house and occasionally jamming with him and working more on the book, testing each of my transcriptions by playing them for him and seeing if there were any corrections to make—and, by and large, there were very few corrections. A lot of the text was generated by Burt Brent, who also wrote "How to Build a Banjo" [near] the end of the instruction book.

After Bill Keith's contribution came to an end in 1963, there was still much more work to be done before the project was finished. Gary Scruggs discusses Burt Brent's participation that led to the manuscript's completion:

The tablatures Bill Keith had produced lay dormant for well over a year as no attempt was made to write instructional chapters. In the autumn of 1964, Dad met Dr. Burt Brent, who was serving as a medical officer in the 101st Airborne Division at Fort Campbell, Kentucky, which is just sixty miles or so from where we lived at that time. Burt had been learning Scruggs-style banjo with the help of a banjo-picking friend of his named Warren Kennison Jr., who taught Burt how to play some of Dad's material.

Burt was a meticulous banjo student and had, as he said, "dissected" Dad's different right-hand roll patterns and other banjo-picking techniques. He convinced Dad that it would be possible to write a step-by-step instructional book outlining how to play Scruggs-style banjo and Dad agreed to give it a try. Dad and Burt worked together on writing teaching chapters regarding details of both Scruggs-style picking and the five-string banjo itself. The instructional chapters were finished within the next several months while Burt was still stationed in Fort Campbell. Bill Keith was then contacted, and he got on board with his tablatures that were incorporated into the book. Burt's friend, Warren Kennison Jr., also provided some tablatures he had previously written out.

The final product wasn't published by Peer International Corporation until 1968. There was an earlier promise of its release that never came to fruition, as indicated in *Flatt and Scruggs '66*, which detailed the book's contents and accompanying album to be available on March 1 of that year.[5] The two-year delay would actually be a blessing in disguise, as Earl was afforded the luxury of promoting his new book on national television via *The Beverly Hillbillies*, as previously mentioned.

Another little side venture that supported his desire to help banjo enthusiasts, also advertised in the Picture Album Song Books, was Earl's reselling of old Gibson banjos. Genuinely caring about the economic plight of struggling musicians wishing for a quality instrument, Scruggs offered an affordable solution. One such individual who purchased a used Gibson from Earl was Bernie Leadon, an up-and-coming banjo player and guitarist who later cofounded pop music supergroup the Eagles. Leadon revisits his excursion to the Scruggs residence:

> I first met Earl in person when a friend of mine from Gainesville, Florida, decided to take up the banjo, and he thought, in order to get a good one, he would call up Earl and ask his advice. We didn't know that Earl had a sort of sideline of work, buying and reselling banjos to folks like us. So my friend and I were soon driving up to Madison, Tennessee, in about 1965. We visited Earl and Louise and their home in Madison, and I remember they showed us around the house, and Gary and Randy were still in school and living at home. Louise and Earl worked out of a den office in the house. The office was filled with photos of Flatt and Scruggs awards and on one wall Uncle Dave Macon's open-back banjo [hung] over a couch. Earl

brought out his Granada for us to play, and he patiently showed us
how he scored the back of his plastic thumb pick with his pocket
knife, so it would stay on his thumb better. He played a bit also, but
after a couple hours, cash was exchanged for the banjo he was selling,
which as far as I can remember, was not an original flathead. But it
came from Earl!

In 1964, a relatively unknown songwriter with a knack for composing
"storied" songs arrived in town and soon became a dear friend to Earl
and Louise. Tom T. Hall emerged as an important fixture in the Flatt
and Scruggs camp by way of the compositions he penned for them, such
as "A Stone the Builders Refused" in 1966, "California Uptight Band"
in 1967, and his multiple songs (including the title track) for *The Story
of Bonnie & Clyde* album in 1968. The storyteller reminisces about his
introduction to the Scruggs family:

> I got to Nashville in 1964, on January 1, in case anyone ever asks me,
> because I'm so terrible with dates, but I can remember that. When I
> got to Nashville, I was on Music Row, writing songs and pitching
> them to people, and Jim and Jesse, and Jimmy Martin, and Flatt and
> Scruggs, and the bluegrass acts around town started recording my
> songs, and I'm sure it was because they could tell by the demo and
> the way I played the guitar on the little demo, they could [tell] by
> listening that I knew what I was doing when I was writing a bluegrass
> song.
>
>   Louise Scruggs really liked my songwriting, and she got Flatt and
> Scruggs to do a lot of my songs, and, of course, I got to know Earl,
> and sometimes I'd go out to where they lived in Madison. They
> rehearsed all these things [at Earl's house]. They would stand around
> and work out every note in the song, eleven or twelve songs. They'd
> rehearse these songs and then they'd go in the studio and they could
> just cut one after the other. Earl didn't like the idea of changing
> anything, once you got an arrangement on it, [and] they made their
> records pretty quick.
>
>   I got to know them because they recorded a lot of my tunes, and
> that's how we got to be acquaintances at that time. I did play some
> television shows with Lester and Earl, because, when I started mak-
> ing records, my first song was "I Washed My Face in the Morning
> Dew," which was a bluegrass tune with a folk attitude, and Louise
> really liked that song, and I'd already recorded it for Mercury, but

she invited me to be on [their] TV show, and I did the TV several times. That's when I [really] got to pick with Earl.

That same year, Detroit-based country music promoter Victor Lewis, along with local filmmaker Victor Duncan, organized a rare concert event for the big screen in partnership with Marathon Pictures Corporation. Filmed in New York City, Flatt and Scruggs joined company with such artists as Buck Owens, Skeeter Davis, George Jones, Wilma Lee and Stoney Cooper, and Hank Williams Jr. in the first-ever country-themed motion picture, *Country Music on Broadway*. Introduced onscreen by emcee Ralph Emery as "just about the best" act in bluegrass, the boys open with their cover of Woody Guthrie's "New York Town," appropriately chosen, given the location (not to mention its lyrics depicting the struggles of being an outsider in the Big Apple), yet it was followed up, in contrast, by the joyfully spirited tune bearing the name of Earl's rural birthplace, "Flint Hill Special."[6]

Before the close of 1964, Flatt and Scruggs incorporated the harmonica of Nashville session musician Charlie McCoy (the future music director for *Hee Haw*, among his many credits), who previously worked with Roy Orbison on his hit song "Candy Man" and was quickly becoming one of the most sought-after studio musicians. McCoy's presence gave the duo's arrangements a richer, more up-to-date sound that kept them on their course away from the traditional style of bluegrass. His participation wouldn't be noticed until after two more Flatt and Scruggs albums came to light: *The Fabulous Sound of Flatt and Scruggs* (Columbia, 1964) and *Kings of Bluegrass—Great Original Recordings Volume 1* (Harmony, 1965). McCoy is first introduced on the back cover of Columbia's *The Versatile Flatt and Scruggs—Pickin', Strummin' and Singin'*, a concept album from 1965 about broken love and regrets as depicted in "You're Gonna Miss Me When I'm Gone," "I Still Miss Someone," and "The Soldier's Return."

In keeping with the spirit of thematic albums, Flatt and Scruggs recorded *Town and Country* in September 1965, where all but one song title contains the name of a real place, such as "Jackson" and "Detroit City," or as in Earl's original bluesy lonesome-sounding composition "Nashville Blues." And yet, at least one fictitious landmark appears, a newly arranged version of "Foggy Mountain Breakdown," complete with a harmonica break. The album hit the streets in January

1966, which marked the beginning of a commercial onslaught of Flatt and Scruggs LPs throughout the next two years: *When the Saints Go Marching In* (Columbia, 1966), *Greatest Hits* (Columbia, 1966), *Strictly Instrumental* with guest artist Doc Watson (Columbia, 1967), *Hear the Whistles Blow: Lester Flatt and Earl Scruggs Sing Songs of Rivers and Rails* (Columbia, 1967), and *Sacred Songs* (Harmony, 1967), their final gospel release.

Despite the saturation of Flatt and Scruggs products from Columbia, sales were beginning to decline as the preferences of record consumers had moved into a more counterculture state of mind. However, a positive explosion was on the brink from Hollywood that would resurrect a classic recording of Earl's and bring forth accolades that were unattainable to him decades earlier.

BONNIE AND CLYDE

In August 1967, Warner Bros. released their blockbuster motion picture *Bonnie and Clyde*. The film was a romanticized depiction of outlaws Bonnie Parker and Clyde Barrow, whose two-year crime spree of bank robbing and murder spread from Texas all the way up to Minnesota during the Great Depression. With Faye Dunaway cast as Bonnie Parker and Warren Beatty as Clyde Barrow, the film sparked a gangster fad across the country and was Oscar nominated for the year's Best Picture. And cruising along for the ride were Lester Flatt and Earl Scruggs with a renewed interest in their eighteen-year-old instrumental "Foggy Mountain Breakdown."

Beatty, who also produced the Hollywood box office hit, was barely thirty years old when the project went into production. Desiring a musical number that would complement some of the fast-paced action sequences, the young producer instinctively thought of Earl Scruggs. In his 2003 interview on NPR's *Fresh Air*, Scruggs depicted how his initial involvement ended with an unexpected twist. "[Warren Beatty] called and wanted me to write a tune. So [then] he called back, I think I'm quoting this exactly the way it was, in a few days, and said he didn't want me to write anything because he found a tune that he thought fit what he wanted."

The tune Beatty found within his music library took root from a seed that was planted in his ear when he was a high school senior in Arlington, Virginia. As part of a civics class assignment at Washington-Lee High School, Warren's classmate Pete Kuykendall (the future editor of *Bluegrass Unlimited*) recalls how he made an everlasting impression on the school's star football jock, who had never spoken a word to him until this one particular day:

> I wanted to be a hillbilly disc jockey. So we had a "What do you want to do when you get out of high school?" And so one day I brought in two or three records from my collection to illustrate what I was going to play when I became a hillbilly disc jockey—one of which was "Foggy Mountain Breakdown," the original 1949 cut of the thing. I played them and didn't pay any attention to it as far as Warren was concerned other than he was in my class. And he kept me after class quizzing me about this music that I had played. And that was the gist of the reason that he apparently heard it either for the first time or at least it stood out to him. And he kept it in his mind when it came to the soundtrack for *Bonnie and Clyde*. I was as surprised as most people were when he used it.

Though Flatt and Scruggs already had an updated version of "Foggy Mountain Breakdown" completed for Columbia in 1965, it was that 1949 recording that Beatty heard over a decade earlier that resonated with him. Earl Scruggs elaborated on the rustic quality of that late-forties recording in his 2003 NPR interview:

> See, we recorded that tune before they got, what I say, good equipment. I mean, just plain everyday microphones in a radio station with no [way] to start making tunes sound fuller or something. It was just raw material. By that, I mean it didn't have no echo chamber or anything on it, so that's what Warren Beatty heard in that tune. So he didn't want to try to record another tune because he thought the equipment they had then [in 1967] was probably—would give it a more modern tune than what we had recorded, which turned out to be "Foggy Mountain Breakdown" and the sound that we got then. He took the Mercury recording and that was it.

Edited variations of "Foggy Mountain Breakdown" appear in three different spots of the movie. Immediately following Clyde's looting of a grocery store shortly after he and Bonnie meet, "Foggy Mountain Breakdown" chimes in as the lawless couple steals a car to flee the scene of their crime. Earl's opening break is all that's used before two obvious edit points appear to sync up the tune's ending with the car's abrupt halt in a remote countryside hideaway. The second installment of the song is its longest, but still heavily edited in a disjointed arrangement. Just as the Barrow Gang escapes from a bank heist, "Foggy Mountain Breakdown" fades up in the middle of its first fiddle break. When the car chase progresses from the city to the rural fields, the fiddle segues into Scruggs's opening notes. The song plays most of the way through with a couple of "talking head" dialog shots intercut that momentarily disrupt the energy of the tune before it climaxes toward its "edited" ending.

And as Faye Dunaway's character finishes reciting Bonnie Parker's poem from a newspaper about their adventures to Beatty's Clyde, the two begin to kiss passionately when a gust of wind blows their paper away. At that moment, "Foggy Mountain Breakdown" whisks in for the last time in the midst of Earl's down-the-neck licks before going slightly up the neck leading into the song's second fiddle break. The balance of the song flows naturally, with the exception of the "shave-and-a-haircut" ending that's dumped by the sound effect of a car engine to coincide with the shot of a passing vehicle, thus ending the music.

Bonnie and Clyde's murderous mayhem ran amok from 1932 to 1934, long before "Foggy Mountain Breakdown" was ever written, well before bluegrass was ever considered a musical genre, and certainly before anyone outside the Carolinas ever heard the three-finger roll on the banjo, yet Beatty's implementation of the signature Scruggs tune worked to enhance the car chase sequences without notice from the general popcorn-eating audience. Not only was the period of the music undetectably inaccurate, so was the spelling of the song during the opening credits, appearing as

FLATT AND SCRUGGS
"FOGGIE MOUNTAIN BREAKDOWN"
COURTESY OF MERCURY RECORDS

According to a liner note written by Louise Scruggs for her husband's 2001 CD *Earl Scruggs and Friends*, Warren Beatty claimed that Earl would get a hit record from his film. In the week of March 2, 1968,

"Foggy Mountain Breakdown" popped up on *Billboard*'s Hot 100 for the next twelve weeks. On April 20, it peaked at number 55, which is an amazing feat for a nearly twenty-year-old bluegrass instrumental, especially when the top five songs in the country were "Honey" by Bobby Goldsboro, "Young Girl" by the Union Gap, "Cry Like a Baby" by the Box Tops, "Lady Madonna" by the Beatles, and "(Sweet Baby) Since You've Been Gone" by Aretha Franklin.[7] The following year Flatt and Scruggs won a Grammy for Best Country Performance, Duo or Group, Vocal or Instrumental with their 1949 recording of Earl's composition "Foggy Mountain Breakdown." It would be the first and only Grammy for Lester, but not for Earl himself, as more Grammy Awards and nominations would come his way in subsequent years, including an unprecedented second win involving "Foggy Mountain Breakdown" in 2002 for Best Country Instrumental Performance.[8] Given the commercial success of *Bonnie and Clyde*, the Flatt and Scruggs team was quick to capitalize on the movie's pop-cultural craze with an album of their own in 1968, *The Story of Bonnie & Clyde*, showcasing Earl, Lester, and the Foggy Mountain Boys in full gangster motif on the front cover. Tom T. Hall would be asked to lend his storytelling abilities for the creation of the LP's title track, in addition to five other *Bonnie and Clyde*–themed songs. Hall reveals just how far he had to go to find the right inspiration for the project:

Columbia Records, Louise, Lester, and Earl decided to do an album, and so I got on a plane and went down to Denton, Texas. I used to go on these trips and just walk around and talk to people, and sit in little beer joints and cafés, and nobody knew who I was in those days. I'd just ask questions about the town, tell them I was passing through, and they didn't really have a very good attitude about Bonnie and Clyde. Most of them were kind of, "Ah, we're tired of hearing about Bonnie and Clyde. They were a bunch of crooks," and stuff like that, you know. So Bonnie and Clyde, at the time I was there, were not big heroes in Denton, Texas, I'll tell you that, but Bonnie and Clyde were not from Denton, Texas; they were from a town a little ways on down the road, which I found out is now a part of Dallas, Texas. Denton is its own town.

It seems to me at one of these places I saw a car, the Bonnie and Clyde car, it was either behind glass, or maybe I was looking outside through a window, but I saw the Bonnie and Clyde car, and it was all shot up and full of bullet holes. I don't know how much the car weighed originally, but I was standing there thinking of all the lead that's in that thing, it probably weighs twice as much as it did when they bought it, or stole it, or whatever [laughs]. I roamed around town, and I got some ideas about Bonnie and Clyde and some atmosphere, and I had a little tape recorder on the seat by me, and [if] I came up with a line, or an idea, for a song when I was driving, I'd hit the button and mostly talk about the song, and maybe later, if I had a little melody line, I'd hum it in there. I went down there for about a week and a half, traveling around in that area looking for Bonnie and Clyde stuff. I never did find out where they buried them, or I didn't ask. I don't remember.

I had a lot of fun writing the album, and they had a good record on it. Louise always told me that her favorite song on that album was "Bang, You're Alive," and I feel embarrassed that I have no idea what that song sounds like now.

The balance of the album's compositions, with the exception of "Foggy Mountain Breakdown," would be filled with instrumentals written by Earl's fourteen-year-old son Randy. The Scruggs's middle son would play lead guitar on the record and cowrite "Reunion" with his dad and Lester Flatt. Earl's eldest son, Gary, also appeared on the vocal tracks singing backup.

Years later in 2008, Earl and his Family & Friends band became an added ingredient in the American Film Institute's tribute to Warren Beatty when Beatty received AFI's Life Achievement Award (the tribute later aired on the USA cable network). Before a night of speeches honoring the screen legend by Hollywood's elite began, and immediately following an opening montage of film clips in which he had appeared, Beatty made his grand entrance to Earl's spirited live performance of—you guessed it, "Foggy Mountain Breakdown."

THE POINT OF NO RETURN

Not only did 1967 produce *Bonnie and Clyde*; it also gave America's hippie movement its Summer of Love. And just like all of the social change around them that year, Lester and Earl were in for a series of transitions themselves—beginning with their health. Still in his early fifties, Flatt experienced a mild heart attack that was potent enough to trigger a series of chronic cardio issues that plagued him for the remainder of his life. Scruggs, on the other hand, was still suffering from hip problems sustained from his car accident in 1955.[9] The time came for him to undergo in-patient surgery while the band was still playing tour dates. With his usual standby, Curtis McPeake, unavailable, Earl needed a replacement fast.

Herb Pedersen was a little-known banjoist out of Berkeley, California, in 1967. His recent move to Nashville while working with Vern Williams and Ray Park (known as Vern & Ray) landed him a spot on *The Early Morning Show*, a local program hosted by country singer Smilin' Eddie Hill. Pedersen remembers how his brief stint on the series led to a meeting with Scruggs that seemed almost surreal:

> Earl saw me on that TV show. After he had heard me, he called me up—he got my number from the Musician's Union—and I thought it was a joke. I thought it was somebody from out here playing a trick on me. So I said, "C'mon, who is this?" and he said, "No, it's Earl Scruggs," and I said, "Oh my gosh, it does sound like him." He said, "I'd like to get together with you if you have some time," and I said, "Of course I do."
>
> So he invited me over to his house, and he said, "Bring your banjo with you," so I said, "Okay," so I did, and you know, at twenty-three years old, you know, I'm just kind of numb by this invitation. So I get there and he said, "Come on into the music room." The thing that I remember walking in the front door was I saw a couple of the portraits that Thomas Allen had painted of their album covers and one of the pictures was the *Foggy Mountain Banjo* cover. It was an oil painting hanging up on the wall and I thought, oh my gosh, this is too unreal.
>
> So we sat and played music. He played guitar and he said, "Let's pick a couple of tunes," so we did, and he said, "Do you know this one?" and I said, "I think I do," so we played and stumbled through some stuff. When we got done he said, "Well, I kind of got you over here under false pretenses." I remember him saying that, and I said, "What do you mean?" He said, "Well, I have to go in the hospital. My hip has been giving me problems. You know I had a wreck in 1955, and there's some bone fragments in there that haven't come out, and I've got to get in there and take care of it, and I'm going to be hung up for a couple of weeks. I was wondering if you'd care to sit in with

Lester and play banjo." My reaction was dead silence. I said, "Are you sure?" He said, "Well, yeah—I've seen you on TV, and you play really well, and you seem to know the tunes, even the Martha White theme, so it would really help me out." I said, "I'd be honored to do that." So Louise came in and we talked business a little bit.

So the following weekend I came over to Earl's and he drove me down to the Opry in his Cadillac and introduced me to Flatt and the rest of the guys at the Ryman. After I met them, I think I played a couple of tunes with them on the show and then got in the [Flatt and Scruggs] bus, and we took off for West Virginia right from the Opry. It was pretty unreal.

I remember coming back, and I would have to go get paid from Louise, you know, and she'd write me out a check. I remember walking up the stairs, and they had a little office trailer off the property. It was in Madison, Tennessee, and they lived a few blocks away from the office where they had this trailer. So I remember going in there and having to walk up, and she says to me, and she has this check in her hand and she's not letting go of it, she's saying, "Do you think you played pretty well this week?" I said, "Yes, ma'am." "You didn't make any mistakes did you?" I said, "I don't think so," as she's tugging back and forth on the check. And then she finally lets it go [laughs]. She was great, she was wonderful, and she was really funny. I was able to play for Earl a couple, or three times, but then he came back. The fact that he even considered me was such an honor.

While the times were indeed changing, both culturally and musically in 1967, Flatt and Scruggs were continuing to perform the same catalog of songs they played endlessly for years, which by this point had grown stale for Earl. They previously made a few unsuccessful attempts at cover versions of easy rock songs like John Sebastian's "Nashville Cats" and Tommy Boyce and Bobby Hart's Monkees classic "Last Train to Clarksville," both produced by their longtime coproducers Don Law and Frank Jones. The pop singles, combined with recent alterations to their sound, may have been indicative of Earl and Louise's desire to move the band into a more progressive mode away from traditional bluegrass. However, it wasn't enough to rescue them out of their slump of declining record sales.[10] A huge makeover was needed quickly, and the brass at Columbia had one waiting in the wings that would permanently alter them from the sound of bluegrass. To boost sales in a market that was gravitating more toward the nation's growing "long-

haired" youth culture, Columbia decided to separate producers Don
Law and Frank Jones from Flatt and Scruggs. Their salvation came
through the ingenuity of Bob Johnston, who recently had transferred
from New York to Nashville. Recognized for producing two of the label's biggest stars, Bob Dylan and Johnny Cash, Johnston proved to be a
valuable commodity for Columbia. Jumping at the chance to work with
Lester and Earl, he convinced the pair to step outside of their comfort
zones by cutting songs from his repertoire of artists, which didn't appear to be much of an issue at first.

"They were receptive to recording anything," Johnston comments. "I
never really asked anybody to record anything that they didn't want to
record or didn't like or something else. They were wonderful players,
and they knew what they were doing. They were really good at what
they did and really good at what they played." Gary Scruggs asserts the
Johnston formula:

> The strategy was to record songs made popular by contemporary
> artists of that era. Johnston was Bob Dylan's producer at the time,
> and he brought a lot of Dylan songs to the table for them to record
> for the albums he produced—there were five Dylan songs on *Chan-
> gin' Times*. Johnston also changed the Flatt and Scruggs sound by
> adding a full drum set and electric instruments to their records.

Appropriately titled *Changin' Times*, this revolutionary LP not only reflected the cultural change that the country was facing; it also signified
the reconstructive musical direction of Flatt and Scruggs as well as the
changes developing within them as individual men. But the superbly
polished arrangements on the album, coupled with its financial success
in early 1968, wasn't enough to convince Lester Flatt, a bluegrass purist
at heart, that the group was justified in their musical transformation.
Appearances at counterculture music venues like the Avalon Ballroom
in San Francisco became bothersome to him, as he disliked and disap-
proved of the long-haired hippie crowds. Yet, on the flipside, Earl
Scruggs loved the challenge that came from this new material along
with the audiences it attracted. Both Earl and Louise understood the
importance of expansion and diversification as an opportunistic means
for growth and marketability—a concept that Lester just didn't want to
grasp, especially since his interest in the business end of the partnership
was nonexistent.

Changin' Times also included a revamped version of "Foggy Mountain Breakdown" (minus the recently added harmonica break from the 1965 arrangement) and another unique piece of artwork from Thomas B. Allen depicting Flatt and Scruggs in pastel-colored clay busts on the front cover. And among the backside's black-and-white photos is a prominently placed reprint of the Avalon Ballroom's psychedelic-style poster for the duo's November–December 1967 shows.

By March 1968, Flatt and Scruggs headed to the Far East for a series of sold-out shows in Japan. They would be the first American bluegrass band ever to tour Asia. Takashi Shimbo, one of the promoters from Shinnichi Promotions responsible for booking the pair, shares his memory of Lester and Earl's historic visit:

> When I look back at the day when Flatt and Scruggs came to Japan years ago, I'm sure their impressive performance meant a dawn of Japanese bluegrass. It was also my first experience as a promoter for [a] foreign artist. Because nobody wanted to take [the] risk for [a] bluegrass act in Japan at that time.
>
> The release of their first record was from Japanese Columbia records in January 1958. It was a 45-rpm single record that contained two tunes: "Jimmie Brown, the Newsboy" and "Blue Ridge Cabin Home." The following release in April of the same year contained "Flint Hill Special," "Your Love Is Like a Flower," "Foggy Mountain Chimes," and "Jimmie Brown, the Newsboy," a total of four songs on a 45-rpm EP. These were the first and second bluegrass releases in Japan. Japanese bluegrass started from Flatt and Scruggs—actually the popularity of "Jimmie Brown, the Newsboy" and banjo picking. Before long, linked with folk music, bluegrass was getting popular among college students in the early '60s.
>
> The band spent a few days in Hawaii, then they got to Haneda Airport at night on the fourth of March in 1968. [At] that time, Narita International Airport hadn't been open[ed] yet. Just after they arrived at the hotel, Mr. Masaaki Yosimura, coeditor of *Country and Western* magazine, and I were invited to the hotel. We had a meeting about the schedule during their stay. Earl Scruggs and his wife, Louise Certain, as a manager, joined us. Lester Flatt was exhausted from the long flight, so he didn't show up.
>
> The day finally came. There was a long line several hours before the concert. The concerts were scheduled from March 3 to 14, held in Tokyo (twice), Osaka, and Kyoto, including several days [on the]

Okinawa U.S. Armed Forces bases. The audience for the concerts filled every hall to overflowing.

Unbeknownst to Flatt and Scruggs, within those massive crowds, a "Beatles-esque" frenzy was brewing for them as Earl described to Doug Hutchens in 1989 on *Bluegrass Today*:

> It was just unbelievable—how they accepted us and the crowds that we did have. It was really—it just blew my mind. I didn't know how popular the banjo—well, I had no idea how popular the banjo was over there, but I met one guy who was teaching banjo, and he had a little over 200 students just himself. So it went real well, and I've had a lot of personal contact with Japanese people ever since.
>
> The first night, we [were] playing this auditorium, and it was equivalent to Carnegie Hall. It was a real elite auditorium. Apparently, there'd been a band there that didn't want to do any autographs. So this manager asked if we would sign some autographs after the show, and we said, "Sure, we'd be happy to." Well, behind the stage they had a little corridor and one side of it was glass, as well as I remember. But they had a table setting to where they couldn't get by us except but one side. In other words, [they] would come by me first, and I'd sign and Lester signed, then go on by [to] the end of the table. Well, we signed until the time was running low and people knew that they wasn't going to have enough time to get an autograph. So they got to trying to push in so fast until they pushed this one glass panel down. Well, that wound it up with the promoters. They rushed us into a room, cut out all of the lights, and it took a couple hours, I guess, before we ever got out—and they got us out with cigarette lighters, showing us down the exits. I had fun with the guy on the rest of the tour while I was over there. Each night I'd say, "Can we autograph tonight?"—"No, no, no, no autographs, no autographs."

One of the many young fans following the band on that tour was Japanese banjoist (of the band Bluegrass 45) and future publisher of *Moon-Shiner* magazine Saburo Watanabe. Flashing back to March 1968, he affirms the overly excited mob that besieged Flatt and Scruggs. "I went to see them at Osaka, Kyoto, and Tokyo. In Tokyo, a lot of young Japanese fans are waiting [for] autographs after the show. The Beatles toured Japan in 1966, and girls were going crazy, but I never thought it happened [to] boys! I was there, anyway."

And for all of the hoopla that came with their arrival in Japan, only one song from their new *Changin' Times* album, "Down in the Flood," made it into their set according to Takashi Shimbo:

> To select the tunes they play on the stage was very important for the Japanese bluegrass fans, who might have no chance to see them live again. On behalf of Japanese bluegrass fans, I persistently negotiated with them about each song. Our requests, which we were eager to [hear] from them, were mostly from the old records at the time. The tunes they recorded at Mercury and early Columbia. In fact, those were the tunes which Japanese fans learned from records. Concerning every tune, Louise asked Earl if they could sing or not. Then he promptly answered, "I don't remember such old numbers. But, anyway, I'll try to recall them."

For as much as Earl Scruggs enjoyed his group's Far East tour, the repeated renditions of the old-school songs, loved by Lester Flatt, were now a huge bore for him personally. His resilience to forge ahead with their covers of contemporary music was met with animosity by Flatt, who was extremely uncomfortable singing the lyrics of most of these songs.[11] So by the time *Nashville Airplane* flew in near the end of 1968, Flatt's disinterest in more material from Bob Dylan, as well as Donovan's "Catch the Wind" and Tim Hardin's "If I Were a Carpenter," was overtly obvious, as his voice lacked energy and conviction. And the best example can be heard on the LP's opening track, "Like a Rolling Stone," which was also released as a single earlier that summer.

THE SCRUGGS BOYS COME OF AGE

Like with *The Story of Bonnie & Clyde* and *Changin' Times*, the *Nashville Airplane* sessions grafted in the talents of Earl's sons, Gary and Randy. Gary provided background vocals and a tambourine, in addition to an instrumental composition, "Frieda Florentine," while Randy played lead guitar and a five-string Dobro. The three Bob Johnston–produced albums from 1967 and 1968 had utterly derailed Flatt and Scruggs off their previous course into uncharted territory.

The presence of Earl's sons on these albums didn't just happen by accident or because their dad thought it would be fun to put them on his records; the boys spent years honing their musical talents, as noted by Gary Scruggs:

> I learned to play trumpet in grade school and continued in school bands until I graduated from high school. Guitar was the first stringed instrument I learned to play, and then electric bass. I later taught myself to play harmonica and keyboards. Randy's first instrument was autoharp, then guitar. He also played trumpet in school bands. He also learned to play banjo and fiddle. Steve played guitar, piano, banjo, and saxophone. We all learned a lot from Dad but were mostly self-taught, except for school band lessons and Steve taking some piano lessons. I taught Randy his first chords on the guitar, but he quickly took it to a much higher level soon after on his own— seems like he always had a guitar in his hands once he started playing. Dad had taught me my first chords on guitar. We jammed occasionally with Dad when growing up.

The skill sets of Gary and Randy (Steve was still very young) began to infiltrate the Flatt and Scruggs ensemble during the early 1960s while the band was at the top of their game. An early instance came in 1962, when at age nine Randy made his television debut on the *Flatt and Scruggs Grand Ole Opry* show playing the autoharp and would continue to do so numerous times afterward, as well as perform with the band in concert. The boys would sometimes spend part of their summer vacation traveling with their dad and getting to better know the members of the Foggy Mountain Boys. "The band members treated us very warmly," says Gary Scruggs. "Josh, Jake, and Paul all had children about the same age as Randy, Steve, and me. Mom was a friend of the band members' wives, and Randy, Steve, and I grew up around the band members and their families."

And when it came to recording with their dad's legendary troupe, the Scruggs brothers got an early start. "I was seventeen, about to turn eighteen. Randy was thirteen, almost fourteen," Gary recounts. "I played rhythm guitar on some tracks but was primarily used on background vocals. Randy played acoustic guitar, both rhythm and lead, on the tracks he played on." Gary eventually received a recording contract of his own from Columbia, and under the direction of Bob Johnston he cut two singles.

As for Papa Earl, the excitement of watching his sons come of age musically filled his heart with a level of joy that made his destination as an artist crystal clear. Scruggs shared his sentimental feelings with NPR in 2003:

> Well, the biggest thing for me—see, I had three boys coming along, Gary, Randy, and Steve was my youngest boy, and they were good musicians. So I just had a band in my home, and one of the biggest thrills a person will ever get is to go onstage with his children, especially if they're good musicians, and I'll have to brag on 'em even though they are my boys. I thought [they were] some of the best musicians that I ever played with. So it was a great outlet for me to start working with my boys.

THE END OF AN ERA

Lester Flatt's disengagement with the recording and performance of their new material proved to Earl Scruggs that there were no more worlds to conquer for the two biggest names to come out of bluegrass over two decades earlier. At the same time, Scruggs's love and admiration for his sons was a constant reminder that a new horizon was within his grasp. The time was quickly approaching for him to make a judgment call regarding his future in showbiz.[12]

By February 1969, only two months following their participation in the Miami Pop Festival and just a few weeks after their appearance in Richard Nixon's presidential inauguration parade, both Lester Flatt and Earl Scruggs were ready to go separate ways. They played their final show together on the Grand Ole Opry on the 22nd of that month, and all of the members of the band were given notice, although Flatt soon rehired those members to be his backing band along with a new banjo player. A few weeks later, the business end of Flatt and Scruggs and their "Foggy Mountain" brand was officially dissolved, but not to the satisfaction of Lester, who sued the Scruggs Talent Agency (Earl and Louise) on April 9.[13] As a consequence, neither man could retain the use of the name Foggy Mountain Boys for their subsequent bands.

Ironically, both Flatt and Scruggs would regroup with their producer, Bob Johnston, in late August 1969 to crank out one last album for Columbia, per their contract. Suitably titled *Final Fling—One Last*

Time (Just for Kicks), the cover art by Thomas B. Allen was symbolic (whether intentionally or subliminally) of the current and future status of the former partners. In the forefront is an invigorated, hatless Earl Scruggs sporting a standard necktie. Behind him is a slightly faded Lester Flatt donning his traditional bluegrass uniform: Stetson hat and Kentucky colonel string tie. Above them, in a cloud of flowers, are colorless images of Leonard Cohen, Bob Dylan, and Johnny Cash, three of the influential figures that came with Johnston, whose songs are not only covered on the album but whose compositions Flatt reluctantly sang on their previous recordings. Scruggs, however, continued to work with Cohen, Dylan, and Cash on later productions as he held their work in high regard. And if the Allen painting wasn't enough, the caption bubbles on the back cover solidified their dissolution in plain English with "So long, Earl . . ." and "So long, Lester . . ."

Though their parting was a sad blow to the loyal fan base that had grown to epic proportions over their twenty-one years together, each man took with him a different element from that sector, as Lester would keep on singing true bluegrass for the older generation while Earl reinvented himself, catering to the tastes of the younger crowd. Both of them experienced a newfound happiness that had dwindled over the last couple of years due to their musical differences. Speaking on behalf of his father, Gary Scruggs cites a few of Earl's most memorable moments from that blessed era of his career:

> Even though the early Flatt and Scruggs years were sometimes a bit of a struggle, they were an exciting time for him because the band was making a name for itself. They won numerous country music industry awards from the mid-1950s on into the mid- to late 1960s. He very much enjoyed making cameo appearances on *The Beverly Hillbillies* TV show. I know he enjoyed the Japan tour, his first appearance on the Newport Folk Festival, and the live Flatt and Scruggs recording at Carnegie Hall. There were many highlights for my father throughout the Flatt and Scruggs years, too many to mention.

With further retrospect, bluegrass banjoist and historian Jim Mills provides an analogy on the legacy of Lester and Earl:

Flatt and Scruggs were a success that came along at the right time in history, and I don't think what they accomplished can be replicated by anyone, not now or in the future. Now keep in mind that I think they were anointed. I mean, everything just fell into place for them through the years, no matter what the decade was. Something good always came along, and they never took a step backward. It was always a step forward for the Flatt and Scruggs band, and for Earl Scruggs.

One day I got to looking back on just how great the Flatt and Scruggs career was, a twenty-one-year period. How many bands can you say have lasted twenty-one years and be successful the entire time? If you separate Earl from the bunch, and look at his life, I don't think honestly that it's a career that can ever be re-created simply because of the timing in life. Flatt and Scruggs played six days a week for fifteen years. These guys knew when the other guy would breathe in or out. I don't think there's a band today, or there will ever be a band in history, that'll be that tight and work that much.

6

PUSHING BOUNDARIES

Earl was very modern in his musical taste and was willing to take
chances in areas of music that had not been explored by Southern
musicians prior to his pioneering spirit.
—Roger McGuinn, folk rock artist

Following the breakup of bluegrass music's most successful act, Earl
Scruggs felt a great sense of relief, after years of boredom with picking
the same old songs with the same old arrangements, over and over
again.[1] He was now free to spread his wings into other genres of music
where the five-string banjo was seldom heard. His liberation from the
shackles of traditional bluegrass (acoustical strings only) allowed him to
include percussion instruments, keyboards, horns, and electric guitars.
This seemingly radical departure from his almost twenty-five-year
mainstay introduced the talents of Earl Scruggs to a new multigenera-
tional audience that he never would've known from inside the garden
gates of bluegrass. Scruggs was determined to diversify his craft by
maximizing all of the resources from his beloved five-string before the
eyes and ears of the world.

This marked the birth of the most rewarding period of his career.
Not only was he attaining satisfaction in his new identity; he was also
experiencing a wealth of personal joy rooted in the talents of his sons,
Gary and Randy (and later on, Steve), whom he missed terribly during
his many years of touring. Noticing how much their musical abilities
had improved, Scruggs felt the time was right for them to become a
band. And reminiscent of the musical family from which he blossomed,

Earl was now at the helm of his own family troupe—the Earl Scruggs Revue.

While his former partner wasted no time in launching a new band—Lester Flatt and the Nashville Grass (consisting mainly of former Foggy Mountain Boys: Paul Warren, Burkett "Uncle Josh" Graves, and English P. "Cousin Jake" Tullock)—Scruggs spent the next couple of years in an experimental mode to perfect the direction of his artistry. With Gary attending college and Randy in high school, the performance schedule for the new group was largely limited to weekends and summer vacations, thereby restricting their exposure.

Despite Louise Scruggs's effort to introduce the Earl Scruggs Revue in a June 1969 press release printed in *Billboard*, it would take another three years for an album to be released under the that name. During these organizational years, Earl would record two albums for Columbia. First came *Nashville's Rock* (1971), featuring cover versions of pop songs, such as the Rolling Stones' "Honky Tonk Women," the Beatles' "Hey Jude," and an angelic-sounding arrangement of Simon and Garfunkel's "Bridge over Troubled Water." The second album was a guest-artist collaboration, *I Saw the Light with Some Help from My Friends* (1972), that included the talents of Arlo Guthrie, Tracy Nelson, Linda Ronstadt, and the Nitty Gritty Dirt Band, along with Revue members Gary Scruggs, Randy Scruggs, Vassar Clements, and Bob Wilson. Concurrently, Gary and Randy put out two records for Vanguard as the Scruggs Brothers: *All the Way Home* (1970) and *The Scruggs Brothers* (1972). But the first true family production to introduce and showcase the Revue resulted from a 1970 National Educational Television network special titled *Earl Scruggs: His Family and Friends*, which effectively captured this critically pivotal moment in Earl's life.

THE EARL SCRUGGS REVUE

In the television documentary, Earl declared himself part of a new generation of banjo pickers looking to climb out of the pigeonhole associated with such relic tunes as "Cumberland Gap" that predated his existence. The further he went with the banjo, the more pleased he became. As his sons Gary and Randy began to evolve musically, he instinctively recognized that a serious makeover was imminent. It was time to reinvent himself: the Stetson hats and Kentucky colonel string ties were laid to rest in favor of dress suits with standard neck ties (in the coming years, he wore suits less frequently and opted for a more casual wardrobe accented by a longer hairstyle). And while Earl's appearance had changed, it would be a few months before the public would hear a peep out of him. Gary Scruggs defines the logic behind his father's delay:

> After Flatt and Scruggs parted ways, Mom and Dad were not so eager to immediately hit the road again. They wanted to think things through, so Dad took some much-needed time off and then he, Randy, and I started working up new material, or rearranging some of his older material. We worked up a variety of styles of music, both materially and sonically. The sound evolved over the next few years.

In molding their band, Earl and his banjo became the nerve center to Gary's lead vocals, electric bass, and harmonica and Randy's lead guitar (acoustic and electric), with occasional fiddle, banjo, and autoharp. The boys quickly became a powerful influence on their father's selection of music. Together they would weave some of Earl's favorite songs, such as "T for Texas" and "Step It Up and Go," into a new repertoire blended from contemporary folk, jazz, blues, and pop-rock rhythms and backbeats.

An early arrival in the new band was future Country Music Hall of Fame member Charlie Daniels. Having grown up in rural North Carolina, Daniels was a longtime fan of the banjo man. Upon his arrival to Nashville in 1967, he went to work at Columbia Records, doing odd jobs for producer Bob Johnston. It was during that time when he met his musical hero, Earl Scruggs, as he was booked by Johnston to play on a number of Flatt and Scruggs sessions. By mid-autumn 1969, Charlie was drafted by Scruggs to join him at the Vietnam Moratorium, and from that moment, he was a full-fledged member of the Revue. Daniels reflects on his brief time with the band:

> They kind of took me under their wing when I came to Nashville, [and] they did, Earl, Louise, and the boys. I didn't have a lot going on at the time. They put me in position to appear in front of a lot of people. Nobody knew who Charlie Daniels was. Of course, Earl was a legend and to be associated in any way with him or anything like

that raised my stature to some degree in that it gave me some validity and some legitimacy. And I'll never forget it. It meant a lot to me at the time. To be a part of the Earl Scruggs Revue was a big deal to me—playing the Grand Ole Opry, the first time I ever played it, and recording with Earl and doing some personal appearances with him was a big, big deal to me.

"In addition to his talent, Charlie Daniels brought a lot of positive energy and showmanship to the band," adds Gary Scruggs. "Charlie was a Revue member for a year or so, playing guitar. He left the Revue in order to pursue what turned out to be a very successful solo career with his Charlie Daniels Band. At that point, Jody Maphis joined the Revue on rhythm guitar." As the son of country music stars Joe and Rose Lee Maphis, Jody would spend the next nine years as an "adopted" member of the Scruggs family. Maphis recounts his induction into the Revue:

> I met Randy Scruggs at Madison High School, just outside of Nashville, and he was a year ahead of me. And he come and got me one day and introduced himself and said, "Are you Joe Maphis's son?" and I said, "Yeah."—He said, "Let's get together and do some picking." So we got together, and Randy's playing "Foggy Mountain Breakdown" [on banjo], and I played rhythm guitar to it, and before I knew it, I'm over at Earl's house—and we're sitting around after school playing with him. It kind of started right there in Earl's living room. For me, working with Earl was kind of like going—that was my college. I went straight from high school right to the Earl Scruggs Revue. I spent more time with the Scruggs family than I did my own.

Shortly after Jody entered the Revue, studio backup singer and pianist Lea Jane Berinati joined for several months and was later replaced on the piano by Bob Wilson, whose Nashville recording session credits included playing on Bob Dylan's *Nashville Skyline* and *Self Portrait* albums. During this shuffling of members, Jody Maphis would experience a switch of his own from rhythm guitar to his permanent post on the drums, as he explains:

> I always just kind of messed around with [the drums]. It wasn't anything planned. Some friends—other kids we went to school with—they were putting a band together to go try to play down in Florida for the summer. And they were going down there to kind of

audition at a couple of places. Two days before they were supposed to leave, the guy who was playing drums backed out. And I just happened to be messing around. I went down there for a week with them and auditioned and came back up, and the next thing I know, me, Randy, and Gary are starting to mess around with some stuff. They were just doing their first Scruggs Brothers album, and we started messing around as a trio 'cause they were wanting to go out and do some stuff with me on drums, and then Earl heard it and, before I knew it, we just started doing it. It just kind of grew from there. It wasn't like there was a set thing. As the new members of the Revue played longer together, and then, other people would come in and out, we just started finding what was working, what was adding to it, you know, what sparks some things. There [were] quite a few people in and out of there. I think the Revue was trying to figure out what it was going to do 'cause nobody got settled into it and locked in. But it was really a magic time musically, you know. It was wide open back then. Everybody wanted to play with everybody.

In 1971, legendary fiddler Vassar Clements graced the Revue, and following close behind for a stint was an old friend from the past, Burkett "Josh" Graves, who signed up for a couple years on the Dobro, after exiting Lester Flatt's Nashville Grass in 1972. Both Vassar and Josh would eventually leave the Revue in order to pursue solo careers. That same year, Earl's youngest son, Steve, began to make appearances on a part-time basis, as he was still in junior high school. However, he became a full-time member in 1976, after his eighteenth birthday, mainly on the piano, with some guitar, saxophone, and banjo. Other comings and goings included pianist Jack Lee for a year or so, steel guitarist and saxophonist Jim Murphy, and drummer Taylor Rhodes, who replaced Maphis during the group's final two years.

Trekking the grounds of America's institutions of higher learning and the stages of its finest music clubs and concert halls, Louise Scruggs also made sure to book dates for the Revue in the popular bluegrass festival circuit. Earl's new sound echoed through the open grounds of such fests held in Bean Blossom, Indiana; Watermelon Park in Berryville, Virginia; and Camp Springs, North Carolina, where the Revue was filmed performing their rendition of Elton John and Bernie Taupin's composition "Country Comfort" as part of Albert Ihde's documentary

Bluegrass Country Soul. The Revue would soon be performing at major rock festivals as well.

At these venues, Scruggs began publically to experience the rewards he'd hope to reap in the rebirth of his banjo with the talents of his sons. The freshness presented a resurrection to many of the old bluegrass standards, and as his nephew J. T. Scruggs summarizes, it coincided with a philosophical belief he held in high esteem:

> I think he was always just proud of doing things different. I mean, he was an innovator in music. He always embraced change. I think he was very proud of the fact that he didn't just do one thing all of his life. He was always changing his music style and trying to do things differently. He said, "If I can see a light shining out there farther, I want to try to find it and see where it leads me."

THE VIETNAM MORATORIUM

On November 15, 1969, just ten months after appearing in President Richard M. Nixon's inaugural parade with Lester Flatt and the Foggy Mountain Boys as representatives of Tennessee, Earl Scruggs stepped outside of his unassumingly quiet demeanor to stand in unison with an estimated one million antiwar demonstrators congregated on the National Mall for the Vietnam Moratorium march in Washington, DC. With his sons Gary and Randy, along with thirty-three-year-old Charlie Daniels, Scruggs broke ranks with his peers in Nashville to make a bold political statement for the first time in his life. Documentary writer/director David Hoffman, who captured the historic event on film, paints a portrait of Earl's bravery in that epic moment:

> Country stars were unanimous at that time in being pro—what used to be pro-American, as though the antiwar movement was anti-American, which it wasn't. But there was a debate in the country, and the prowar community set it up so that, if you were an American, you wore an American flag and supported the war. And the country [music] people were completely like that; the Grand Ole Opry was totally like that. There was no break until all of a sudden Earl pops up out of nowhere, with no one directing him or leading him. He decides on his own the war is wrong. We are killing American boys for no good reason—he didn't like that. So, typical of him, he informs

the press in some way or another, they pick [it] up, he makes a statement about it, which upsets his community in Nashville—really upsets his community in Nashville—and the antiwar movement asks him to come to the largest demonstration in the history of American demonstrations to perform. He didn't care what anybody else thought. He didn't care what it would do to his career, which, people said, it will hurt your career—it will reduce your sales and they may not invite you to the Grand Ole Opry again.

Charlie Daniels reiterates Earl's conviction and the massive reception they faced on that frigid Saturday:

> This was a big step for Earl. This was an act of courage for Earl. This was kind of a step out from his, what was considered at the time, his base, his bluegrass base of older people—of course, Earl had a big following of younger people too, but I thought it took a lot of courage for him to do that. And when he called me and told me that "they have been trying to get me to go to Washington for this Vietnam thing, and I'm going to go—I've decided I'm going to go and I'd like you to go with me." And I, you know [said], "Yes, I'm there. I'm with you. Let's go." I was very honored that he asked me to go.
>
> I remember that day. It was so cold you couldn't even feel the strings under your fingers, and it was impossible to keep an instrument in tune. It was brutally cold! I had never seen the [National] Mall where we were, across from the Washington Monument, that many people—it was just a sea of heads from one side of the Mall to the other and up and down. It was a moving experience. Especially for Earl, this was a big step out for him, in my opinion. I think it was something that he probably had to think about a lot.

"There was quite a bit of criticism directed toward us regarding our appearance at the Moratorium," remembers Gary Scruggs. "The Nashville music community was generally very politically conservative back then, and our appearance there surprised a lot of people. We were the only Nashville act, I'm aware of at that time, to speak out against the Vietnam War."

EARL SCRUGGS: HIS FAMILY AND FRIENDS

During the formation of the Revue in 1969, Scruggs became a subject of discussion at the front offices of the National Educational Television (NET) network, just as it was undergoing absorption by the Public Broadcasting Service (PBS).[2] Independent filmmaker David Hoffman was pitching an idea to feature the banjo man in a documentary showcasing music along with interviews. Hoffman outlines the scope of the TV special:

> It was a time when [NET] was kind of interested in broadening its base out of the northeast, and I came in the door with my partner at the time with a proposal that they do Earl Scruggs, who had a vision that he was going to move out of bluegrass and interact with other great musicians. And since he was seen as kind of—everyone who had ever met him liked him—he was a good guy and a guy without an ego. We came in with money from a grant—I think it was a fundraising grant. They were going to use it to raise money for [NET], and Earl said, "Fine."
>
> We made a list of all of the people Earl wanted to play with. There was no one who said no, but there was a few whose schedules didn't allow, but everybody said yes. And then we traveled with Earl, and that was the idea—my idea and Earl's idea—we could've seen Joan Baez, other than at her home, we could've seen Doc Watson, other than at his home. They could've been in a studio or in any other place, but we decided we were traveling to them to their place. It was let's just sit down together—Earl's view and mine. And the Vietnam story, which is a part of my film, is a key moment because it was how we started. We started with the Vietnam story and then filmed all of the other scenes.

Though the Moratorium was the first sequence shot, it wouldn't appear until a little more than a third of the way into the final cut, just before Gary's interview about his dad's personality and playing together as a family, which segued into the Scruggs Brothers Vanguard recording session with Charlie Daniels. The film opens with Earl, Gary, and Randy jamming with folk rock legend Bob Dylan at the home of Thomas B. Allen in Carmel, New York.

According to Gary Scruggs, they played four songs with Dylan that day, but only two of them appeared in the final cut of the movie. And out of the two tracks, just "Nashville Skyline Rag" made the groove on the vinyl disc. Another two-song segment in the movie that flew into Earl's nest came from the Byrds. The band's leader and founding member, Roger McGuinn, shares his affinity for Earl Scruggs along with his memory of the program:

> I admired him greatly for his musicianship, and he was such a gentleman. He always dressed up, wore a suit and tie and a diamond stickpin that I thought, you know, this guy is really a class act. I thought he was wonderful. I just enjoyed his whole personality. He was so gracious he had that sort of southern hospitality, inviting you to come to his house and everything. It was amazing.
>
> What sticks out in my mind is doing that little film that he did with his sons, Gary and Randy and my band, the Byrds, with Clarence White. I remember that, and doing "You Ain't Going Nowhere." There's a clip of that that sticks out.

Earl's desire for the Byrds to participate in the film resulted from a previous jam session he had with them at his house in 1968. Gary Scruggs describes in detail the backstory of his family's relationship with the pop band:

> It was in the spring of 1965 when I first heard the Byrds on the radio, and it was their recording of "Mr. Tambourine Man." I loved the vocals and the jingle-jangle of Roger McGuinn's electric twelve-string guitar on that record. The Byrds quickly became one of my favorite rock bands. Even when the Byrds went through major personnel and stylistic changes over the next few years, I continued to like their music. Roger was the constant for me.
>
> I met Roger at Nashville's Columbia Records' Studio A in March 1968 when the Byrds were there working on their *Sweetheart of the Rodeo* album. He told me he was an Earl Scruggs fan, so I invited him and the band over to Mom and Dad's house to meet Dad. The meeting turned into a jam session and a friendship that led to Dad inviting Roger and the Byrds to take part in the made-for-TV documentary *Earl Scruggs: His Family and Friends*.
>
> Along with taping "You Ain't Going Nowhere" with the Byrds, we also played Doc Watson's tune "Nothing to It," a great instrumental which had appeared on the Flatt and Scruggs with Doc Watson album *Strictly Instrumental*. Both my brother Randy and the Byrds' Clarence White had been influenced by Doc's flat-picking style on

acoustic guitar, and the tune gave Randy, Clarence, and Dad a chance to really shine on the solos.

Although the Byrds were considered to be a rock and country rock band at the time, Roger had a strong folk music background and Clarence came from a solid bluegrass background. Roger, who was formerly known as "Jim," had played acoustic guitar and longneck five-string banjo for folk groups in the folk boom era such as the popular Chad Mitchell Trio. Clarence had been a member of the Kentucky Colonels along with his brother Roland, a mandolin player. So both Roger and Clarence were well aware of Dad's contributions to the music world.

Dad reciprocated the respect shown to him by the Byrds as well as other musicians from various genres. He enjoyed the often impromptu jams that occurred in those days, whether at his house or on the road at concert venues. His enthusiasm for jamming with other musicians, both young and old, carried over for the rest of his life.

Perhaps one of most redemptive moments in bluegrass ever caught on camera is the dressing-room jam session between Scruggs and Bill Monroe at the Ryman Auditorium as the Grand Ole Opry was being broadcast on WSM radio. More than twenty years earlier, when these two giants were bandmates in Monroe's Blue Grass Boys, they were frequently announced on the Opry stage by the "Solemn Old Judge," George D. Hay, as "Bill Monroe and Earl Scruggs and his fancy five-string banjo." When Scruggs quit Monroe's band, along with Lester Flatt, in 1948, things were friendly, or at least cordial, the few times they crossed paths during their travels, but when Flatt and Scruggs joined the Grand Ole Opry in early 1955, Bill Monroe was furious and refused to speak with either man for the next fourteen years. His loathing for them even went as far as refusing to make eye contact with them whenever both acts were present at the Opry. The NET documentary crew captured the very first performance between the two men (with their respective bands), which visually chronicled the end of their long-standing rivalry, as confirmed by Gary Scruggs:

> I visited the Grand Ole Opry at the Ryman Auditorium fairly often in the latter years of the Flatt and Scruggs partnership. I spent most of the time backstage in the area where the dressing rooms were located or standing in the wings offstage. I witnessed firsthand how Bill

Monroe totally ignored Lester and Dad, even to the point of avoiding eye contact if they were nearby.

The Revue made its first appearance on the Grand Ole Opry several weeks after Flatt and Scruggs had split up in February of 1969. I was shocked when Bill came up to us with a big smile on his face, welcoming Dad back to the Opry. I later noticed he was just as friendly to Lester after the Flatt and Scruggs split. So there was no real "reconciliation"—at least there was no mention of any past animosity that I know of. Rather, Bill's mood and attitude just changed out of the blue when Flatt and Scruggs split up. It was as if there had never been any grudge or ill will at all.

Other aspects of the television production included a trip near to Earl's birthplace in North Carolina, where Scruggs reunited with family. Audiences witnessed him in action with his brothers Horace and Junie in a rendition of "Cripple Creek" (Junie on the banjo with Horace, Earl, and Randy on acoustic guitars). The Morris Brothers, Zeke and Wiley, whom Scruggs affectionately respected and performed with on WSPA in Spartanburg, South Carolina, back in 1939 at the age of fifteen, are introduced in a jam session with Earl and Randy. Viewers were also taken to the homes of Doc Watson and Joan Baez, two of Earl's favorite songwriting musicians whom he absolutely adored, for picking sets, along with his sons. Spectators followed Randy Scruggs to Madison High School and were welcomed inside the Scruggs family's modest home for a sampling of Earl's cover version of the Beatles' song "With a Little Help from My Friends," on his then upcoming instrumental LP *Nashville's Rock*.

And yet, with all of this attention bestowed upon Earl Scruggs for the NET television audience, the banjo man, in all of his humility, found ways through his musical genius to deflect the honor away from himself, as articulated by David Hoffman:

> Earl liked what was happening in contemporary social cause[s] [and in] new music. He was interested in great talent, whether it be famous or not famous. If you watch him in any single scene, he is doing his best to listen to the other musicians and to play into and support what they're trying to do—not to be his own man, stand out and stick out, you know, but to play into the other guy's music and enhance it. He wasn't driven by ego. He was driven by great music.

Not long after the NET special aired, Hoffman directed two documentary shorts for Mobil Oil: *Spike: A Montana Horseman* and *Travelin' Men*. Both were produced with a little help from the Earl Scruggs Revue on the music tracks.

THE REVUE'S SHOWS AND REVIEWS

With the success of *Earl Scruggs: His Family and Friends* to jumpstart Earl's new musical direction, the 1970s proved to be a banner decade for his new family-centered band. It was an era packed with memorable live performances, innovative albums, film-worthy events, and national television appearances. Flanked by the youth of his sons, forty-six-year-old Scruggs Sr. was attracting a younger crowd of college-age kids at a time when many entertainers his age were frowned upon by youngsters, who saw them as their "parents' music." The hard-driving sound of the Earl Scruggs Revue shattered that stigma and paved the way for Earl to be relevant among a new breed of fans half his age. Gary Scruggs details a number of key venues for the Revue that had a profound impact on Earl's reinvention of himself:

> We performed in Carnegie Hall in New York City and in Wembley Arena in London, England. We played on the Grand Ole Opry in the early years of the Revue. In the Revue's early years, we performed in several nationally known music clubs, including the Troubadour in Los Angeles, the Cellar Door in the Georgetown area of Washington, DC, and the Great Southeast Music Hall in Atlanta. There were also the Lone Star Café in New York City, the Quiet Knight in Chicago, and the Great American Music Hall in San Francisco. We appeared on many music festivals—both rock festivals and bluegrass festivals, even though we were never truly a rock band or truly a bluegrass band. We played on many college campuses, big and small. It seems like it was during the 1970s that big-city "street fairs" started happening, and we were booked on quite a few of them. Outside of the USA, we performed in several provinces in Canada, as well as Bermuda and England.
>
> As for television, we performed on NBC's *Midnight Special* two times, once on a show featuring country music that was cohosted by Loretta Lynn and Marty Robbins, and once on a show featuring rock and blues music, hosted by Ray Charles. Radio legend Wolfman Jack

was the show's announcer. We played on Phil Donahue's show when it was based in Dayton, Ohio. We performed on several Country Music Association's network shows. We also did the PBS show *Austin City Limits*. We did NBC's *The Today Show* in, I think, 1971 or 1972, when the late Frank McGee anchored the show. We did *The Tommy Hunter Show* in Canada and shown on the CBC network. There were other TV shows, including Nashville-produced programs, but I don't remember the names of them all.

Along with the many clubs, college campuses, festivals, and television shows the Revue played, they also found themselves in harmonious alignment with a number of artists appealing to the youth crowd, as Jody Maphis elaborates:

> The young kids really took to Earl, and I don't know exactly what the magic was, but they loved him. It was just a great time. All of a sudden it just started, like we'd be on the road and then we'd be doing four or five dates with the Doobie Brothers, or we'd be out with the [Nitty Gritty] Dirt Band, or doing stuff with the Byrds, or doing these big rock festivals. It was just amazing. You never knew what—I mean, we did a little short tour opening for Steppenwolf, and we even did some gigs with Edgar Winter and the James Gang. We did a little short tour with Three Dog Night. We did a lot of stuff with Linda Ronstadt, the Eagles, and of course Charlie Daniels. We played Central Park several times with, like, Emmylou [Harris] and Asleep at the Wheel. We did Willie Nelson's first Dripping Springs Reunion [in March 1972]. Everyone wanted Earl. He had that kind of appeal.

In the town of Manhattan, Kansas, just northwest of Topeka, is the campus of Kansas State University, the site of two milestones in the Earl Scruggs Revue's portfolio. In March 1972, Columbia recorded and later released *Live at Kansas State*, the band's first concert album, featuring a diverse range of songs that covered almost every musical genre. Not only were old tunes like "Bugle Call Rag," "Sally Goodin," and "Foggy Mountain Breakdown" revamped for the college crowd; the Revue proved just how much they could jive with Earl's "Carolina Boogie" before getting down deep in the blues with "Everybody Wants to Go to Heaven."

Their performance was a big enough hit that the university invited them back to the campus for an Earl Scruggs tribute concert the following January, to be filmed by Michael C. Vorhol and Richard Abramson. The event included performances from Joan Baez, the Byrds (just prior to their disbanding), the Nitty Gritty Dirt Band, Ramblin' Jack Elliot, Doc and Merle Watson, Tracy Nelson and Mother Earth, David Bromberg, and the Earl Scruggs Revue. Intercut with interviewed segments of the performing artists, the concert made its movie premiere two years later in 1975 as *Banjoman* at the Kennedy Center in Washington, DC, although it would be another two years before the soundtrack LP from Sire Records made its way to store shelves.[3] Country music artist Vince Gill was just getting his feet wet when he first crossed paths with the Earl Scruggs Revue and vouches for the generous compassion the senior Scruggs had for numerous beginners seeking guidance:

> I started learning to play mandolin, I started to learn banjo and trying to play fiddle and all the stuff on guitar and Dobro. I started playing in all the bluegrass bands. But, I think, at eighteen probably, eighteen years old, I [ran] into Earl and Randy and Gary and all those guys when they had the Revue going in the midseventies, and we were playing a lot of the same festivals, so we got to be friends all those years ago. I loved how welcoming [Earl] was to all musicians— the person that he was, and how kind he was to all the young musicians that were obviously going to start tripping around his feet and admire him and love him like we all do and did. I think when you're a young person, and someone you admire is kind to you, I don't think you ever forget it for your whole life. That's what I saw in Earl every time a young turk would come sniffing around. He was always, always welcoming. You'd be hard pressed to find a kinder guy than Earl.

For all of the adulation Scruggs was receiving with his new band, there was a large group of fans who felt abandoned by the banjo man and were not so quick to embrace the musical change that came with the Earl Scruggs Revue. Jody Maphis reveals the disgruntled feelings among steadfast bluegrass music fanatics:

> The purist bluegrass people, they weren't real pleased with us at all. Especially with me playing the drums and Earl when he went electric. Oh my goodness, they hated that. But, I mean, for the most part,

a lot of the other bluegrass [people], they saw that it was opening the door for everybody. Everybody was getting to participate a little bit more, but there were some that just didn't want to go through the door. It was a touchy time 'cause there were some people like [from the magazine] *Bluegrass Unlimited*, when an album came out, oh they'd crucify us. Earl was taking it. I think he understood it, but it was, like, he thought it was pretty silly.

Banjoist and *Bluegrass Today* host Doug Hutchens corroborates the sentiment voiced by bluegrass fundamentalists:

They were getting so much bad press—there wasn't that many bluegrass periodicals, but he and the boys weren't that popular with the hardcore bluegrass people. So much of the time, it didn't go over that well with the audience because people were coming expecting to hear Lester Flatt and Earl Scruggs. Even though it was called the Earl Scruggs Revue, he came out with his banjo with a pickup in it.

The installation of an electric pickup on Earl's banjo that stirred so much controversy among bluegrass fans was completely misunderstood, as Gary Scruggs clarifies:

He added it in the early 1970s with the Revue. Why? We had drums, electric bass, and on some songs, Randy would switch from acoustic to electric guitar—our concerts were high energy, and there were times when we were fairly loud and performing on large stages. Dad installed a pickup so that he could plug into an electric guitar amplifier placed behind him in order to better hear his banjo onstage—feedback from an acoustic instrument, especially in that era, could easily become an issue if front-of-mic monitors are relied upon on a loud stage in a large venue. Many bluegrass "purists" complained that "Earl has gone electric," but what they didn't realize or understand was that what the audience always heard was his banjo being played into a microphone, not the guitar amplifier sound we heard onstage.

Perhaps one of the most agile attributes to Earl's musicianship that was passed along to his sons and their band was the ability to record entire albums in short blocks of time, a practice that was becoming less common as pop LPs were beginning to take months to record. Much of it had to do with their readiness prior to entering the studio. A lot of their arrangements were worked out on the road in front of audiences, as every song required a lead break from someone in the band. The more they experimented on the road, the more organized they were in the studio. Much of the material recorded was songs they played live, so they'd be ready when the engineer rolled tape.

They did their homework for the studio, unlike groups that would record brand-new songs, never played nor rehearsed, causing them to spend long hours and days recording—one song. "You didn't go out and just waste a lot of studio time," says Jody Maphis. "You go in there and do the best you can and knock it out. And also, you start losing the magic of it doing it over and over and over. We knew to catch the first couple of takes." Gary Scruggs further comments:

> Typically it took a few or sometimes several three-hour sessions to record a studio album, depending on how much overdubbing we did after the tracking. Additional time would be needed to mix the sound. A couple of live albums only took an hour or so to record, but then additional time was needed to mix them. We recorded an instrumental album, titled *Dueling Banjos*, in one day, doing so during two three-hour sessions.

It was on March 9, 1973, when the Revue capitalized on the popularity of "Dueling Banjos" with their own version, along with an all-instrumental collection of new material and a revitalization of oldies. In addition to Earl and Randy's banjo/guitar duel, the band picked their original country-styled "String Bender" and a rearranged version of an old fiddle tune, "Black Mountain Blues," along with their progressive banjo-fiddle-based "Peking Fling." Among the old catalog of Flatt and Scruggs tunes, "Reuben" (revamped and retitled "Lonesome Ruben") and "Fireball Mail" were, without doubt, the most radically transformed from their previous versions on *Foggy Mountain Banjo*. Both are played in a combination of jazz and blues, hence reflecting the musical revival Scruggs wanted to achieve with bluegrass tunes from a decade earlier.

WILL THE CIRCLE BE UNBROKEN

Unquestionably, one of the most innovative musical productions assembled on vinyl is the Nitty Gritty Dirt Band's epic album from 1972, *Will the Circle Be Unbroken.* And at the epicenter of this phenomenon in country music was Earl Scruggs. At the dawn of the seventies, the Dirt Band released their *Uncle Charlie* LP, which scored a top-ten single for them, "Mr. Bojangles," a cover version of Jerry Jeff Walker's 1968 ballad, backed with their rendition of Earl's "Randy Lynn Rag."

While still making a name for themselves, the Dirt Band captured the attention of Gary Scruggs during his senior year at Vanderbilt University. Near the end of his fall semester in 1970, the group held a concert at the university that sparked a relationship between themselves and the Scruggs family, which led to the production of their musical masterpiece. Gary Scruggs provides an in-depth account of *Circle*'s evolution:

> I invited Mom and Dad to go with me to the concert, and with the help of a Vanderbilt dean of students, I arranged a meeting beforehand with the Nitty Gritty Dirt Band in the dressing room before the concert. We had a fun visit, and we also got together with the band in their dressing room following the concert. We quickly became friends and ended up working several concerts and festivals together over the years.
>
> In June of 1971, the Earl Scruggs Revue played for a week at a music club in Boulder, Colorado, called Tulagi's. Most of the Nitty Gritty Dirt Band members lived in Colorado at that time, and John McEuen, the multi-instrumentalist who played mostly five-string banjo and fiddle in the [band], didn't live all that far from Boulder. He came to see us just about every night. He would come back with us to the motel in which we were staying after the shows, and there would be jam sessions well past the wee hours of the morning. John asked Dad if he would consider recording with the Dirt Band. Dad said yes and returned the invitation for the Nitty Gritty Dirt Band to record on his next album, and the Dirt Band agreed.
>
> For the original *Will the Circle Be Unbroken* album, the Nitty Gritty Dirt Band came up with the idea to record with older country music artists they were fans of. The Dirt Band asked Dad to help with inviting some of the artists because they had never met some of those artists. Dad was particularly helpful in getting Roy Acuff, Maybelle Carter, and Jimmy Martin involved. The Dirt Band also asked Dad to recommend some musicians for further support on certain instruments—Dad helped in getting Vassar Clements on fiddle, Roy "Junior" Huskey on upright bass, and Norman Blake on Dobro guitar

booked on the sessions. Randy and I also appeared on several tracks of the three-record set.

The album was recorded in the summer of 1971 and was significant for a number of reasons, including [that] it merged what was considered to be a pop or rock act, the Nitty Gritty Dirt Band, with traditional country music artists. It involved younger artists performing with older artists at a time when there was much discussion, concern, and debate over the so-called generation gap. It was also a triple-disc album, which was very unusual in country music, if not unprecedented. All in all, I think it's fair to say that it was the first of its kind, at least the first I know of.

Not to be left out, the rest of the Scruggs family, Louise and Steve, were invited to be a part of the large chorus assembled to sing background vocals on the title track. Two more *Circle* volumes arose from the Dirt Band, both produced in participation with Earl Scruggs: one in 1989 and the other in 2002. As part of the thirtieth anniversary of *Circle*'s original release, PBS aired a concert special called *Will the Circle Be Unbroken, Farther Along*, in which Earl and Randy Scruggs, Vassar Clements, and Jerry Douglas (on Dobro) appeared onstage with the Nitty Gritty Dirt Band for a rendition of "Earl's Breakdown" that went on to win a Grammy for all the artists in 2005 for Best Country Instrumental Performance.[4]

WHERE THE LILIES BLOOM

Based on the novel of the same name by Vera and Bill Cleaver, *Where the Lilies Bloom* was a low-budget feature film written for the screen by the creator of *The Waltons*, Earl Hamner Jr., produced by Robert B. Radnitz, and directed by William A. Graham. Shot on location in Watauga County, North Carolina, the movie depicts the heartfelt courage of four backwoods children (three girls and a boy) determined to stay together as a family following the death of their widower father, who struggled to make a living as a sharecropper on a primitive farm at the foot of the Great Smoky Mountains.[5] While much of the onscreen talent recruited for the production was picked from a crop of local actors in the Appalachians, the services for the soundtrack were rendered straight from the Scruggs Talent Agency outside of Nashville, as Gary Scruggs recalls:

> The film's producer, Robert B. Radnitz, invited Dad to do the soundtrack. Radnitz brought the raw and unfinished film to Nashville. Dad, Mom, and Revue members viewed it in a rented movie theater in downtown Nashville. Not long after the viewing, we recorded the soundtrack in a studio in Los Angeles. The studio had a large screen and we watched the action on the screen as we recorded the music.

Along with the United Artists theatrical release of the film in 1974, Columbia issued the *Where the Lilies Bloom* soundtrack album, headlined by the Earl Scruggs Revue. A single of the title track (backed with Randy and Earl's original "All My Trials") was also cut under the Revue's name, featuring the high-pitched lonesome vocal of Barbara Mauritz, who wrote the song, which is heard during the movie's opening credits. Interestingly, the small black-and-white image of the Revue appearing on the album jacket's front cover was a photo taken by Nashville photographer Wilmer "Slick" Lawson that is similar to the photo used on the cover of the band's 1973 self-titled LP *The Earl Scruggs Revue*. In that still on the *Lilies* cover, Earl is surrounded by Revue members Josh Graves, Randy Scruggs, Gary Scruggs, Jody Maphis, and fifteen-year-old Steve Scruggs. The photograph misrepresents Steve's participation, as he didn't play on any of the *Lilies* tracks, while Vassar Clements, who was part of that project, is not pictured at all.

Where the Lilies Bloom was the second theatrical feature to showcase instrumental compositions by Earl Scruggs, such as "Stash It," which fit perfectly into the mountain ambience of the movie, as did an updated version of his classic "Flint Hill Special." It's also the first (and only) motion picture to be scored by the Revue.

ANNIVERSARY SPECIAL

More than a year after the Revue's *Rockin' 'Cross the Country* landed on store shelves, producer Bob Johnston collaborated with the Scruggs family in the early fall of 1975 to create a celebratory two-volume *Anniversary Special* album honoring Earl's twenty-fifth year with Columbia

Records. The records highlight the talents of Earl and the Revue with an array of guest artists and their respective songs.

Some of the guest artists, like Joan Baez, Charlie Daniels, Tracy Nelson, Roger McGuinn, and Johnny Cash, were already established fixtures in the Scruggs camp, while others, such as piano man Billy Joel and the rhythm and blues trio the Pointer Sisters, came from a talent pool of rising stars and studio musicians assembled by Johnston, with some help from guest vocalist Don Nix. Two of the coveted musicians who participated in the sessions at Nashville's Quadrafonic Studios were keyboardist L. Leon Pendarvis, the future music director and conductor for the *Saturday Night Live* band, and drummer Willie Hall, who went on to play for such performers as Isaac Hayes and the Blues Brothers. Unlike most of the other guests, who came from genres that had Nashville ties, both men were rooted in rhythm and blues. Pendarvis tells of his experience as part of that unique compilation:

> I was brought there because of Bob Johnston, who produced it. For about a couple of years or so, I was kind of like one of Bob's guys, so to speak. So when that project came up, he thought I would be suited for it; so that was my first Nashville recording. I was doing studio recording in New York, which is, I think, how Bob and I met, but I had never done any recording in Nashville. It certainly was an album that I was proud to be a part of—certainly because of who Earl was. He was just a legend. And also, it was somewhat novel for me, because of the nature of the kind of record that it was, considering that most of what I was doing in New York was in the pop or R& B vein. So it was different in that regard and a learning experience in that regard too. That album was kind of, for lack of a better word to put it, an all-star cast of folks. It didn't feel like your typical studio record. So it was kind of unique in that regard.
>
> Willie and I were the only [instrumental] players of color that I recall, at least, on that project. In some respects, I didn't pay a lot of attention to that, but I did pay attention to it because it's kind of hard not to. And you know, it meant nothing in terms of what the rapport was like with the players there because musicians, the way I look at it, is we tend to transcend that stuff. There's kind of a camaraderie and kind of this unspoken bond that musicians have, and that's a lot of what I felt, you know, being like the outsider in a way.

Willie Hall revisits his invitation to play on the record along with his discovery of Earl's musical diversity:

> The way I became involved: a friend of mine, Don Nix, who's a noted guitarist and songwriter, who was actually a friend of George Harrison of the Beatles—Don and I are old friends, and Bob Johnston, who was the producer on that session, he wanted to change musicians, you know, he wanted a variety of different musicians on that particular session. And at that time, my reputation was pretty hot as an R&B player—and Don came to me and asked me if I wanted to do a session with Earl Scruggs. And we both laughed about it because it was so far-fetched from the Stax Studios—the R&B stuff. So, naturally, I agreed. I thought it would be a great privilege to be a part of that. So Don and I flew up to Nashville, and there were a host of musicians involved in that—some real great players.
>
> One thing that impressed me about Earl Scruggs: the musicians in between takes or on a lunch break, everybody would just get in the studio and start jamming. And Earl was the first banjo player that I ever heard play the blues on the banjo. I thought that was so impressive, man, so he gained my total respect from that point. It was so impressive to hear him actually bend notes on the banjo. Most of the blues consist of a lot of single notes, but you know, some of the guys had tendencies to bend their notes, and Earl really impressed me with that, man. I didn't know many banjo players at that time, but hearing him do that, it just blew us away, man.

On the morning of Monday, September 29, 1975, as Bob Johnston and company were assembled in the studio listening to playbacks, they received startling news that Earl Scruggs had suffered injuries from an airplane crash the night before. While flying his single-engine Cessna 172 into Nashville's Cornelia Fort Airpark after operating hours, Scruggs encountered dense fog that caused him to overshoot the runway. His landing gear clipped a fence that flipped the small aircraft upside down in a nearby soybean field. With fractures to his left wrist, left ankle, and nose, he was stranded within the wreckage until sunrise.[6] Earl's niece, Grace Constant, depicts how the family searched for and rescued him:

> One night I received a late phone call from Gary. Uncle Earl had driven his car to the airport. Uncle Earl was flying his plane to a

[Revue] show out of town, then returning to Nashville. When it was apparent Uncle Earl was late getting back home, Aunt Louise and Gary went to the airport to look for him, but Uncle Earl wasn't there. My son, Jeffrey Davis, and I got up and dressed, and I drove as fast as I could to Cornelia Fort Airpark. We got out of the car and ran down the runway calling for him and finally heard someone faintly calling for help. I knew that was my Uncle Earl's voice. I took off to call Gary so he could get help. We didn't have cell phones [back then], and it was so dark that you could not see anything without lights.

Scruggs spent the next few months recovering from the crash, which eerily occurred four days shy of the date of his horrific car accident twenty years earlier. During his recuperation, the first volume of the *Anniversary Special* was released before the end of 1975. Willie Hall relives the thrill of it all:

When the product was released, man, I was really surprised to see the list of people that participated, because a studio musician, usually he'll come in and they work hard on the basic tracks. And once those are finished, you know, they usually go on back to their regular life. So I was only there for the recording of the basic tracks. But then when the product came out and I got to see all the people that were involved—all the background people and different musicians that would come in to do overdubs and stuff like that—I was really pleased with the product. I tell a lot of people that I speak with, you know, they ask me about my accomplishments in the music field and I say one of my most cherished accomplishments was the Earl Scruggs project. Because of the fact that, you know, growing up as a child in Florida, I was an avid fan of *The Beverly Hillbillies*. I thought that kind of comedy was new, and it was so funny at that time, man— and that theme just sticks in your head, you know. So I grew up memorizing and humming that theme for years, and then to actually meet this man, and to be a part of one of his projects, and for that project to make such an indentation, I cherish it as one of my most memorable participations in a recording.

The *Anniversary Special*'s second installment hit the streets in 1976 under the title *The Earl Scruggs Revue Volume II*. America's bicentennial year also brought the release of *Family Portrait*, a country rock production that heavily spotlighted the talents of Gary, Randy, and

Steve, with Earl mainly backing them up. And while their studio recordings were changing, they continued to perform much of their noted material on the road, as captured on *Live from Austin City Limits*. Only four more albums awaited the Revue in between booking dates during its latter few years: *Strike Anywhere* (1977), *Bold and New* (1978), *Today and Forever* (1979), and *Country Comfort* (1980).

A DYING MAN'S REQUEST

In the spring of 1979, Earl's former partner, Lester Flatt, was in need of hospitalization due to chronic cardiac problems that dated back to a heart attack he endured twelve years earlier. This would be Lester's final trip to the infirmary, as the severity of his illness was too great for him to overcome. Understanding that he may never see his old friend again, through the urging of Marty Stuart (who was their mutual friend and member of Flatt's Nashville Grass at the time), Scruggs went to the hospital and he spent more than an hour visiting the deteriorating Flatt.[7] In his 1989 radio interview on *Bluegrass Today*, Earl responded to his dying bandmate's special request:

> I went to see Lester—I don't know how many days it was before he passed away, but he was really in bad shape; he was in the Baptist Hospital here in Nashville. And he could hardly talk loud enough for me to tell what he was saying. And he wanted to know if we could play some dates together—some reunion dates together. And my answer immediately was, I said, "Lester, number one: I want you to get well. Number two: yes, we'll play dates together when you get well. But my biggest concern now is for you to get more strength and get to feeling better, then we'll talk about doing a reunion." So that was kind of the way it was left.

Soon afterward, on May 11, 1979, Lester Raymond Flatt, one of the pioneers of bluegrass music and cofounder with Scruggs of the legendary Foggy Mountain Boys, passed away at the age of sixty-four, just over a month short of his sixty-fifth birthday. In 2003, Earl spoke endearingly about his relationship with Lester on NPR's *Fresh Air* with Terry Gross. "Though he's been dead for several years, I still have a warm spot in my heart and cherish the days we worked and traveled together."

THE REVUE COMES TO A CLOSE

Shortly after the passing of Lester Flatt, Earl summed up his future plans in an interview with Tim Timberlake on May 19, 1979, in Lanexa, Virginia:

> I don't have any thought of retiring. I have cut back. I used to travel seven days a week, and I just don't want to do that anymore because I'm enjoying grandchildren and my own children and family. I want to still stay in the business but, you know, not at a hard pace like I used to—but my health, thank goodness, is still good and as long as it is, and I love music, so I'd like to stay with it as long as I can.

By the early spring of 1980, Earl's recurring back pains were reaching an all-time high in frequency and complications. Traveling became increasingly difficult for the banjo man, who at only fifty-six years old was still in the prime of his life. But while the patriarch of the Scruggs family was battling health issues, Randy was eager to launch a production company he founded through his investment in a recording studio (which later included a partnership with his brother Steve). That September, the Earl Scruggs Revue played their last show in a North Carolina city street festival.

After eleven years of riveting performances, the family troupe that was voted the number one musical act among colleges consecutively for two years officially disbanded.[8] Though Earl Scruggs performed and recorded under his own name in the coming decades, sons Gary and Randy continued to be a presence by his side, keeping the spirit of their father's Revue alive for the rest of his days. In retrospect, Jody Maphis conveys the essence of Earl's leadership through this transitionally gratifying juncture of his career:

> He took some stands on things at a time when it wasn't popular to take those stands—and he was the same way with his music. If it was something he believed in, he was a hundred percent behind it, and it was going to be out there. He never held anybody back, especially

with the music, and he defended everything that we did, which I find very admirable 'cause he believed in what we were doing. He let us all grow musically in the process, and that's something that I'll cherish forever.

7

EARL, EARL, EARL

I learned to play the banjo a little bit. Obviously, all of us that ever picked one up, we go straight to the source, and everybody tries to play like Earl. I mean, that's pretty profound actually—hands down, the largest majority of all people who play that instrument are going to be pointed to and defined by Earl.
—Vince Gill, country music artist

SCRUGGS AND COMPANY

After the breakup of the Earl Scruggs Revue in September 1980, Earl entered into a long period of semiretirement. The serious back pains that were plaguing him thwarted any chance of maintaining a full schedule of tour dates. Though he may not have had the health to sustain extensive travel, he did have the desire to continue performing and recording on a part-time, at-will basis. The first project to emerge came about as a friendly offer from Scruggs's pal Tom T. Hall, who remembers the circumstances that led to the Columbia release of *The Storyteller and the Banjo Man* in early 1982:

> I had a recording contract with Mercury Records, and my manager came to me and jokingly said, "You're going to be out of a recording contract for a while," and I said, "What happened?" He said, "I'm negotiating with the record company, and it'll be about a month

before we get the negotiations wrapped up, so right now, you're not on a recording label"—and he was sort of laughing about it.

But I had an idea. I had been working with Lester and Earl on all these songs all these years, and for some strange reason I picked up the telephone and called Earl. I said, "Earl, I've got an idea." I said, "I'm in between recording contracts and I'm not signed with anybody right now," and I said, "Why don't you and I get together and do an album together?" It was quiet on the phone for a minute, and he said, "Tom T., the hair is standing up on my arms," and I thought that was a great compliment, and I said, "Well, let's get it done." I knew Louise was running the show. I said, "See what Louise thinks."

So they called me back and said Randy Scruggs was a producer at that time and was producing some nice things, so Randy Scruggs produced the album, and we went into the studio and we recorded it, and we had a great time. We had success with it, and it sold some albums. I didn't collaborate with Earl on any more projects other than that, but Louise had called me up and wanted us to go on tour together, but, you know, I had a manager and a booking agent, and I had a full-load schedule of tours, but I'd like to brag and say that I did.

Out of the album came the singles "Song of the South" and "There Ain't No Country Music on This Juke Box." Even though both 45-rpm labels note that the songs were taken from the Columbia LP *The Storyteller and the Banjo Man*, the word "banjo" is misspelled in capital letters on "Song of the South" as "BANGO." The tone of the album signaled a less electrifying progressive sound than that of Earl's Revue days. His return to more traditional country arrangements was announced publically by Associated Press writer Joe Edwards in an article on August 20 of that year.

By autumn of 1982, Earl temporarily traded his suit and tie for a pair of denim overalls in Kornfield Kounty to make a surprise appearance on the long-running country music variety series *Hee Haw*. Without any fanfare, Scruggs participated, briefly, in two episodes as part of the Real Hillbilly Band. The popular syndicated program was taped behind the Grand Ole Opry stage at the Opryland Complex in Studio A, then produced in segmented pieces that were later assembled into a season's worth of episodes. *Hee Haw*'s producer, Sam Lovullo, explains Earl's unannounced presence:

One thing that made this show was that it was an impromptu show. In other words, things happened suddenly. And Marty Stuart, that day, was in the back room of the Grand Ole Opry visiting with Roy Clark. He was not listed as a guest, and so the bottom line is that, I have recollection now, that Earl Scruggs was there [too]. Roy Clark—and this is something very exciting which was the way *Hee Haw* was done—Roy Clark said, "Let's go out there and put these guys together and do something." And that's the way this event came about.

Earl kicks off the opening lick for their vocal rendition of "I Like Mountain Music" and then plays a break in the instrumental "Soldier's Joy." In a star-studded lineup, Scruggs is visible at the far left top of a riser with Marty Stuart on mandolin, Roy Clark on Dobro, and Opry upright bassist Billy Lineman, all standing behind front-row fiddlers Byron Berline, Roy Acuff, and John Hartford, with flattop guitarist Norman Blake. *Hee Haw* cohost and country music star Roy Clark elaborates on the band's arrangement:

> We had all those great musicians, and all of them, maybe, never had a chance to play together before. They had Earl playing banjo, of course, and they put me on a Dobro. And Earl said, "Can you really play that thing?" I said, "I'll only know when we get through." I never played that much Dobro, but I wasn't about to play banjo in front of Earl [laughs]. All I had to do was turn around and look at whoever was there and point to have them do it. I was like the leader of the band, only because they wanted to know where to aim the camera.

Keeping his collaborative momentum going with guest artists, Scruggs recorded *Top of the World* in 1983. With Rodney Dillard, Ricky Skaggs, Lacy J. Dalton, and the Burrito Brothers in the mix, the record would be the second of Earl's to be produced by his middle son, Randy, along with John Thompson. Scruggs brothers Gary and Steve also contributed their talents, Gary with background vocals and Steve as assistant engineer. Another single for Earl was cut from this album, "Sittin' on Top of the World," featuring Dillard's vocals.

In 1984, Scruggs composed the cheerful-sounding "American Made—World Played," which became the title track for his final LP with Columbia. The album's outcome was similar to his first post–Flatt and Scruggs project, *Nashville's Rock*, in that it primarily contained instrumental cover versions of recent popular tunes, only this time it favored some of country music's hit songs. And after thirty-four success- ful years with Columbia Records, Earl Scruggs remained silent for the next seventeen years before returning to the recording studio to appear on a brand-new medium—compact disc.

During this long break from recording, Earl and Louise Scruggs suffered their greatest loss as their youngest son, Steve, and his wife, Elizabeth, died tragically in their home on September 23, 1992. The shock of losing his son at thirty-four years of age sent Earl into a mourn- ing period where he didn't pick a single note on his beloved five- stringed instrument for eight consecutive months.[1] The healing for him, musically, didn't begin until his dear friend John Hartford stopped by with his fiddle offering to "pick." The invitation helped to close the wound in his heart as Earl slowly began to play again that night.[2]

A little more than a year later, after he rejuvenated his banjo, Scruggs received a request to participate on Byron Berline's forthcom- ing album. The longstanding rift that existed between Flatt and Scruggs and Monroe (which started in 1948 and worsened in 1955) was clearly over when Flatt and Scruggs split up in 1969, as demonstrated by their willingness to share the stage at various shows. Yet it had been decades since the public heard them together on a recording. Berline describes his success in the studio homecoming for the two biggest names in bluegrass:

> In 1994, I asked Earl to play on my album *Fiddle and a Song*, and he said he would, and then I asked Bill Monroe if he would play on it, and he said he would as well. So I got the both of them in the studio at the same time. That was the first time they'd been in the studio together since the forties. [We] told Earl that Bill was going to be there, and Bill that Earl was going to be playing as well, and they didn't seem to mind. I filmed the whole thing—I had my nephew film it—and I still have it. I haven't put any of that footage out, and of course the Nashville Network heard about it, and they came down and filmed some of it too.

Two years later, while in the hospital for back surgery, Scruggs took an unexpected turn that nearly claimed his life. "In September of 1996 he was hospitalized in hopes of getting his back problems solved," says Gary Scruggs. "The back surgery turned out to be successful, but, while in the recovery room, he had a heart attack. It was found that he needed a quintuple bypass. It took a while to recover, but after a year or so, he felt a hundred percent better than before the heart attack."

Upon full recovery from his near-fatal encounter, Earl was energized enough to make a musical comeback. At the age of seventy-four, he assembled a new band that included his sons Gary and Randy along with a rotating ensemble of friends. Gary Scruggs illustrates some of the highlights from this new chapter in his father's career:

> In 1998, he started touring a little, now and then, with his Family & Friends band. I was always a part of it and felt very grateful and excited over the next several years to be performing with him again. We didn't tour full-time, just occasional dates, so the band's personnel varied, depending on which musicians were available at any given time.
>
> Over the next thirteen years or so, Earl Scruggs with Family & Friends performed at several major music festivals, including Warren Hellman's Hardly Strictly Bluegrass Festival in San Francisco, California; the Stagecoach Festival in Indio, California; MerleFest in Wilkesboro, North Carolina; the Newport Folk Festival in Newport, Rhode Island; the Telluride Bluegrass Festival in Telluride, Colorado; the Huck Finn Music Jubilee in Ontario, California; the Bonnaroo Music and Arts Festival in Manchester, Tennessee; the Calgary Folk Music Festival in Calgary, Alberta; the Winnipeg Folk Music Festival in Winnipeg, Manitoba; the Vancouver Island MusicFest in Courtenay, British Columbia; and the Johnny Keenen Banjo Festival in Longford, Ireland.
>
> Other highlights included performing at the Country Music Hall of Fame and Museum in Nashville, Tennessee; the Kennedy Center in Washington, DC; the Ryman Auditorium in Nashville, Tennessee, and playing some co-billed concerts with friends such as Steve Martin, the Nitty Gritty Dirt Band, and Charlie Daniels. We also performed at a couple of well-known music clubs, B.B. King's Blues Club in New York and the Birchmere in Alexandria, Virginia. Dad appeared as a guest on recordings or live performances with several other artists, including Dwight Yoakam, Patty Loveless, the Chieftains, Béla Fleck, Loretta Lynn, Marty Stuart, Tony Trischka, and the Dixie Chicks.
>
> In 2001, a CD titled *Earl Scruggs and Friends* was released on MCA Records. There were several guest artists involved with that album, including Elton John, Sting, Johnny Cash, John Fogarty,

Steve Martin, Travis Tritt, Vince Gill, and Billy Bob Thornton, to name just a few. "Foggy Mountain Breakdown" was re-recorded for that MCA album. Featured performers were Earl Scruggs on banjo, Glen Duncan on fiddle, Randy Scruggs on acoustic guitar, Steve Martin picking the second banjo break, Vince Gill on the first electric guitar break, Marty Stuart on mandolin, myself on harmonica, Albert Lee playing the second electric guitar break, Paul Shaffer playing piano, Jerry Douglas on Dobro, and Leon Russell on organ. A video of us playing along with the recorded track was released and went to the number four spot on the CMT cable channel video chart. In 2002, the featured performers all won Grammy Awards in the Best Country Instrumental Performance category.

Dad made television appearances on *The Tonight Show with Jay Leno* and *The Late Show with David Letterman*. Earl Scruggs with Family & Friends [also] appeared on a PBS special, *All-Star Bluegrass Celebration*.

And tuning in to Earl's first late-night spot from November 2001 was Paul Henning's authorized *Beverly Hillbillies* biographer, Stephen Cox, who recalls the excitement of the banjo man's revival:

The most impressive thing I've ever seen on David Letterman was the night that Earl was on there with about eight other guys, and they all played. And of course they were plugging the new CD. But, holy mackerel, when they played "Foggy Mountain Breakdown," and you have all those guys, including Paul Shaffer and Steve Martin and the rest, playing that thing—one of the best things I've ever seen on David Letterman in all those years there. It was quite amazing. It was just a sight. It was historic on that show. That was some good television right there.

According to Steve Martin, performing "Foggy Mountain Breakdown" on the late-night program was the result of a subtle admission by Earl: "I remember when we were going to do the Letterman show, everybody thought [since] 'Foggy Mountain Breakdown' is played so much, we shouldn't do that, let's do something else. They asked Earl and he said, 'Well, I think you should always go out there with your best.' And that's why we ended up doing 'Foggy Mountain Breakdown.'"

Shortly after his return to television, Earl Scruggs made a cameo appearance, with his son Randy, in the heartwarming motion picture

Changing Hearts, released in April 2002. Based on the award-winning play *Colored Eggs* by Daniel Wright, the screen adaptation's star, Faye Dunaway, personally requested Scruggs as a wedding musician for her matrimonial scene with costar Tom Skerritt.[3] This would be the second time that Earl had a presence in a feature film with Dunaway—the other, of course, being *Bonnie and Clyde* (1967).

In late July 2003, PBS's long-running *Great Performances* series aired an epic concert hall production that was a countrified spin-off from the international operatic sensation the Three Tenors. Gary Scruggs discusses the televised event:

> Earl Scruggs performed a live concert billed as "The Three Pickers" that featured him along with the great guitar player from Deep Gap, North Carolina, Doc Watson, and bluegrass artist Ricky Skaggs. Alison Krauss also took part as special guest, playing her fiddle and singing harmony on a few of the songs. The concert was held in Winston-Salem, North Carolina, and was recorded for CD and DVD release on Rounder Records. The CD and DVD were released in 2003.
>
> Before the Three Pickers united to pick and sing for the bulk of the concert, Earl was joined by his Family & Friends band for a couple of songs; Ricky was likewise joined by his band, Kentucky Thunder, and Doc performed a couple of songs with his grandson, Richard Watson. When the Three Pickers began their trio performance, it turned out to be a great combination of picking, singing, and storytelling.

The historic performance brought two Grammy nominations by the year's end: Best Traditional Folk Album and Best Country Instrumental Performance for "Pick Along."[4] The following years brought even more attention to Scruggs, beginning with Sony Music's two-disc compilation *The Essential Earl Scruggs*, released on March 2, 2004, and showcasing the banjo man's body of work from 1946 to 1984. In September 2004, he was named Resident Artist at the Country Music Hall of Fame and Museum, where his residency gave way to four concert programs. That same month, Scruggs traveled to Ireland with his Family & Friends band for the Johnny Keegan Banjo Festival. Christine "Chris" Keenan, the event's organizer and widow of Johnny Keenan (one of the greatest four-string banjo players to come out of Ireland, for whom the festival was named), speaks eloquently about Europe's emotional reception of the American banjo icon:

> Earl's appearance in Ireland made the national main evening news. Thousands of people came from all over Europe to get a close-up glimpse of their hero. When he walked onstage in our specially erected concert tent—incidentally, the largest seated event ever to be held in the town of Longford—the whole crowd stood up in unison, unheard of in Ireland *prior* to a performance—with several rows of grown men clutching Flatt and Scruggs albums, crying their eyes out. The earth shook.

On April 30, 2005, he joined a host of veteran bluegrass musicians at MerleFest's Blue Grass Boys' reunion honoring Bill Monroe. Former Blue Grass Boy guitarist Peter Rowan recites an "Earlism" that's exemplary of his well-known dry sense of humor:

> There was a quote from Earl that really blew my mind. We had a Blue Grass Boys reunion at the MerleFest years ago, and Earl was part of the band. During the rehearsals, it was bliss, it was heaven. During rehearsal, standing in a circle at the Hampton Inn, I asked Earl if he wanted us to play the song "Heavy Traffic Ahead," the same structure on his solo as the verses, and he just looked at me and said the most drop-dead thing I've ever heard anyone say—he said, "Well, follow the leader is all I know." That has got to be the most classic bluegrass statement of all time, because when you take the solo you're the leader. That's another thing people don't understand about bluegrass: you've got to get up there and lead the band.

"He had a good sense of humor," adds Steve Martin. "He loved little phrases like, 'He's one knife short of a full set,' meaning a set of cutlery, when he's talking about somebody being dim." Scruggs enthusiast and *Banjo Newsletter* columnist Bob Piekiel used to spend time with Earl via his friendship with John Hartford. It was Hartford who introduced Bob to Earl, which morphed into regular visits to the Scruggs house for jams and conversation. "When I would go to the jam sessions, I would always have my banjo in hand," says Piekiel. "But I would much rather sit, and watch, and listen to Earl than actually play. Sometimes Earl would say, 'Why don't you pick?' and I would say, 'Well, the priest

doesn't say grace when the Pope is around [laughs].' Earl would laugh
and say, 'Well the Pope isn't here.'"

During a break at another such picking session, Bob recalls an incident Earl recounted from his childhood that could've changed the
course of history:

> Earl was a storyteller himself, and a fountain of information, and he
> just loved to tell stories about everything from his early days on the
> farm and growing up to music and so on, and how he approached
> playing. He told me a story that when he was just a boy, back in
> [Flint Hill], three men and their wives, they were called the Gaines
> Brothers, came to his church, and they were teaching gospel singing
> and piano, among other instruments. They were offering ten lessons
> for approximately three dollars to anybody who wanted to come to
> this event and to try out with these people to see if they were any
> good to be worthy of these lessons. So they had songbooks and so on,
> and Earl showed up with his banjo. They happened to pull a tune
> from one of the songbooks that Earl sort of knew, "The Chinese
> Serenade," which now has been turned into a fiddle tune that we
> know of as "Chinese Breakdown." It's kind of a lesser-known blue-
> grass song, but it's out there. So they told Earl to play it, and Earl
> played it the way that he would on his three-finger banjo. He did a
> very good job at interpreting the melody and, when he finished the
> tune, one of the guys said to him, "There ain't no use in you taking
> lessons. You're never going to be any good," and told him to leave.

In addition to his wit and storytelling, Earl also had an uncanny ability
to create little oddities from novelties dating back to his youth. Longtime friend and devoted student of Scruggs Pete Wernick (aka Dr.
Banjo) admits how one such instance became a magical moment:

> Visiting him once in his later years, he was wailing away on a tune I'd
> never heard before. I asked what it was and he just said, offhandedly,
> "Obelisk Flour." It was really catchy, up the neck, and unmistakably
> "Earl," but unlike anything I'd heard him play. I asked where it came
> from and he ended up singing this little jingle about Obelisk Flour
> and let me record it, singing and all. "It's songs and music for a
> quarter of an hour, a few kind words about Obelisk Flour. . . ." I
> learned it from my recording, and after that when I'd visit, he'd ask
> how I was coming on Obelisk Flour. I'd play it and he'd say I didn't
> quite have it and would show me again, but my recordings show he

kept changing it slightly. I know my version is pretty close, and I love playing it and thinking about him. At one point I googled "Obelisk Flour" to get some background and was a bit shocked to learn that the company, which was based in Louisville, had shut down in 1940! So Earl must have heard the song on the radio in the 1930s as a teenager, and here he was past eighty making a banjo tune out of it. I don't know of anyone else playing the tune, so I have a special feeling about having learned this little gem from him.

Less than a year after the Blue Grass Boys reunion at MerleFest, Anne Louise Certain Scruggs, Earl's wife of fifty-eight years, lost her lengthy battle with an illness at Nashville's Baptist Hospital on February 2, 2006. The woman most responsible for the success of her husband's remarkable career passed away just fifteen days prior to her seventy-ninth birthday. Earl and Louise's sixty-year relationship came full circle as the banjo man bid his final farewell to the love of his life at the Ryman Auditorium, where they first met.

On November 13, 2007, the Country Music Hall of Fame and Museum held its first annual Louise Scruggs Memorial Forum to honor businesswomen in the music industry who are reflective of the pioneering spirit established by Mrs. Scruggs.[5] Three years later, on September 30, 2010, Louise would join her husband, who was listed in 1991 as an inaugural inductee into the International Bluegrass Music Association's Bluegrass Hall of Fame.[6] Earl, Gary, and Randy paid tribute to Louise's memory during the induction ceremony with a touching rendition of "You Are My Flower," an appropriate choice from the old Flatt and Scruggs catalog, as voiced by Gary Scruggs:

> It was my mother's idea for Flatt and Scruggs to record the album *Songs of the Famous Carter Family*, which was released in 1961. One of her favorite songs on that album was "You Are My Flower," a song on which Dad played guitar whenever he performed it. So that's the song we decided to play in memory of her at her induction. Joining Dad, Randy, and me that evening were Jon Randall Stewart and Dierks Bentley on harmony vocals and Rob Ickes on Dobro guitar.
>
> The 2010 IBMA awards show was held in Nashville at the Ryman Auditorium where Mom and Dad had met in 1946. We thought it was fitting that the other Bluegrass Hall of Fame inductee that year was the late John Hartford, who had been a very close and dear friend of Mom and Dad's.

The Ryman was also host to Earl's last recorded album. Gary Scruggs looks back at the recorded performance and identifies many of the talented artists who contributed to the Family & Friends troupe over the years:

> In 2007, Earl Scruggs with Family & Friends played a concert at the Ryman Auditorium that was recorded for future CD release. The band consisted of Earl Scruggs on five-string banjo and picking his three-finger style on acoustic guitar on a couple of songs, Hubert "Hoot" Hester on fiddle, Rob Ickes on Dobro, John Jorgenson on electric guitar, mandolin, and clarinet, John Gardner on drums, Jon Randall and Randy Scruggs on acoustic guitars, and myself on electric bass. The live CD, titled *The Ultimate Collection Live at the Ryman*, was released on Rounder Records in 2008. The album was nominated for a Grammy in the Best Bluegrass Album category.
>
> There were other musicians who played at least several dates in the Family & Friends band, including guitarists Albert Lee, Keith Sewell, Bryan Sutton, Jeff White, and Brad Davis—fiddlers Bobby Hicks, Stuart Duncan, and Glen Duncan—Dobro players Jimmy Stewart, Jennifer Kennedy Merideth, and Jerry Douglas—drummers Harry Stinson and Mark Beckett. Guest artists who sat in with Family & Friends included Vince Gill, Emmylou Harris, Travis Tritt, Marty Stuart, Charlie Daniels, Dierks Bentley, and Kris Kristofferson.

As Earl's career (and health) was beginning to slow down, his ear for musical perfection remained strong. Veteran banjoist Tony Trischka remembers one experience that taught him a lesson not only about how Scruggs could truly pull tone out of his instrument, but also about how easily he could play songs in other keys and tunings:

> I was out in Missouri with Earl, I don't know, maybe five or six years ago, and his road manager came over to me and said, "How would you like to play Earl's banjo?" I said, "Ahhh ya!" This was the banjo he recorded everything on, though it had a different neck, but it was that banjo. So I went back to Earl's dressing room, and he handed me the banjo, and it felt terrible and it sounded terrible, but he sounded great on it, I couldn't get a sound out of it. Steve Martin was on the show also. Earl hands me the banjo and I started playing "Ground Speed," then I hand it to Steve, who likes to play in double-C tuning. He plays and then hands it back to Earl without retuning

it, and Earl starts playing "Brown's Ferry Blues" without picks in double-C tuning, without batting an eyelash. I've never heard him play in double-C tuning, and he just did it. I thought, I need to record this, but I couldn't because he played it just one time through.

Scruggs's final performance occurred at UCLA's Royce Hall on November 5, 2011. Retrospectively, Earl's thoughts about the vast number of musicians he performed and recorded with since the genesis of his career is expressed by Gary Scruggs. "He got a big kick out of jamming with others, and it's really amazing to look back and note the many musicians with whom he collaborated—and the diversity of all those artists."

GIBSON'S EARL SCRUGGS BANJOS

Just as Earl's recordings with Columbia were heading toward a close in 1984, the Gibson Guitar Corporation (prior to their name change, Gibson USA) sought to create an Earl Scruggs–model five-string banjo. Nearly twenty-five years after Scruggs first approached Gibson and they declined to carry his name on a line of banjos, he was now fully unified with the company to revitalize his coveted Granada complete with nickel-plated hardware, not gold-plated hardware as was originally on the banjo. The new model was called the Earl Scruggs Standard. In 1989, Earl summarized the development of his signature model to Doug Hutchens on *Bluegrass Today*:

> Well, let's see, I guess about three or four years ago, it started with the idea to do a Scruggs-model banjo. And that's what they did. They came out [with] one and it was very good. But about a year and a half or two years later, Greg Rich and some other people came in—he's a perfectionist and not [to be] throwing off on the first banjos that they made because the sound was there—but Greg has put it back to the old prewar style. I mean, you can't tell it, or I can't tell it, from the prewar banjos, and I believe—I've had a lot of prewar banjos over the years, and I believe the Scruggs banjos that they're building now just lay down a dozen of them. I believe just about every one of them will come up to what the best old prewar banjo would come up to. I've never seen anything like it. They just don't miss a trick, and I think a whole lot of it is—is the perfection that goes into it and how

well they put it together. They've got the very best of metal that goes in it, they use the best wood, and I just don't know what they could do to improve it. And even to the inlay, it's all just like the best you could ever ask for.

Subsequent models were introduced after the nickel-plated Earl Scruggs Standard: there was the '49 Classic, which was like the Earl Scruggs Standard model except for the "bow tie" style inlay on the fingerboard, followed by three gold-plated engraved editions—the Golden Deluxe, the Flint Hill Special, and the Earl Scruggs Special. On July 19, 2002, Gibson saluted Scruggs with the unveiling of a unique limited edition collectible banjo simply called The Earl. Featuring a hand-drawn portrait by artist Randall Martin on the back of the resonator, the very first model was personally presented to Earl Scruggs, compliments of Gibson's chairman and CEO Henry Juszkiewicz, at the Gibson Bluegrass Showcase in Nashville.[7]

THE SCRUGGS HALL OF FAME

With all of the awards given to Flatt and Scruggs during their prosperous reign in the 1950s and 1960s, the crowning achievement for the duo came in 1985, when Earl and Lester were inducted into the Country Music Hall of Fame. They joined the ranks of their legendary predecessors Gene Autry, Tex Ritter, Hank Williams, and the Carter Family, as well as their peers, Roy Acuff, Chet Atkins, Merle Travis, and Johnny Cash, in addition to their old boss Bill Monroe and a fellow banjoist whom Scruggs held in high regard, Uncle Dave Macon. "I've had a lot of honors that has made me feel as good, but, I guess, the greatest one would have to be the Country Music Hall of Fame," admitted Scruggs to Doug Hutchens in 1989. Being a man of few words, he confessed, "I didn't have [a speech] prepared. I just went up and smiled and bowed and walked off. To put me out on a stage to make a speech, I just go speechless, so I just accepted it and walked off."

The following year, Scruggs returned to his old stomping ground in Boiling Springs, North Carolina, to receive an honorary doctorate of humanities from Gardner-Webb College. An honorary doctorate of music followed in 2005 from the Berklee College of Music in Boston, Massachusetts. In 1989, he was awarded a lifetime honor, a National

Heritage Fellowship from the National Endowment for the Arts
(NEA), before visiting the White House, where he was presented with
the NEA's National Medal of Arts by President George H. W. Bush in
July 1992. In the inaugural year of the International Bluegrass Music
Association's Bluegrass Hall of Fame (1991), Scruggs was one of three
inductees—the second, following Bill Monroe, with Lester Flatt as the
third. Upon his out-of-retirement return in 1998, Scruggs picked the
notes from his locomotive-sounding "Reuben" at the end of "Same Old
Train" (from the CD *Tribute to Tradition*), which won him a Grammy
in the Best Country Collaboration with Vocals category in 1999 along
with twelve other country music artists.[8] And Gibson Guitars once
again recognized Earl in February 2002 with their Orville H. Gibson
Lifetime Achievement Award.

Pop music singer-songwriter Ray Davies wrote a number for his
band the Kinks about seeing all of the stars on Hollywood Boulevard in
1972. And while "Celluloid Heroes" names a few actors from the
Dream Factory's golden age, the glamorous sidewalk in the heart of
Tinseltown added the name Earl Scruggs to its illustrious Walk of Fame
in 2003. Gary Scruggs reminisces about the day the banjo man was
immortalized in concrete:

> He was presented his Hollywood star on February 13, 2003. Several
> celebrities attended, including *The Beverly Hillbillies* cast members
> Max Baer Jr. and Donna Douglas. John McEuen of the Nitty Gritty
> Dirt Band and Kevin Nealon, formerly of the *Saturday Night Live*
> cast, who also plays five-string banjo, were there. The date was the
> one-year anniversary of Waylon Jennings's death, and Waylon's wid-
> ow, and our friend, Jessi Colter, was also there. Other celebrities
> attended, including musicians Keb' Mo' and Dwight Yoakam. There
> were other celebrities present. I just don't remember them all.
>
> Dad's star was embedded in the Hollywood Boulevard sidewalk
> almost directly across the street from the Roosevelt Hotel, the hotel
> he and Lester always stayed at whenever they were in Los Angeles to
> film shows for *The Beverly Hillbillies*.

And among the *Hillbillies* clan, Max Baer Jr. served up a "Man of the
Hour" roast when he was reunited with the Clampetts' "old friend from
back home" on that Thursday afternoon:

When he had his star on the Hollywood Walk of Fame and they asked if I would show up there, and I did, if I would say something, I said, "Well, we did seven years of *The Beverly Hillbillies* before I realized that Louise was not a ventriloquist"—because Earl never said anything, and he was laughing. I said, "If everybody talked about as much as Earl, this would be the shortest party that you've ever had. There would be a lot of silence," you know, because Earl didn't talk. And when he finally did, he had to get up and say something— when he did at this thing [laughs], he didn't say very much, I can tell you that.

The man directly responsible for hiring Scruggs to perform "The Ballad of Jed Clampett" as well as casting him in guest appearances, Paul Henning, was too ill to attend. His authorized biographer, Stephen Cox, was on hand to witness Earl's reserved excitement:

Earl's wife, Louise, invited me to the star ceremony. He was proud and everything, but he's on a smooth road there. He's not getting too excited. You can tell he was excited in seeing that star, and he was all smiles, and he had lots of friends with him there, and all that, and it was a big honor, but anybody else would be jumping for joy, but Earl was just, sort of, on one speed, you know, and it was "medium."

I was impressed that Max drove in from Vegas for it. Donna was here; she went to it, and that, to me, was a really nice touch. And I think that Earl was visibly, not that he got up and screamed or any-thing, but just from his face, when they introduced both Max and Donna there, that he was very proud to have them by his side. Be-cause they, at that point, were the surviving stars from the show.

And after leaving a permanent impression on the streets of Hollywood, Earl Scruggs continued to receive numerous honors, including the Academy of Country Music's Pioneer Award (2005), the Country Music Hall of Fame and Museum's special exhibit *Banjo Man: The Musical Journey of Earl Scruggs* (2005–2006), induction into the Nashville Songwriters Hall of Fame (2007), the Folk Alliance's Lifetime Achieve-ment Award (2007), the Recording Academy's Grammy Lifetime Achievement Award (2008), and an induction into the North Carolina Music Hall of Fame (2009).

In 2005, Junie Scruggs's son J. T. was employed as a manager of the PPG Industries plant in Shelby, North Carolina, when he was asked to

spearhead a monumental project that would become the ultimate preservation of his famous uncle's legacy. J. T. Scruggs expounds upon the
evolution of the Earl Scruggs Center: Music & Stories from the
American South:

> I was actually at work and got a telephone call from a gentleman who
> said, "You know, we got two people in Cleveland County that have
> done well, and we need to do something to recognize them." And
> that was Earl and [country music singer-songwriter] Don Gibson. I
> said, "What do you want to do?" and he said, "Well, we ought to do a
> museum. We got this old courthouse [built in 1907] sitting up there
> empty and nothing going on." And I said, "Fine, what do you want
> me to do?" and he said, "Would you help me talk to the family?"
> That's kind of how we got started. We went and talked to both
> families: to Ms. Gibson and to Earl and then we made a decision
> later—it sort of died for just a little bit, and through some work that
> we'd done with the community, we brought in a guy from North
> Carolina State University to help us with the city of Shelby from a
> standpoint of revitalization. It was basically dying. We actually had
> forty different people who volunteered and came in three different
> days for meetings over a three-month period. We'd done a lot of
> research, and he told us we just needed to do something, and out of
> that we came up with something called Destination Cleveland
> County and adopted the two projects: one was the Don Gibson
> Theatre and one was the Earl Scruggs Center.
>
>   We started our fundraising campaign, and we then formed a
> board, and we said, "Well, we need to really do something to make
> sure our donors know that we're for real," and the easiest thing to do
> first was the theater; it didn't require as much research. So we actual-
> ly borrowed some money and renovated an old theater for an event
> center and opened it and then continued to do research and work on
> the Scruggs Center. We spent a lot of time and effort on research
> because, when we first started, we met with the Department of Cul-
> tural Resources in North Carolina at Raleigh. They told us that only
> seven percent of museums in the state of North Carolina were in the
> black and asked us, "Why do you want to do a museum?" We told
> them that we had this person we felt we needed to recognize, and
> they said, "Before you do it, make sure you go research that seven
> percent that's actually doing well so that, when you do open up,
> people will come and want to come back again." So that's kind of
> how we got started.

For as much of an interest as Earl had in the development of the center, the sands of time ran out, and he didn't survive long enough to see the opening of the museum bearing his name. It took an additional two years before the grand opening occurred on January 11, 2014. Elevated into the center's chairmanship, J. T. Scruggs details the spectacular event, which was nearly washed out:

> We assembled a group of volunteers who led everything, and they put together a heck of a grand opening. We had planned this big thing for musicians to come out of the crowd and out of buildings to do a flash mob appearance on the outside, and guess what? We had this humongous rain. I mean, it must've rained four inches—and they didn't let that bother them. They went over to the Methodist church, right across the street from the Scruggs Center, which held about 800 people. They got permission to use it, and they moved in there and had the music and all [of] the ceremonies and everything inside, and we probably crammed an extra 150 people in above what they really wanted us to have in there. But it was really good! And then that night we had a great show for the grand opening, with Travis Tritt, Vince Gill, and a lot of other people that were there. It was grand. It was really good.

Other performers appearing in the grand opening concert were Sam Bush, Gary Scruggs, Randy Scruggs, Jim Mills, Rob Ickes, and John Gardner. Eddie Stubbs of Nashville's WSM radio emceed the event. Gary Scruggs comments on how the facility honoring his father exceeded his personal expectation and became a valuable asset to the community:

> I expected to see great things when I visited the Earl Scruggs Center just prior to its grand opening, and what I saw was even greater than I had imagined. Memorabilia and artifacts that help tell the story of my father's life, and also the history and cultural traditions of the region are exhibited on the first floor. But the Earl Scruggs Center is much more than just a museum.
>
> Civic and private events are held on the second floor, and the facility hosts educational events for schools. Limited-time special exhibits are also displayed on the second floor. The center hosts community events held outdoors on its grounds.

That same year, another hall of fame enlisted Earl Scruggs into its honorarium. "Dad became the first five-string banjo player to be inducted into the American Banjo Museum's Hall of Fame," notes Gary Scruggs. "Previously, only four-string banjo players had received that honor."

With all of the numerous accolades (some of which are mentioned in preceding chapters, while others remain unnamed due to the extensiveness of his merits), Gary specifies the ones (both tangible and intangible) most dear to his father's heart:

> I think as far as awards and honors are concerned, being a member of the Country Music Hall of Fame was probably number one. His Grammy Lifetime Achievement Award was also special to him. I know he was proud that he inspired the term "Scruggs style," which became widely known. Though he didn't live to see the opening of the Earl Scruggs Center, he was justly proud and honored that the facility located so near his birthplace would bear his name. As far as a collective accomplishment, he often said the highlight of his career was playing music with his sons.
>
> I have to add that likewise, the highlight of my music career was the years I spent performing with my father in the Earl Scruggs Revue and his Family & Friends band.

THE WORLD LOSES THE BANJO MAN

After battling a number of health issues that brought him to St. Thomas Hospital in Nashville, Earl Eugene Scruggs, the youngest and only surviving child of George Elam and Lula Ruppe Scruggs, died peacefully on Wednesday morning, March 28, 2012. He was eighty-eight years old, thus making him the longest-living member of the family from which he was born. Earl's funeral service was held on Palm Sunday, April 1, at the place where he stood sixty-six years earlier and brought to the world a revolutionary new sound on the five-string banjo.

Many of Nashville's most recognized names and faces filled the seats of the Ryman Auditorium to pay their respects to a man who was both so much admired and so well loved. The service, billed as "A Celebration of Life," was emceed and officiated by Grand Ole Opry announcer and WSM air personality Eddie Stubbs. Many of country and bluegrass music's finest musicians took to the stage to eulogize and perform in honor of the banjo man. "Gary asked me to play on it," professional banjoist and Scruggs historian Jim Mills recollects. "I played a tune with John McEuen, and I also went to the graveside service just for the family and friends he invited me to. It was surreal for me, you know, to think that he was gone, but it was still a beautiful service, very reverent. It was a long service, but it was great. You didn't want it to end, that kind of thing."

Country music star Charlie Daniels, who was one of the many eulogizers of Scruggs, speaks eloquently about the assembly that brought the music world together to pay their final respects:

> I was very impressed. I think Gary was the one that probably put it together. At Earl's funeral at the Ryman, it was so classy. It was so well done. It was not underdone, it was not overdone, it was just perfect. The people who were involved in eulogizing, and the music that was played, the things that were said, and the ending was one of the most poignant I've ever seen at any funeral.
>
> In the middle aisle, they had Earl's casket set at the front. They had his banjo sitting on a stand behind the casket, and when the service was over, the pallbearers came and took the casket. A gentleman came out, and if I'm not mistaken, he was wearing white gloves, he took Earl's banjo, put it in the case. They wheeled the casket out, and the middle aisle, it was like a graduation at West Point, where they hold the swords up; they held five-string banjos up.
>
> And it was such a poignant moment. I mean, it's something that I'll always remember. I've never seen more of a tribute to what this man was about and what he meant to us than that. Here's all these banjo pickers. We're all Earl Scruggs fans and admirers, and they were standing there holding their banjos up there like swords. I don't know how many there were, but there were a bunch. They lined the aisle and they took the casket out. The last thing was that Mastertone went out in the case.

Though Earl's music brought an abundance of joy to millions of people around the world, many of whom idolized the banjo man as a legendary musical genius, there are those who saw him as an inspiration, a mentor, an innovator, an aviator, a friend, and of course, a devoted family man. Collaborative friend and country music's "storyteller" Tom T. Hall recounts some of his visits to Earl's house that, unwittingly, spoke volumes without uttering a word:

> Earl used to call me, you know, and tell me to come by and visit, and I would go out there, and go into Earl's house, and Earl would go to the refrigerator and get us a couple of Coca-Colas, and we'd take the tops off them, and sit on the couch and we would talk. The thing that always made it very interesting was that we were sitting, not looking at a TV or out a window; we were just sitting looking at a wall. The couch we were sitting on faced the wall, and there were paintings on [it], and as much as I'd looked at it, you'd think I'd remember, but I don't. We'd sit there and talk awhile, and we'd talk about fifteen or twenty minutes, and Earl would get very quiet. I would sit there for another fifteen or twenty minutes, and we wouldn't be saying anything, and I'd get more and more uncomfortable. And this happened on several occasions, and then I'd say, "Earl, I got to be getting down the road," and Earl would turn to me and say, "Oh, Tom T., don't leave. We're having a good visit." I always rather marveled at that, and that was part of the charm of Earl Scruggs. You know, me being a storyteller, you know, I'm just running my mouth all the time, but Earl had enough class and southern manners to know you could sit on the porch and just visit without running your mouth all the time. I regret somehow that I never got the hang of that.

Grace Constant, daughter of Earl's sister Ruby, also shares a few thoughts of endearment about her uncle and his family:

> Uncle Earl always encouraged me to be true to myself, follow my heart, and take time to stop and smell the roses. Uncle Earl was a father figure to me. I was very close to Uncle Earl, Aunt Louise, and the boys. Gary and I have been extremely close, and I love him like a brother. That bond grew even tighter as Gary and I took care of Uncle Earl the last years of his life. Being able to travel with Uncle Earl, during his last years, was a great experience for me. I always made sure he was properly dressed and on time for his shows. Gary and I alternated living with Uncle Earl in his last years so he would have someone with him at all times to assist with whatever he might need. We were a team. I will always cherish all the stories Uncle Earl told me about growing up on the farm and his life after he started making music and traveling on the road.

One of the highlights of every year was Uncle Earl's birthday party. Aunt Louise planned huge celebrations and invited politicians, such as the governor and mayor of Nashville, and lots and lots of celebrities. After Aunt Louise passed away, Gary and I continued this tradition. Uncle Earl also enjoyed "working" in his little garden, which consisted of tomato and pepper plants. He had a garden until his last year of life. Uncle Earl always had a dog. He named all the male dogs Clyde and all the female dogs Bonnie, except for one, which he named Pepsi. I still have his last dog, Bonnie.

Uncle Earl always took time to talk with his fans and sign autographs. He commented several times that, if it weren't for his fans, he would not be where he was, and that making time for them was the least he could do.

Earl's eldest son, Gary, who assumed all of his father's managerial duties after the passing of his mother, also reveals some of his fondest memories about the Scruggs family patriarch as both a celebrity and a dad:

It was great fun performing with him in the Earl Scruggs Revue and, in later years, in the Earl Scruggs with Family & Friends band. He had a very appealing stage presence, and it was fun to perform alongside him.

We both shared a love for baseball. When I was young, I played Little League, Babe Ruth League, and high school baseball. When in town, he not only attended those games, he was also ready and willing to get out in the yard and spend time playing catch with me and hitting ground balls, line drives, and high fly balls to me. He did the same with my brothers. He was good with the bat. In his later years, we watched many baseball games on television together. He was a great conversationalist and always fun to talk with. I also have many fond memories of him interacting with my mother and other family members.

I learned early on that he was very quick to share his musical talents and knowledge with younger people, or anyone else, for that matter, who wanted to learn his style of picking five-string banjo or just get some tips about music and the music business in general. Many times I saw him giving advice and demonstrations to others when asked about how he played a particular lick or riff on the banjo. He was very generous with his time and talent.

Dad was also a gifted guitarist, a true icon in the world of music, and an inspiration to countless musicians. As far as I know, he accomplished what he set out to accomplish, and then some.

8

THE INFLUENCE OF EARL SCRUGGS

My biggest influence from the start to this day has always been Earl
Scruggs. I then began to listen to the disciples of Earl, and that
included J. D. Crowe, Sonny Osborne, and Bill Emerson. They became a new group of banjo players to learn from after spending my
first few years listening only to Earl. Of course Earl was their hero as
well.

—Jim Mills, professional banjoist and Scruggs historian

It's been said that imitation is the highest form of flattery. In the case of
Earl's disciples, one of the best representations of that saying occurred
at Carlton Haney's bluegrass festival in Camp Springs, North Carolina.
As part of the muggy-weathered Labor Day weekend event in 1971, a
banjo line performance, featuring a roster of pickers that was a literal
who's who of bluegrass banjo virtuosos, paid tribute to their musical
idol—Earl Scruggs. Independent producer and director Albert Ihde
captured the historic moment on film and used it as the finale for his
documentary *Bluegrass Country Soul.* Among the many players visible
were Sonny Osborne, Bill Emerson, J. D. Crowe, Alan Munde, Jimmy
Arnold, Don Stover, and Randy Scruggs, along with a few other lesser-
known banjoists: Rick Riman, A. L. Wood, John Farmer, and Saburo
Watanabe of Japan.

After a flattering introduction by Osborne, a noticeably sheepish
Scruggs compliments all the banjo players onstage before hammering
the opening lick to his iconic instrumental, "Foggy Mountain Breakdown" (followed up by "Dear Old Dixie" at the close of the movie).

From the moment Earl pinched the strings on his banjo, all of those standing by him knew the game was on. The master had, once again, set the standard they knew couldn't be matched. It was a privilege for these devoted followers of Scruggs to pay homage to him the best way they could, yet most of them felt inferior performing in front of him before a live audience. One of the many in that lineup, Alan Munde, recalled the moment when Earl led the charge of battling banjos:

> I'll tell you what my sense of the whole experience was for me. As soon as Earl pinched the banjo strings, I wished I wasn't there. His tone was so, so good, and the playing sounded so brilliant. It sounded like Earl Scruggs for sure. I played because I was standing there and they put me in the line. It was, for me, the best tribute to Earl Scruggs just to listen to him play. We should have all sat down in chairs and just listened to him, which would have been a good tribute. I appreciate what they were trying to do, but for me I just felt like, oh man, I just feel so useless.

Opinions about the experience vary from player to player. Some admit to feeling humbled and nervous about following Earl, while others, like Bill Emerson, expressed relief that Scruggs chose a tune they could each play with confidence:

> When he said, "Let's pick one," and kicked off "Foggy Mountain Breakdown," it was a little bit of a relief [laughs]. It was a relief because that was one that I knew and had played a thousand times, and I guess everyone else kind of felt the same way. It's a standard banjo tune, and everybody knew how to play it. For me it was not intimidating. I had a lot of confidence at that particular juncture in time. I was with the Country Gentlemen, and we were, kind of, at a peak, and we were playing almost every day all summer long, and I knew I'd have no problem playing "Foggy Mountain Breakdown." So there I was onstage, and there was Earl Scruggs playing "Foggy Mountain Breakdown," and I was going to get to play it too, so I was sort of happy.

Most of the featured banjoists knew from the beginning that they were not going to beat Earl at his own game and that the best they could do was to show respect by attempting to play "Foggy Mountain Breakdown" as close to the way he played it as possible. One of the earliest disciples, J. D. Crowe, learned quickly that he was never going to be Earl Scruggs, but he always tried to play like him simply out of admiration. Crowe affirms that point through his recollection of the banjo lineup:

> If you're going to honor the man, then you should try to play as close to the way he played it as you can. I wanted to show Earl that I learned how to play from him, and I tried to play it like he played it. During that jam, I played the melody and not a bunch of hot licks and other stuff. I mean, there were some guys that got up there, and you couldn't even tell what they were playing.

Without question, it was a thrill for these musicians to play with their mutual hero. It's an amazing thing to consider that the platform was filled with banjo masters in their own right, who themselves felt humbled in the presence of this musical legend. The disciples of Earl Scruggs all seem to share similar narratives of his influence on their musical development and lives in general. Almost anyone you talk to about Scruggs will immediately reference *The Beverly Hillbillies*, the 1949 recording of "Foggy Mountain Breakdown," the old Martha White television show, and local concert venues as the catalysts that propelled them into the world of the five-string banjo. It was also possible, in those early days of bluegrass, to get a one-on-one conversation with Earl, and many of those aspiring young banjo players speak of such encounters as life-changing experiences.

The disciples highlighted in this chapter have been placed by when they began playing professionally, regardless of the year they first picked up the banjo. Not all practitioners of the Scruggs style are mentioned, as they are countless, although many of the major players are included as a testimony to the fingerprints left on them by the hands of Earl Scruggs.

THE NEW FRONTIER

As primitive string music began to evolve into early country and gospel music before the refinement of bluegrass, old-school banjoists such as Charlie Poole, Uncle Dave Macon, Dave "Stringbean" Akeman, Grandpa Jones, and Snuffy Jenkins played either clawhammer, two-finger, or

various forms of three-finger banjo, often within the context of comedic
buffoonery. The banjo wasn't thought to be a serious instrument, and its
players weren't considered serious musicians. All of that changed literally overnight in early December 1945 because of a young man from
the Piedmont region of North Carolina. The three-finger rolls that Earl
Scruggs spent endless hours refining jettisoned every one of his predecessors. "All the old banjo players were jealous of Earl, the new guy on
the block," bluegrass banjoist Eddie Adcock says candidly. "Earl was
extremely talented for his day, and a very nice, soft-spoken person who
would always treat you nice." His peer group of three-finger stylists was
very limited in the 1940s, the other primary players being Don Reno
and Ralph Stanley. Without any thought of what he had started,
Scruggs was simply doing what he loved most, but in the homes of rural
Americans, seeds were being sown in the young hearts and imaginations
of his first crop of pupils.

The 1950s wasn't just the first decade of rock-n-roll; it was also the
premiere decade for the disciples of Earl Scruggs. Many within this
rudimentary batch of five-string banjo pickers, despite having previously heard Scruggs in the mid- to late 1940s, did not begin professionally
until the 1950s. One of the earliest to hail from this group, Sonny
Osborne, started at the age of eleven in the winter of 1948 after en-
countering Larry Richardson, who played banjo with his older brother
Bobby as part of the Lonesome Pine Fiddlers. In a *Frets* magazine
interview, Osborne acknowledged that he copied Earl closely and could
play every break and background note from Flatt and Scruggs's 78-rpm
recordings. He further credited Scruggs's backward roll patterns as the
resolution to the timing problems he was experiencing at the outset of
his picking. By 1952, the same year he began his stint with Bill Monroe,
Sonny claimed he truly understood the mechanics of the right hand,
which intensified his duplication of Earl.

Though having heard Scruggs's recording of "Randy Lynn Rag" in
1957, Sonny had an epiphany to distinguish himself from the man he so
much admired.[1] The separation led to the development of his own fiery
drive, which became the main ingredient in a countrified bluegrass
sound he perfected with Bobby as the Osborne Brothers for more than
fifty years. "Sonny Osborne, to me, is the first that went progressive
while sort of staying in the Earl Scruggs style," claims bluegrass musician Sam Bush. Bluegrass historian Fred Bartenstein backs up that

point by referring to Osborne as "kind of a 'mad scientist' on the banjo" due to his experimentation with a six-string banjo that had five long strings and his early controversial use of an electronic pickup.[2] Osborne is widely recognized by bluegrass aficionados to be one of the post-Scruggs giants of the five-string banjo and has been a lifelong student of Earl's music.

Before attending a Flatt and Scruggs performance at the Kentucky Mountain Barn Dance in Lexington, J. D. Crowe had never witnessed the banjo played with such command. This made him want to get a banjo of his own so he could imitate Earl. Flatt and Scruggs had recently based themselves in Lexington, which gave young J. D. access to Earl anytime he and his family came to the shows they played in the area. Though his father tried to set up lessons for him directly with Scruggs, Crowe confesses that Earl's advice produced a better result for him:

> My dad would talk to Lester and Earl, and of course they were grown men, and I was just a kid. I was just in awe of everything. I wouldn't say nothing, but my dad asked Earl if he could give lessons, or show me some things, and I remember him saying, "Well, I really don't know what I'm doing myself. I just play whatever I hear that comes to my mind. He can watch and pick up anything he can, but I can't sit down and show him." Earl was probably just too busy being on the road, you know, but he did say I was welcome to pick up whatever I can by watching him play. All those guys were just so gracious in those days.
>
> I was still too young to comprehend what Earl was doing, but it did help to fix my eyes on the hand positions on the neck. You know, it really did help me some. I just watched him. He did what he was supposed to do. He did his job. He just played what he normally played, and all I did was watch and take in all I could. I learned it all by just watching Earl, and listening to records. Maybe if I'd had a teacher, it might have been different for me. Who knows? I'm just glad it happened the way it did. I was lucky to have the chance to be around Flatt and Scruggs because they lived here in my hometown, so I was very fortunate. Otherwise, I would not have been able to do that.

By 1955, J. D. had learned how to play well enough to go on the road with Mac Wiseman during his summer vacation. This gave him the necessary experience of playing professionally. A year later, Jimmy Martin was passing through Lexington when he heard Crowe on a live show on a local radio station and offered J. D. a job on the spot. After his stint with Martin, Crowe teamed up with mandolin player Doyle Lawson and legendary guitarist and singer Red Allen. Together they formed the Kentucky Mountain Boys, wherein J. D. developed a unique sound all his own. In 1975, he founded the New South, a band that became a nurturing ground for some of bluegrass music's greatest talent. Crowe's popularity got a significant boost with the founding of the Bluegrass Album Band in 1980, with the help of Tony Rice, Jerry Douglas, Doyle Lawson, Bobby Hicks, and Todd Phillips.

Like other Scruggs disciples from the 1950s, Bill Emerson was introduced to Earl's banjo through old 78-rpm recordings. Some people had the opportunity, in various places, to hear Flatt and Scruggs on the radio, but that luxury wasn't available to Emerson, growing up in the Washington, DC, area. After hearing cuts from Flatt and Scruggs, along with Bill Monroe, from his neighbor's record collection, Emerson purchased the same records as well as a few of the Stanley Brothers from a record store by special order. And of all the things on those records, it was Earl's banjo that stood out most to young Bill. When Flatt and Scruggs came to town, Emerson finally had the opportunity to see his new idol in action. He admits to the everlasting impression it left on him:

> Lester Flatt and Earl Scruggs had come to town here. There was a ship that was docked in Washington, DC, called the SS *Mount Vernon*, and it went down to Mount Vernon on the river and back again. It was a tour. They might have a jazz band, Louis Armstrong, or somebody like that, and this time they had Flatt and Scruggs, and I went down there and was able to sit right in front of the stage and watch Earl Scruggs close up. That's the first time I ever saw him play, and of course I was thrilled at that and just became obsessed with playing the banjo. I really noticed the power and the attack Earl had when he played. I used to get upset when the fiddle would play and say, "Why is that guy playing when Earl could be taking that break."
>
> I never dreamed I would be able to get up and play in front of people. I just wanted to give it a shot. I got to where I could play one song, then two songs, and then the whole thing kind of snowballed. Then it got to where people wanted to hire me to play.

Yet, as Bill developed his own banjo skills, he came to realize, like so many other budding banjo players, that he was not going to *be* Earl Scruggs. "I finally figured out that I wasn't getting very far trying to play exactly like Earl," says Emerson. "And not only could I not do that, but he'd already done it. I kind of had to do my own thing, whatever that is, you know. [I] just tried to play what I'd heard."

Bill Emerson evolved into one of the most original-sounding five-string banjoists in this first tier of Scruggs disciples, especially during his tenure with the Country Gentlemen, as he's considered, by many, to be a maestro at playing out of the open C position. This was unusual in bluegrass music, since most banjo pickers played in G tuning.

A number of musicians who blossomed in the 1950s started on less expensive instruments, typically Kay banjos (as did J. D. Crowe) or sometimes homemade banjos that almost never stayed in tune. The goal, nonetheless, was to pick like Earl Scruggs, regardless of the instrument's quality. Such is the declaration of disciple Roni Stoneman:

> I was living in Maryland in a one-room house with everybody playing music night and day with instruments my daddy made for all of us. Daddy made me my first banjo. The neck was so short it looked like a mandolin neck, but that was to work on the rolls that were so important, and they were Earl Scruggs rolls, the rolls of Earl. Scott [my brother] said, "You have to learn that. That's the only way to do it right." Daddy made me a second banjo, but it wasn't very good and it stayed out of tune a lot, but I was able to keep it in tune when I played one of Earl's tunes like "Down the Road." Scruggs kept the strings ringing, and you don't stop and start. You don't have a jump in your roll. My right hand is marvelous because of the Scruggs roll.

Veronica Loretta, nicknamed "Roni," is the youngest daughter of Ernest Stoneman (who was affectionately known as Pop), a multitalented musician who decided he was going to try his hand at music and became best known for his song "The Sinking of the Titanic," which became one of the most popular recordings of the 1920s, selling around one million copies. Pop and his wife, Hattie, formed a family ensemble with their children—the Stonemans. By the time her father built her a second banjo, Roni was beginning to learn a number of Earl's tunes, and the second time she saw Flatt and Scruggs perform, she had the opportunity to briefly chat with the banjo man himself. Stoneman spoke about her awkward meeting with Scruggs that eventually led to a more teachable moment years later:

> So I went to see Earl, and he was in the dressing room, and there I am just standing there looking at him, just staring at his hands, and I said, "I play too," and he said, "You play? Do you play clawhammer?" I said, "No, I pick it like you." He said, "You do?" I said back to him, "Yes, well, I'm working on it, working on playing the rolls like you do." He just looked, and I thought, here was my hero. Here was my future for whatever I had coming up the road. He smiled and never said anything else. A few years later, I saw him again at some festival, him and Flatt, and I loved them both. I never talked to them. I was too shy, but Earl Scruggs would watch me. He would watch every move I made.
>
> Then several years passed, and the Stonemans were at the Opry, and I'm about seven months pregnant, though I don't look it because I only weighed 118 pounds. Well, I'm standing there at the Ryman, and Earl Scruggs walked over to me and said, "You play the banjo?" I was real shy, but I said, "Yes, but I play real simple." He said, "Keep it simple—keep it that way and you'll never have any trouble. Keep the rolls clean and simple." It gave me courage to go out onstage and play the "Orange Blossom Special," and I had to kick it off, and I thought, please, God, give my fingers the rolls to make it clean, and I did good on it.

By the 1960s, the Stonemans' success had expanded significantly as they would appear on top venues like the Grand Ole Opry and *The Jimmy Dean Show*, and in 1966 they had their own syndicated show, *Those Stonemans*. The family also had the opportunity to appear in feature films before disbanding. Roni embarked on a solo career and is perhaps most remembered as a regular cast member of television's long-running musical variety series *Hee Haw*.

With his young ears attuned to the jangling sound of clawhammer-style banjo, Haskel McCormick was only nine years old when he first heard Earl Scruggs in 1946. From the moment he heard the crispness of Scruggs style, his perception of the five-string banjo was forever changed, and he was determined to copy Scruggs. McCormick explains:

> Earl's the one who got me going. He got me interested in the banjo. When I first heard his style, I just loved it. It just took hold of me,

and I had to learn how to do that. My dad played the clawhammer style, and was good at it, but when I heard Earl the first time, I wasn't interested in the claw-hammer style anymore. I like the cla-whammer style; it's a good style, but I just never got interested in it much. I followed Earl, and Earl was my hero, and I looked at him and tried to follow him as close as I could. It was just out of this world. It was exciting. It was something. It was like icing on the cake, you know. You've heard the old-time style of banjo, and that's all I had heard up till that point, and I thought, how can anyone be that different and that good?

And just like Osborne, Crowe, and Emerson, it became obvious to Haskel that trying to imitate Scruggs note for note and tone for tone was simply out of the question. "Later on, after I got going pretty good, I tried to make my own style," says McCormick. "I didn't want to be exactly like Earl because he's already done it his way. I wanted to try to be a little different, and I think I did." Haskel and his brothers, known as the McCormick Brothers, started playing music as early as 1945 but made a name for themselves by the 1950s. As mentioned in chapter 3, McCormick was one of three pickers to have the honor of filling in for Earl Scruggs, for a short time, while he was recovering from his car accident in 1955 (the other two being Don Bryant and Curtis McPeake). Many years later, he would join Scruggs's former partner, Lester Flatt, in the Nashville Grass from 1971 to 1973.

SPREADING WINGS

The 1950s proved fertile years for the development of bluegrass banjo. Earl Scruggs opened the floodgates to a new generation of creative banjo players who were building, not only on his style, but also on the approaches of his contemporaries, like Don Reno and Ralph Stanley. During the 1960s, a fresh group of Scruggs devotees began to carve out their own techniques, yet their musical senses were being influenced by the increasingly popular genres of folk and rock-n-roll. Bluegrass banjo had not changed a great deal from the late 1940s through the 1950s; however, the ears of this latest brand of banjoists were being adjusted to the pop culture to which they were now exposed, and that meant unlimited possibilities for the five-string, as Earl himself quickly discovered.

Despite the plethora of sounds emerging from this turbulent decade, Scruggs continued to be the chief motivator for people to play the banjo. The influence and appeal of his style was no longer confined to regions east of the Mississippi River. During the 1960s, banjo enthusiasts were popping up all over the landscape, from coast to coast.

For many aspiring musicians in the 1960s, inspiration came from a contemporary innovation known as the concept album. One of the decade's earliest examples, spearheaded by Louise Scruggs in 1961, was *Foggy Mountain Banjo*. Though it was a Flatt and Scruggs production, many consider it the first "unofficial" Earl Scruggs solo album. The instrumental compilation showcased Scruggs style at its best and drew a clear distinction between Earl and his folk counterparts. Native Oklahoman Alan Munde is one of the many Scruggs disciples who couldn't believe his ears after listening to *Foggy Mountain Banjo*. Munde describes its relevance in near mind-blowing terms:

> The first time I heard Earl play the banjo, I thought it was inhuman, or extrahuman, or superhuman. I just couldn't imagine in my wildest dreams how that could be done. The other impression I had was that it was the best I'd heard in my whole life. I just couldn't believe it. It was overwhelming. The Christmas after I started playing the banjo, one of my friends gave me the *Foggy Mountain Banjo* album by Flatt and Scruggs, and that was the huge kick in the pants for me, and that's no new story. It's the story of almost every banjo player, to a certain extent, and it started in my era. The year *Foggy Mountain Banjo* came out was the first time, in my recollection, that I heard him. I'd heard the style before, just on TV and, you know, my family wasn't particularly musical, and they certainly weren't into country music, but, you know, folk music was big in the late fifties and early sixties, and there were banjo players in among them who played a Scruggs-ish style, and I was really liking the banjo then. The only banjo player I could identify by name was Pete Seeger.

In perfecting his own instrumental technique, Munde gravitates more toward the melodic style popularized by Bobby Thompson and Bill Keith in the early 1960s, as much of it stems from his exposure to the fiddle players in the Oklahoma-Texas region where he grew up. The banjo's melodic approach is to play fiddle tunes in a way that mimics the fiddle, note for note, utilizing flowing scales rather than playing melodies out of chord positions, which is more in line with Scruggs style.

Alan played banjo for Jimmy Martin from 1969 to 1971, and during that time he learned how to play solid, Scruggs-style banjo, which explains his ability to play melodic tunes with the same kind of intensity and drive.

When his tenure with Martin ended, Alan Munde joined up with fiddler friend Byron Berline to form the legendary bluegrass band Country Gazette. His creativity can be observed in the seemingly effortless way he plays tunes in keys like F, B-flat, E, and D while in G tuning without the use of a capo. Though firmly connected to Earl Scruggs, Alan has drawn from a number of musical genres to create a methodical technique that echoes classical, jazz, blues, and rock-n-roll. While never claiming to be a jazz banjoist, Munde was one of the first players to experiment with elements of jazz.[3]

After the breakup of Flatt and Scruggs in 1969, Lester Flatt hired all of the members of their former Foggy Mountain Boys to launch his new band, the Nashville Grass (as mentioned in chapter 6). The only vacancy that needed to be filled was the spot occupied by Earl Scruggs. "I was the first banjo player after he and Earl split up," remarks Vic Jordan. "Josh Graves asked me if I might be interested in playing with Lester, so I auditioned, and he liked it. After the audition, Lester said, 'Do you have any questions?' I said, 'Only one question: do you want me to try to play just like Earl, because I don't think anybody can do that.'" Flatt gave Jordan assurance that he could play the tunes as he felt them.

Though he played with Earl's old bandmates, Jordan fancies himself a disciple of both Earl Scruggs and Don Reno. He was encouraged to study them both and to pick up whatever he could from their distinctive styles: Reno had a more single-string guitar technique, in sharp contrast to Scruggs's syncopated roll patterns. As Vic began picking the banjo in his late teens, he acknowledged that his initial preference for Reno's approach was soon invaded by Scruggs:

> I actually started out trying to do a little more Reno style than I was Scruggs style at the time. I got into both of them, and they were both influential on my playing. I graduated from high school in 1957, when I met a banjo player named Harlan Baumgardner, and he had a band called the Cripple Creek Boys. This guy took me under his wings. He showed me how to use picks, how to tune the instrument, and showed me some chords. He used to invite me over to his house

when the Cripple Creek Boys would practice, and I would sit over on
one end of the living room and plunk on my banjo while they played
and practiced. Harlan pushed me in the direction of Earl Scruggs
and Don Reno and the Stanley Brothers. This would be about the
time that I learned about Scruggs and Reno.

As time went on, Vic was able to develop his own style of playing that
incorporated the things he had learned from Scruggs and Reno. He
knew that he would never be able to play exactly like Earl, yet he loved
the tone and sound of Earl's attack on the banjo, and he goes on to say,
"I just liked the sound of Earl's playing overall. I didn't know much
about timing and tone; it just sounded good to my ear, the way he was
playing it, you know. It sounded good and I simply wanted to play just
like that. I was very impressed with it."

The California connection to bluegrass music developed mainly
through the folk boom that was taking the world by storm in the 1960s.
The banjo had united with folk music fans via Pete Seeger and the
Kingston Trio. Earl Scruggs only helped to popularize it even more
within the hootenanny circuit through such venues as the Newport Folk
Festival. In 1962, Flatt and Scruggs furthered their folk identity with
the subtitle *Folk Music with an Overdrive*, a phrase coined by
American folklorist and musician Alan Lomax, as printed on the cover
of their latest songbook.

Out of that awakening came a number of banjo enthusiasts who
would become converts to bluegrass music after hearing it for the first
time. Anybody listening to Dave Guard of the Kingston Trio and Earl
Scruggs side by side could hear the major differences between these
two banjo players. And for many, it was the sound of Earl's banjo that
raised the bar. California banjoist Herb Pedersen (who substituted for
Scruggs in 1967 due to his medical issues at the time) rose out of the
folk music scene in the early 1960s and justifies how bluegrass swayed
him away from folk music. "About 1959 [or] 1960 I heard bluegrass for
the first time. It was just very infectious, and anybody who likes bluegrass knows exactly what I'm talking about. At the time, I was more into
folk music, and then, when I heard bluegrass, you know, that really
turned the corner for me." He further reflects upon his introduction to
the banjo of Earl Scruggs:

There was a local record store that I'd go into to get the latest folk music that was out and that sort of thing, and this guy came up behind me and said, "Do you like banjos?" I said, "Yes," and he said, "Well try this record," and he pulled out the *Country Music* album with Flatt and Scruggs on the cover; they had the red coats. The title of it just said *Country Music* across the top. It didn't even refer to bluegrass at all. I brought the record home and put it on the turntable, and that was the first time I'd ever heard Flatt and Scruggs play. It was just amazing. It sounded so smooth, and Earl was just so precise at what he was doing, you know, and the note value of each string he was playing was phenomenal. I'd never heard anything done that well.

After a few stints in West Coast bands, Herb Pedersen played a significant role in the cross-pollination of bluegrass, country, folk, and rock-n-roll. His musical dossier includes a three-year period with the Dillards (1967–1970) as a replacement for banjoist Doug Dillard, and he performed with other bluegrass groups such as Country Gazette and the New Kentucky Colonels. His career as a musician reached a pinnacle when he recorded and performed with Linda Ronstadt, Emmylou Harris, and John Denver. Pedersen's success continued to grow when he, along with guitarist John Jorgenson and mandolinist Chris Hillman, formed the Desert Rose Band in 1985.

As one of the original founders of the legendary pop group the Eagles, Bernie Leadon brought to the table a rich background in folk and bluegrass music, which can be heard in a number of Eagles songs recorded during his tenure with them (1971–1975). Like many others of his generation, Bernie was first influenced by folk artists such as the Kingston Trio and Pete Seeger. He talks about how he was introduced to Scruggs-style banjo via Pete Seeger. "I bought Pete Seeger's book *How to Play the 5-String Banjo* and, although Seeger was not a Scruggs-style player, he had a photo of Earl in that book and a decent explanation of how the three-finger bluegrass style was played with finger and thumb picks." While living in Southern California, Bernie had the chance to befriend other bluegrass musicians like Chris Hillman, banjo player Kenny Wertz, and Dobro player Larry Murray to help whet his appetite for bluegrass.

"In late 1964, my family moved to North Florida, where there was more bluegrass music in the local culture," notes Leadon. "I met some good players there and was taken one evening to fiddle player Vassar Clements's home in Tallahassee to play with him. Vassar was driving a Charles Chips truck for a living because his wife had made him give up touring. Luckily for everyone, he went back to music." Eventually, he would pick up a few Flatt and Scruggs and Don Reno LPs in an attempt to gain more instruction. "I had purchased and studied by then the Flatt and Scruggs record *Foggy Mountain Banjo* and had slowed the old record player down to half speed to get all the notes right," explains Leadon. Being one of the few disciples of Earl to successfully cross over into the cultural world of pop music, Bernie Leadon's command of Scruggs-style banjo is prominently evident in such Eagles songs as "Take It Easy," "Earlybird," and "Outlaw Man."

After tenures with local bands in Columbus, Ohio, and an enlistment in the Marine Corps, banjoist John Hickman began his professional career when he joined Earl Taylor and the Stoney Mountain Boys. By 1969 he moved to Los Angeles, where he and his brother started a band called the Hickman Brothers. John initially started off playing guitar in 1957, but after hearing Earl he shifted his attention on the banjo. Hickman paints a picture of the scenario that altered his course:

> Earl Scruggs was the first banjo player I had ever heard. There was an older fella in the neighborhood who had all of Earl's records, and so on, at that time, and I became interested in it through him. It was a 45[-rpm] record; it was "Shuckin' the Corn," I believe. His name was Burley Blankenship. I was really impressed by how much in control Earl was with the banjo, more than anybody else, I imagine. That impressed me right off the bat; everything was where it should be, it seemed like, you know. I think more than anything it was the way Earl heard the music and was able to project it. Pretty much the way he heard things.

Though Hickman never tried to imitate Earl note for note like other players did early on, he mainly strived to make his own sound from the outset. He illustrates that point with an example from his favorite Scruggs tune, "Dear Old Dixie." "I really like the kickoff introduction to it. I was never able to get that exactly right, of course. I don't play anything exactly like anyone else." John soon met up with fiddler Byron Berline during his days with the Hickman Brothers, but it wasn't until 1976 that he and Berline began playing together. In the late 1970s, John

Hickman gained high recognition within the community of bluegrass banjo players for his unique style, which was a creative mixture of Scruggs, Reno, and melodic styles. His 1978 solo banjo album *Don't Mean Maybe* is still a favorite of many aspiring and established banjoists.

The 1960s proved to be an experimental decade for music, and bluegrass was no exception. The advent of alternative forms of music gave birth to fresh sounds that would be taken even further by the time the 1970s rolled around. The decade would also become a breeding ground for a more progressive type of bluegrass, known as "newgrass." This advanced approach had been adopted with the Bluegrass Alliance band in the late 1960s, yet there were a number of musicians prior to the Bluegrass Alliance who experimented with contemporary music à la bluegrass.[4] The winds of change could be felt with such groups as the Country Gentlemen and the Seldom Scene, who brought into bluegrass pop tunes like "Mrs. Robinson," "Rider," and "Sweet Baby James."

As already observed, Flatt and Scruggs also dabbled in folk and rock with cover versions of songs by Bob Dylan, the Monkees, and the Lovin' Spoonful. The difference with some of the ensembles that preceded the newgrass generation was that they only peppered their albums and performances with rock-n-roll and folk tunes, whereas the newgrass bands pulled all the stops out and created entire performances and albums around such songs. No matter how progressive bluegrass music became, Earl Scruggs never lost his place as *the* principal banjoist to be mimicked.

One such Scruggs disciple, Terry Baucom, became a dominant force in bluegrass banjo in the 1970s as he introduced his Scruggs-based picking in such bands as Boone Creek and Doyle Lawson and Quicksilver. He is known for a powerful, driving banjo style that earned him the title "The Duke of Drive." Terry learned his craft by listening to Earl, which is how most everybody else learned to play, yet, like J. D. Crowe, he also learned by watching what Earl was doing with his hands. Often he would observe photos of Earl, and he tells a story about the placement of his right hand for optimal picking:

> I was so eaten up with Earl that, when I was in grade school, I'd go to the library and look up "banjo," and I forget when it was, probably the early sixties, but when you would find "banjo," you see a picture of Earl sitting there, and he had the red string bowtie and the hat.

He had his pinky and ring finger of his right hand down on the banjo head, he had the picks on the strings. So, when I saw that, man, that's exactly what I did. I just put my little finger and my ring finger down, and it felt natural, and that's how I play to this day. Seeing that picture of how Earl held his hand got me in the right program.

When Baucom was ten years old, he played in his father's band, the Rocky River Boys, and it was right around this time that he had the opportunity to meet Earl Scruggs at a local show not far from his home. He details the experience as one of those unforgettable moments of a lifetime, and how Lester Flatt brought out the best in Earl:

> The first time I saw Earl, it was in the early 1960s, and we had this little school a few miles from my house, though I didn't go to that one. I was in another district, but it was in Fairview, North Carolina, and they were playing on a Sunday afternoon, I think it was, but it could have been Saturday. It was on the weekend, I do know, and that was the first time I ever saw him in person. It was in a gymnasium, and it was packed out, and I remember Earl got off the bus, and he came into the gymnasium, and he had to cross the whole floor to get to the dressing room. And man, everybody broke into this wild cheer! I mean, it was like Elvis had walked out. He just took his hat off, held it out, and nodded to the crowd and went on backstage. I was just a kid. I didn't know any better that you couldn't go backstage, but I went backstage and I didn't say a word to him. I just stood there and looked at him for a while. I'm sure he felt my eyes burning a hole in his back. I just stood there, and I was in awe of how he could play like that.
>
> Earl played like he did because he was Earl, but I'll tell you one thing, Flatt was the perfect guitar player for him because he laid the drive on Earl. I mean, Earl didn't have to do it all by himself because Flatt was on him all the time. Man, that's why they sounded so good together. As a banjo player, you know well how fun it is to play with a really good guitar player. It's just great, man, and that's what made Earl want to get it. I just had to point that out, you know. How did Earl play with that much drive? Well, he had it in his right hand, but he also had Lester standing there jamming with him.

Baucom would eventually go on to play with a number of award-winning bands, many that have helped define the direction of bluegrass music in the 1980s, 1990s, and 2000s, and which led to his own band, the Dukes of Drive.

As established earlier in this chapter, Earl's disciples understood that they were never going to *be* Earl Scruggs; however, it's not uncommon to hear banjo players discussing the question of who "sounds" most like him. Among the small number of banjoists people mention, Kenny Ingram's name seems to come up more often than others. Ingram credits Earl as his main influence, but he's also drawn from the styles of several early disciples, like Sonny Osborne, J. D. Crowe, Bill Emerson, Allen Shelton, and Walter Hensley. As a young boy, Kenny used to watch *The Flatt and Scruggs Grand Ole Opry* on Saturday afternoons with his dad. He recalls the day his father made him an offer that caught him off guard:

> He just made a comment to me, one day, that if he bought me a banjo, would I learn to play it? I was just a dumb kid, so I said, "Sure," and that's how I got started. I was about eight years old, or even younger, when I first heard Earl play the banjo. You know, I watch those old TV shows now and I can remember watching them when I was a kid. I remember seeing [seven-year-old] Ricky Skaggs on the show with Lester and Earl. It's hard to say, as a kid, what my impression was, but it got my attention for sure.

Ingram first met Earl at the Culpepper Bluegrass festival in 1972 when he was playing with Jimmy Martin and the Sunny Mountain Boys. However, it wasn't a significant one-on-one conversation at that particular moment. Later, he had the chance to spend some quality time with Earl, reminiscing that, "The first time I got to meet him up close and personal was about the time Lester passed away, and Red Allen had done a tribute album to Lester, and that was cut at Earl's house. Earl was there, and, of course, Louise, and his son Stevie was doing the engineering."

Kenny continued learning his chops throughout the 1960s and played with bands in his hometown of Nashville, Tennessee. He would eventually get the opportunity to put his banjo experience to the test on a professional level. "I picked banjo locally for a while, and in 1971 I went to work for James Monroe," remembers Ingram. "I was one of the original Midnight Ramblers, and in May of 1972 I went to work for Jimmy Martin and stayed with him until October 1, 1973. I then went to work for Lester Flatt and stayed with him until the end of June 1978. I went back to work with Jimmy and stayed until, I think, the spring or winter of 1980."

Kenny Ingram gained significant recognition as a banjo player when he joined up with Lester Flatt as the third banjoist in a direct descent from Earl Scruggs, preceded by Haskel McCormick, who was preceded by Vic Jordan. He laid a thumb to the banjo that was sometimes reminiscent of the way Earl performed.

Another banjo player often referenced for his similarities to Earl Scruggs is Charlie Cushman. When he was just a small child, Charlie had developed an interest in music from watching various country music shows on WSM television, and like Ingram, *The Flatt and Scruggs Grand Ole Opry* made the biggest impression on him. The allure of Earl's five-string had captivated him noticeably enough for his grandfather to purchase a used banjo.[5] Cushman characterizes the origin of his fascination with Scruggs:

> In comparison to the fiddle and the steel guitar and stuff, here comes Earl Scruggs with this banjo, playing these breakdowns, and that really caught my attention because it really stood out compared to fiddles and steel guitars. That banjo just jumped out at me. By age four, I was asking for a banjo. I was bitten fairly early. The first exposure I had was on television, and I don't know if the same thing would have happened if it had been on radio or not, you know. It probably would, but the ability to watch this guy, and to watch his fingers, and watch him walk up to the microphone, you know, just the whole package. I remember all of that, the way they worked the microphones and took turns playing, you know. It's all very obvious when you hear those guys play, even to a little kid.

Charlie took lessons for a while from a guitar player, who knew a little bit of three-finger-style banjo. Soon he would develop the ability to play by ear from Flatt and Scruggs records and was showing new licks to his teacher, consequently ending his lessons.[6] He went on to enter banjo contests in the Nashville region and also pick with other musicians in the area. He continued to earnestly study Earl Scruggs's banjo technique as he progressed in performances with some of bluegrass music's biggest names. After appearing on the Opry one night in the 1990s,

Cushman was pleasantly surprised by a complimentary phone message that awaited him at home:

> I was on there one night with [banjoist and fiddle player] Mike Snider. We had about five minutes left in the show, and he asked me if I had my banjo picks, and I said yes I did. So he took the banjo off, handed it to me, and it was during a commercial break he said, "You play us out of here." We came back on the air and they introduced Mike and he introduced me and I played "Earl's Breakdown." Anyway, I went home that night, it was about midnight, and there was a message on my answering machine. Well, it was Earl saying, "I just watched you on the Nashville Network doing the Opry, and you really played that old tune really well, and I just wanted to let you know I saw that, and we'll talk to you later." That was a high point in my career, and if I never played again, I got a compliment from Scruggs. The next day I made sure I didn't erase that message. I went and got my cassette recorder and I copied it.

Though Charlie Cushman enjoyed a prosperous career in bluegrass, in addition to becoming an authority on prewar Gibson banjos, fate ultimately led him back to his Scruggs roots as a key member of the Earls of Leicester (pronounced "Lester"), a Flatt and Scruggs tribute band.

In 1962, young Marc Pruett came home from school, as he usually did in the late afternoon, and sat down for a snack while listening to a music show called *The Cornbread Matinee*. He only had a half hour to snack and listen to the radio before his mom would make him do his homework. It was during one of those breaks that Pruett claims he received a spiritual calling:

> One day, the deejay played Lester Flatt and Earl Scruggs's "Flint Hill Special," "Earl's Breakdown," "Dim Lights, Thick Smoke," and it covered me up. I was eleven years old and I asked my mom, "What's that instrument they're playing?" She said, "Son, that's a banjo." I said, "I want one for Christmas." That's how I became interested in the banjo. When I heard him play, it was like God said to me, that's part of who you are too. Earl's playing spoke straight to my heart, and I've never heard any banjo music come close to moving me the way his did. There have been a lot of great players that I admire and emulate, but Earl Scruggs did the whole thing. I'll say this—his music has given my life a quality that few things equal.

As an early adolescent in 1965, Marc worked up the courage to approach Earl Scruggs for an autograph at the Old Asheville City Auditorium, where Flatt and Scruggs were performing. Pruett relives the day when he knocked on their bus door and was greeted by their bassist, Cousin Jake Tullock:

> I asked if Earl was there, and I was invited into the bus, and there he was. He was so cordial to me. I chatted for a couple of minutes and got an autograph. I asked Earl, "Where's Mr. Flatt?" And he said, "He walked down the street with Josh to get a sandwich." Later, I sneaked backstage to a room where I heard them practicing. In those days, I guess the artists weren't so heavily guarded, and I just walked up the steps to the dressing room—and walked in. And it was me, alone with Lester, Earl, Jake, Josh, and Paul. They played "Gonna Have Myself a Ball." That year, that was a current release for them.
>
> Earl was sitting down in a chair that didn't have much of a bottom in it because I remember he was sort of hunched over as he played. I always thought it was brilliant how he tuned his fifth string up to G-sharp for that one song, which was in the key of E. He played the song in open G with the fifth string tuned up one fret. That's the only song I've ever heard in that tuning. At the end of rehearsing that one song, it was real quiet for a few seconds, and Lester said, "Let's get this damn thing over with." The mood was somber. No one else said a word, and they all put their instruments away and left the room.
>
> As a thirteen-year-old kid, I didn't know what to think, but many years later I heard that the promoter for that show collected all the money and left town without paying the band. I can only imagine how they felt playing to several thousand people—and not getting paid. One last thought on that show. On my way out of the dressing room, I lightly brushed Earl's banjo with my left hand and listened to that silvery, rippling, pinging sound. I wish I could do that one more time.

In February 1968, Marc Pruett would again see Flatt and Scruggs perform at the old Asheville-Biltmore College. "It was cold and icy, but they put on a hot show," says Pruett. "And that was just a year before they broke up. It was fabulous. I would call it controlled power with feeling." Oddly enough, that night he was bitten by an English bulldog while entering the auditorium to find a seat. The dog actually took off the end of his index finger of the right hand, but he was patched up at the school infirmary and was still able to catch the show. Upon reflection, Marc whimsically quips, "I had come to hear Flatt and Scruggs and was bitten by a dog." At the end of the show he was able to talk to the band again and to Earl specifically. Pruett remarks, "I asked him to show me how he played 'Sally Ann,' and he did, but I couldn't play for a month or so."

During the Earl Scruggs Revue's early touring circuit, Earl met a banjo-pickin' comedian from the greater Los Angeles area named Steve Martin. Long before he reached mega-stardom, the young comic was reminiscent of the Uncle Dave Macon era, when the banjo was used as a prop to support comedy bits. While his stage presence at the time was one of endless streaks of zaniness, offstage his knack for the five-string was serious business. Martin speaks about his fascination with the banjo and the man who inspired his musical talent:

> I was about sixteen or seventeen when I got interested in the banjo. I got interested through folk music: the Kingston Trio—and where the banjo was used a lot. But it was not played like Earl played it. There were people who were okay, you know. They kind of strummed it. So I picked it up with that in mind, and through Pete Seeger's book, but when I heard Earl I realized that the banjo was significantly advanced from what I had heard so far. That's when I seriously got interested in playing Scruggs style.
>
> I bought the album *Foggy Mountain Banjo* and that, I would say, changed my life. Earl's playing really changed my life and gave me a whole new creative outlet—and it was really because of Earl. I was a comedian as soon as I was eighteen, and at that point I had only been playing about a year, but I put [the banjo] in immediately and did some comedy with it, and every once in a while in the show I'd play a whole tune.

As a high school friend of banjoist John McEuen, Martin was afforded the opportunity to meet his idol when McEuen invited him to a performance of the Earl Scruggs Revue in the seaside community of La Jolla, California. "I met Earl and was backstage with him, sort of in awe," Martin admits. "It's very hard to be a normal person when you idolize Earl Scruggs and you find yourself with him." While perfecting his comedic skills on the road as a self-described tagalong with the Nitty

Gritty Dirt Band, Steve would occasionally serve as the emcee and opening act for shows that the Revue shared with the Dirt Band.

Like many of the other disciples, "Foggy Mountain Breakdown," "Reuben," "Shuckin' the Corn," and "Sally Ann" ranked high on Steve's list of favorite Scruggs instrumentals. However, he acknowledges that Earl gave him a more personal touch with one particular tune. "He taught me how to play 'Sally Goodin' his way," says Martin. "I actually recorded it, and it was on the back of the single of 'King Tut' [in 1978] as a matter of fact. And I felt really good knowing that I was playing it exactly the way Earl played it."

Martin's ties to the Dirt Band also brought him to the recording studio during their historic *Circle* sessions in 1971, which he fondly remembers being graced by an unexpected visitor:

> When the *Will the Circle Be Unbroken* album was being recorded, my manager William McEuen had assembled all these people, at least this is my impression of it. So I got a recording session after their day was done. I could go in and use the studio. I had written about five or six original banjo tunes that I was going to record, with no intent actually [other than] just to record them. They actually were released on my last comedy album called *The Steve Martin Brothers*. I have photos of Earl dropping by the session. I didn't play with him, but he just dropped in and listened and was very encouraging.

Martin's original compositions recorded in 1971 (not heard by the public until ten years later) had all of the earmarks of a contemporary sound that was gaining momentum among some Scruggs disciples who were creating a more modernized form of bluegrass music.

THE PROGRESSIVE HARVEST

During the 1960s folk boom, alongside Pete Seeger and the Kingston Trio, Flatt and Scruggs were making huge inroads with the genre's musical fanatics. The change that began under that influence continued to gain a large following among younger audiences into the 1970s and 1980s. It was during this time that progressive banjo pioneers like Pete Wernick, Tony Trischka, and Béla Fleck started redefining the limits of the bluegrass banjo. With all due respect to their Scruggs ties, they began to experiment with newer forceful rhythmic patterns on several ancestral bluegrass tunes. For many traditionalists, this did not set well, and they began drawing lines in the sand. They felt that newgrassers were attempting to change the music from its foundational structure, but as time passed there seemed to be fewer people bickering about the conventional versus advancing forms of bluegrass music. More and more festivals were beginning to feature traditional and progressive bands on the same stage, and it became more apparent to promoters that their growing fan base was in the significant numbers of young people who were showing up to their events.

Pete Wernick was steered toward the banjo, via Pete Seeger, by a friend who also introduced him to the music of Mississippi John Hurt, Flatt and Scruggs, and others in the realm of folk music. Shortly thereafter, Pete's own banjo journey would begin. "My friend, Jake, showed me a bit of frailing on the banjo, and we had an old five-string in our house," Wernick recalls. "So I started practicing and got hooked. I started with Seeger-style banjo and his book and playing folky stuff with my friends." Pete also recounts the day he heard Earl's blazing banjo and how it changed his direction:

> Sometime around thirteen or fourteen years old, my friend Jake played me "Shuckin' the Corn," and my first comment was, "That's one guy?" It sounded so dazzling. It was unbelievable and magical. I still remember exactly where I was standing when I heard that. Once I'd gotten a handle on Seeger-style banjo, I decided to try to learn what Scruggs was doing. It seemed impossibly hard. There was no written or recorded help available at the time, and nobody teaching it. It was just trial and error, find the melody and chords by ear, listen and experiment, listen and learn.

After a brief introduction to Earl by John Hartford in the late 1970s, Wernick didn't have any further contact with the banjo man until 1981 when his band, Hot Rize, played the Grand Ole Opry with Scruggs in attendance. After the evening's performance, a friend of Pete's conducted an interview with Earl, asking what he thought of Hot Rize, to which Scruggs replied that he liked the way they sounded. That was motivation enough for Wernick to roll the dice and call Earl on the phone, hoping that he might get an invite to his musical role model's house. He explains the payoff from his gamble in venturing to the House of Scruggs:

> I was nervous, but he was so pleasant and welcoming [that] I relaxed. After that, I'd visit him and Louise about any time I was in Nashville, and we'd have long visits, talking about all kinds of things, and getting to play together sometimes, one-on-one, something I never would have dared to dream. It was hard to put out of my mind that my absolute musical hero and I were taking turns chopping chords for each other. One time it was after midnight, and he and Louise and I were still yakking away, and they invited me to stay over. That was cool!

Becoming a teacher of bluegrass banjo with the publication of numerous instructional books and videos, Pete Wernick has come to be known as Dr. Banjo, which is a play on the fact that he has a PhD from Columbia University. He runs banjo camps and programs for evolving players to learn how to jam and keep good timing in a band situation. He's devoted his life to the teaching of Scruggs style and continues to commit himself to teaching the craft to anyone willing to do the work. Wernick surmises how his mentor, Earl Scruggs, felt about the widespread attraction to his musical aesthetics:

> He would say he's honored that people want to learn his style and leave it at that. His music was so appealing, its influence was dominant, and his musicianship brought a completely new life to the five-string and to bluegrass music. By far the majority of people wanting to play banjo over the last fifty years have wanted to sound like Earl. I do think Scruggs-style banjo is one of the big reasons that bluegrass music will live as long as there are human beings. I count as one of the most significant accomplishments of my life that I have helped many people learn to play Scruggs-style banjo, worldwide. I'm amazed and happy that I've been able to play it myself for over fifty years and counting. I feel grateful to Earl every day for that, and it gives me satisfaction that he knew how I felt about it. I told him I'd never be able to repay my debt to him, no matter how I tried, and I have tried.

When fourteen-year-old Tony Trischka of Syracuse, New York, first heard Earl Scruggs play the banjo, he could never have imagined the overpowering effect it would have on the rest of his life. His discovery of the banjo occurred during the folk boom of the early 1960s. He was first attuned to the banjo of Dave Guard of the Kingston Trio, which didn't last long, as he heard a sound with a more hypnotic effect that made him think, "Okay, this is it, the mother lode, or the father lode maybe." Tony admits that his thirst for the banjo intensified after he began listening to Flatt and Scruggs records:

> The first time I heard Earl was on the Flatt and Scruggs album *Folk Songs of Our Land*. I imagine Louise Scruggs had a hand in this album because they were trying to go more commercial, so they did *Folk Songs of Our Land*. That was, I think, the second bluegrass album I ever owned. It was just like, holy smokes, this is too amazing. This is just what I've been looking for. I remember thinking, oh my gosh, this is too much, but the subtleties were lost on me at that point. But, I mean, I was playing his style at that point, and I got it, but I didn't get it on the deeper levels that I would understand today, which comes from a lot of transcribing his solos at half speed, digging into what he's doing.

More than thirty years after meeting Earl in the mid-1970s while playing on the same festival circuit as the Earl Scruggs Revue, Tony Trischka was honored to have his musical role model record on his 2007 *Double Banjo Bluegrass Spectacular*, along with guitarist Tony Rice and banjoists Béla Fleck and Steve Martin. Tony has contributed greatly to the world of the five-string banjo, from classic recordings in the 1970s as part of the bands Country Cooking (with Pete Wernick) and Breakfast Special, to some of the most comprehensive teaching DVDs and books available on the market today. As noted, both Trischka and Wernick are Scruggs disciples who were some of the first to push the envelope of what was acceptable for the banjo. Their more obscure chord combinations (and instrument arrangements) of bluegrass, jazz, and rock produced an avant-garde sound that foreshadowed the emergence of another disciple who took the banjo beyond everyone's imagination.

If Earl Scruggs invented an entirely new vocabulary for the five-string banjo, then Béla Fleck built a second language. When people first heard Earl play the banjo, they had no idea the instrument could ever produce such a sound. Many years later, when Béla started gaining acclaim, folks responded in much the same way. They couldn't believe what he was pulling out of the banjo. Fleck has raised the stakes for progressive banjo playing, just as Earl did when he set the standard that made Béla's style possible.

Fleck gained a reputation in the band New Grass Revival from 1981 to 1989 with his creative approaches to Scruggs and melodic-style banjo. Along the way, he began incorporating single-string methods that allowed him to venture into jazz, funk, and classical music. His professional career actually began in 1976, with the New England–anchored group Tasty Licks, and he later moved to Lexington, Kentucky, to join the band Spectrum in 1979. Fleck was instrumental (no pun intended) in helping to create and define progressive bluegrass. It was during his tenure in New Grass Revival that he developed a more radical interpretation of the banjo that laid the foundation for the growing number of advancing banjo players in today's generation.

When Fleck began playing the banjo he initially used Pete Seeger's banjo book, yet he readily grasped that it was not reflective of what he was hearing Earl play, though he didn't feel the book was filled with inaccuracies. He eventually purchased a copy of *Earl Scruggs and the 5-String Banjo* and began to devour everything in it, though Fleck confesses, "I wasn't a Scruggs-a-holic in the beginning, but in the very beginning, when I first heard the banjo, it was Earl, and he had that profound effect on me that he's had on so many people."

In the reawakening of his Scruggs state of mind, Fleck began to work hard at emulating Earl's timing and tone after he moved to Lexington in the late 1970s. His intellectual perspective toward the various nuances and intricacies in Earl's musicianship may be due to his highly technical understanding of music theory. Béla outlines a few examples reflective of his ability to make connections in Earl's stylistic bond to things most people would never consider:

> Earl's playing is even better than perfect, because perfect is boring. What I think Earl had was the sound of the high-tech primitive. There's something so earthy and real about Earl's playing that sounds as old as the hills, and he had the modern quality with that speed and dexterity and that bright silvery sound, which sounds very modern and high tech. It's the combination of the two that makes it stand out so much.
>
> I think Earl was a great unconscious player, and I mean that in a most positive light. When you talk about jazz musicians who impro-

vise, they really do their best work when they let their unconscious take over, and Earl was so unpretentious, and unself-conscious, when he played the banjo. He just played what he felt. He wasn't thinking about all the little notes, and that leaves all of us to try and figure out all the little notes.

Like so many other disciples, Béla was afforded the opportunity to jam with the father of the bluegrass banjo at his home. The mutual admiration and respect he and Earl shared was characteristic of Earl's relationships with the disciples he had come to know. "Every time I was at a jam session with him, he was very aware of every single player in the jam, and he made sure that everyone got a solo before he ever came back in," Fleck confirms. "He felt a duty to make sure that everybody was treated equally in jam sessions. He was no prima donna."

IN THE SPIRIT OF SCRUGGS

Earl Scruggs loved to play contemporary music, which became most evident during the 1970s. By the dawn of the 1980s, his seniority with the Earl Scruggs Revue was coming to a close. His touring days ended, and his recordings were beginning to wind down. And while the music around him was continuing to change, a new generation of disciples, born out of the Vietnam War era, were primed and pumped to carry the torch that Scruggs lit some forty years earlier. By this time, banjoists playing newgrass incorporated some melodic techniques into their Scruggs-style picking, as opposed to such veterans as J. D. Crowe, who remained loyal to Scruggs style even within the context of more progressive rhythms.

Rising up through the ranks during this period is, perhaps, the most dedicated Scruggs disciple to date—Jim Mills. Having spent most of his life trying to capture the essence of Earl's playing, he's become a living embodiment of the Scruggs legacy. It was Jim's father who first encouraged him to alter the course of his banjo heritage. "I'm a third-generation banjo player from the state of North Carolina," says Mills. "My grandfather played clawhammer style, my dad played a locally popular two-finger style while I was growing up, and I kind of followed in his footsteps, playing two-finger style. He told me just put that finger pick on the third finger and it will come to you."

Jim's first discovery of Earl Scruggs occurred when he was just six years old. After hearing the original 1949 version of "Foggy Mountain Breakdown" from his older brother's record collection, the song resonated with him, and he told his sibling to "play it again, play it again." Four years later, he dedicated himself to Earl Scruggs exclusively over other banjoists who were cultivating discipleships of their own. And as Mills candidly admits, the popular styles of the day weren't enough to lure him away from Earl:

> I got serious trying to learn what Earl Scruggs was doing when I was about ten years old. From that period on, I was consumed with Earl Scruggs. It's funny to say, and I'm almost embarrassed to say this, but I was very sheltered when I was learning to play. I'm not that old. I was born in 1966. It wasn't like I was born in the forties, but I learned to play like a kid would have learned in the forties or fifties. I did not realize that J. D. Crowe existed, that Sonny Osborne existed, the Seldom Scene, the Country Gentlemen. I didn't even know that Flatt and Scruggs had busted up when I was a kid. Like I said, I was sheltered as a kid. I was tunnel-visioned into Flatt and Scruggs.
>
> I even tried to fool with some of the melodic stuff of Bill Keith and Bobby Thompson, but my ear always took me back to the root, to the foundation of Earl. So I very much patterned my playing after the Scruggs style, and these other guys gave me some new ideas as well. I found Scruggs style to be more natural for my ear.

Jim's respect for Earl Scruggs, and the impact he made on the world of music, radiates from his life story and every tale he tells about Scruggs. His detailed knowledge of Earl's life shows a commitment that is mirrored in the intensity with which Jim plays the banjo and in his passion to know everything there is to know about prewar Gibson banjos. Earl Scruggs was more than the master of the five-string banjo for Mills, and he makes clear the level of impact he's made musically:

> As a musician playing his particular instrument, I believe in all my heart that Earl Scruggs will go down in history as being the most emulated musician, on his particular instrument, of any musician you can think of. What other musician can you think of, on his particular instrument, seventy years after they started playing, is still considered top of the line on their particular instrument?

In the autumn of 2006, a number of Scruggs disciples recorded *Foggy Mountain Special: A Bluegrass Tribute to Earl Scruggs*. One of the devoted followers, who received an International Bluegrass Music Association (IBMA) award for Instrumental Performance of the Year for his rendition of "Foggy Mountain Rock," is Pennsylvania banjoist Tom Adams. Like many Yankees, he initially regarded the "hillbilly" records from his father's collection as "the whiny, singing-through-their-noses sound that came out of our stereo."

By fourth grade, he was interested in playing the snare drum in his school's band, but was never selected, so his dad thought it might cheer him up if he taught him some chords on the guitar, thus marking the beginning of a new direction for him. Adams details how he segued from the guitar to the banjo with an indirect hand from Earl:

> One thing led to another, and I went from playing some rhythm guitar to having [Dad] show me some chords on the mandolin, and then my younger brother, Dale, also learned to play guitar and mandolin. In June 1968 Dale and I played onstage for the first time at a local firemen's carnival. At that point, my dad borrowed a banjo, with the intention of learning it, and the three of us would be a bluegrass group. My dad never got the hang of the banjo, and prior to there being a banjo in our house, I never had any desire to play one. But something clicked when I heard the 1949 cut of "Foggy Mountain Breakdown" on one of Dad's Starday sampler LPs. That was the sound that called me to the banjo. And then I found one of his records, called *Foggy Mountain Banjo*, with nothing *but* banjo tunes on it. I started learning to play the banjo in January 1969 when I was ten years old.
>
> My first and lasting impression upon hearing Earl Scruggs play the banjo was simply Earl Scruggs equals banjo. We had lots of records with banjo on them, and I learned to love many of the tunes and players. But the thought that Earl Scruggs equals banjo was always first and foremost, followed by the thought [that] other people play the banjo too. But not like Earl Scruggs.

Adams had only been playing banjo a year when he had the opportunity to meet the banjo man himself at a show he was playing with the Earl Scruggs Revue. "I first met Earl at Sunset Park [in West Grove, Pennsylvania] in July 1970. It was magic. I will never forget the feeling of watching and listening to him play that day. He autographed my banjo after the show." Tom also reflects on the influence Earl Scruggs had on the world and credits him with motivating so many people to learn the banjo and start playing. "I think that the most special thing about Earl's playing is its power to inspire others to take up the banjo, to bring more music into the world."

Best known for being Alison Krauss's banjo player (though he cuts a good amount of time on the guitar also) Ron Block has a unique style that has captured the attention of banjoists worldwide. Though planted firmly in Scruggs, much of Block's appeal to his five-string fans is the way he chokes the strings, not only to move through melodies different- ly but to add some electric-guitar-like effects to his playing. In some ways, he has created his own verbiage on the banjo.

Block grew up in Southern California, though for a few of those years he lived in the Grass Valley region of Northern California, and in his own words says, "It was a Huck Finn existence, and living in that kind of rural environment has affected me for life." The first record he remembers hearing was Marty Robbins's *Gunfighter Ballads and Trail Songs*, in addition to the music of Fleetwood Mac, the Beatles, and Paul McCartney (post-Beatles). When he was eleven years old, his dad got him a guitar, but as Ron concedes, it didn't take long for the banjo to get a chokehold on his musical interest:

> I first heard bluegrass at around twelve or close to thirteen. It was Lester Flatt on television. I think Haskel McCormick was the banjo player. I hounded my dad nonstop until he got me a banjo for my birthday. Now he likes to say he bought me a banjo when I was thirteen and I didn't come out of my room until I was twenty-one, which is partly true.

Block's journey into the world of bluegrass music was in full swing as he attempted to learn what Earl was doing on the banjo. Prior to any formal lessons, he taught himself how to play from the instructional books and records he began purchasing. Ron opens up about the trans- formation he underwent after discovering the sound of Scruggs:

> I had no bluegrass education at first. I did buy Earl's book early on, and Pete Wernick's book, and learned from both of those and began to get some sense of what was good. I'd order three or four records from County Sales. This was in the very early eighties. I don't re-

member exactly when it was, but it was early in my banjo journey. When I heard Earl for the first time, it was a revelation. I thought, "That's how it's done!" Two or three years into playing, Dad brought me for some lessons with John Hickman. John is a good guy and was patient with me. I remember when he pulled out some live Flatt and Scruggs on his old reel-to-reel tapes. Earl's playing live blew me away. John piled up a box full of reel-to-reels and let me take them home. I had to borrow a reel-to-reel machine and then taped them all off. I've still got a lot of those on cassette. Back then the live shows were hard to come by. I love Flatt and Scruggs live shows because, at times, it seems Earl risks more than on record—he'll do things that still really surprise me.

Despite his own success, Ron Block continues to be a devoted disciple of Earl Scruggs. He likes to contrast the way Earl played to that of other banjoists he has spent time studying. He often argues the case for Scruggs's influence on the music world:

His influence is far-reaching. Is there a bluegrass banjo player, traditional or progressive, who has not been directly or indirectly influenced by him? Earl Scruggs wasn't a traditional banjo player. He was one of the pioneers of a brand-new genre. He created the tradition by innovating, by making something radically new and, to a large degree, previously unheard. He soaked up the traditions of his day as a youngster, learned from players around his home, listened to the radio, played with different people, explored sounds on his own, and came up with a style that continued to grow and evolve. To me, Earl Scruggs exemplifies the spirit of what bluegrass is all about.

As the five-time Banjo Performer of the Year for both the IBMA and the Society for the Preservation of Bluegrass Music of America (SPBGMA), in addition to being the 2011 recipient of the Steve Martin Prize for Excellence in Banjo and Bluegrass, Scruggs disciple Sammy Shelor has an impressive list of accolades to his credit. As the banjo player for the Lonesome River Band for more than twenty-five years, his professional career was launched in the early 1980s.

The beginning of his interest in the banjo dates back to when Sammy was a young lad at the age of four. He was fortunate to have grandfathers who were dedicated to his success in learning to play the banjo and to exposing him to "real-deal" bluegrass musicians who would make that extra difference in his journey. Sammy briefly tells of his first exposure to Earl Scruggs:

> My introduction to the banjo was my grandfather, but I would say that my introduction to bluegrass was Flatt and Scruggs. When I was four, or maybe five years old, my grandfather took me to Hillsville, Virginia, to the VFW, and Flatt and Scruggs were playing, and that's the first time I ever saw a bluegrass band. That would have been around 1966. Visually I remember that show well, but musically I didn't comprehend it. It did impact me and made me realize what music was, and that there was such a thing as a band, because prior to that I [had] just heard my grandfather playing banjo on the couch.

Most any professional bluegrass banjo players will tell you straight-out that they learned from the get-go the impossibility of trumping Earl's legacy. Such a statement is merely a confession that Scruggs had that certain *je ne sais quoi*, and Sammy echoes the same sentiment:

> Well, my first impression was, when I was trying to learn it, I figured out pretty quick that I wasn't going to get it like he did it. He had his heart, and his brains, and his hands, and I didn't, and that's all you can say. I've tried to emulate that the best I can, and like I say, he just had his own thing with it, J. D. has his own thing with it, and Baucom has his own thing with it, and, you know, everybody's got their own heart, and that's what you have to discover. I discovered early on that I couldn't be Earl, so I just tried to find something else. Every banjo's got a voice. Every banjo player has their own voice as well. If Earl hadn't come along, the music would have gone off in another direction.

It goes without saying that banjo players, in any generation, learned at the feet of the masters preceding them. The bluegrass stars that came out of the late 1970s and the 1980s sat at the feet of the second generation of bluegrass champions. The banjo players that came out of the 1990s were beginning to sound more bluesy in their playing, and much of it was influenced by predecessors such as Terry Baucom, Sammy Shelor, and Ron Block, though we can go back further to J. D. Crowe and find examples of bluesy playing in the 1970s.

There's also a great deal to be said about bands that keep the original members around for twenty or more years (as with those of Sonny

Osborne and Sammy Shelor). Jason Burleson is yet another one of those long-termers and has been with Blue Highway since 1994. His style is driving and bouncy, which has helped create his group's distinctive sound. By the time he first took up the banjo at eleven years old, the field of potential mentors in bluegrass banjo was plentiful. But it was his father's love of Flatt and Scruggs's repertoire that drew young Burleson toward the ole five-string. The original Scruggs recordings, which were reflective of a past generation, had stood the test of time when he first heard them in 1978. And regardless of the music's age, Jason notes how significant Earl's body of work was, not only to him but to the longevity of the banjo and everyone who plays it:

> My first influence was definitely Earl. I first heard Earl play on some of my dad's old Flatt and Scruggs records. I loved the way Earl played on the vocal songs. "My Cabin in Caroline" and "We'll Meet Again Sweetheart" come to mind as textbook examples of Earl's genius when it came to playing behind the vocal and how to "play the words" on a solo.
>
> The best way I can think to describe Earl's playing: it's the perfect combination of tone, timing, taste, and touch. To me, he [refined] it and perfected it at the same time. All of us bluegrass players are still trying to get there. We all speak this language he created on the banjo, just with a little different accent. I don't think banjo playing will ever completely shift away from Earl. I think there will be generations that will continue to be inspired by him and will pursue that path of trying to re-create what Earl did. There will always be players that will take what Earl did as their foundation and create something of their own. Players like Béla Fleck and Noam Pikelny come to mind as examples of incredible musicians who were inspired by Earl but found their own voice. I think that pattern will continue indefinitely.

As another disciple who can master both traditional and progressive styles, Kristin Scott Benson plays with immense drive and timing that pops as good as can be found. Kristin comes from a musical family that played bluegrass, and both her father and grandfather were mandolin players. When she was very young, her grandpa took her to see the Earl Scruggs Revue perform at Gardner-Webb College in Boiling Springs, North Carolina. Since her grandfather was playing the same show, Kristin was afforded the chance to meet Earl backstage. "Even though I didn't know anything about music," she recounts, "I realized I was meeting someone important. I mean, it felt different to see him play. I could tell it was special, that this was an important guy to the banjo and to bluegrass, and I remember it. I remember the room and can remember feeling that something big had just happened."

Despite her initial brush with Scruggs, Benson's interest in the banjo didn't surface until a few years later when she was nine years old. Interestingly, she confesses that it wasn't triggered by Scruggs. "What got me into the banjo, specifically, was seeing Doyle Lawson and Quicksilver in 1985, and I got to see Scott Vestal play the banjo, and it was just really something. That's what sparked my interest in that particular instrument, and it was years before I got one, but from that point on, I wanted to play the banjo." With Vestal as the vehicle that brought Kristin to the five-string, she quickly comprehended the significance of the man she had once seen as a youngster. Her analysis of Earl's relevance is summed up by the way she places the banjo learning process into a historical context:

> The thing that I think characterized his playing above everyone else's playing was the level of perfection. I can't think of any other instrument in the world where the goal of your playing is so focused on the past. Oftentimes, in bluegrass, the weight of your musicianship in a bluegrass context is how closely you can do what Earl did. The part that's so impressive about Earl is that no one has done it that well since. Now, people have since done different things, and have added intricacies to their playing, but as a whole bluegrass banjo playing has not changed very much, and the foundation of it all is still his playing, and to this day no one can execute the way he did, as well as he did.

Having played with a number of groups over the years, including the Larry Stephenson Band, Sally Jones and the Sidewinders, Honi Deaton and Dream, Larry Cordle and Lonesome Standard Time, and most recently the Grascals, Benson is also involved with some of the banjo camps that are offered throughout the United States, where she asserts to her students the principles of Scruggs:

> I continually tell people this, because I teach a lot of lessons, as well as playing, and I continually remind people that Earl created this, and has done better than anyone else has. He was making it up. He created this system that was so flawless that it remains relatively

unchanged all these years. I try to tell people that Earl was playing what came naturally to him. There are some phrases and characteristics of his playing that I avoid, if at all possible, because I just can't seem to make it sound like that, and so I try to remind people that he did what came naturally to him. So after we learn a certain amount of material, then we have this word bank, essentially, of solid phrases that can give us the tools to be a solid bluegrass banjo player, and where does that come from? Well, it comes from the playing of Earl Scruggs. With this particular instrument, you really do have to adhere to rights and wrongs, and if you want to be taken seriously as a bluegrass banjo player, you have to adhere to the right way as being Earl's way.

INTERNATIONAL SENSATIONS

Many people think bluegrass music appeals exclusively to those living in rural America, yet amazingly, the attraction is widely shared throughout the world. Since music is a language that needs no interpreters, individuals can understand each other through harmonies without ever comprehending one another through the verbal tongue. In chapter 5, Earl Scruggs spoke eloquently of the banjo's popularity in Japan in the 1960s, which spawned some of the finest bluegrass banjoists from Asia, such as Tamotsu Miyamoto, Kazuhiko Murakata, and Hiroshi Yasuda.

Following the end of World War II American music of many varieties became widespread in Japan. A big part of this growth was due to the U.S. servicemen who were part of the American occupation force from 1945 to 1952. Armed Forces Radio broadcast everything from big bands to swing, country, and bluegrass. Japanese civilians were exposed to these new forms of music. Bluegrass especially gained momentum with the Japanese, perhaps because of the similarities between the musical instruments of Japan and America. It's easy to understand why the five-string banjo is so well liked among the Japanese when you consider the prevalence of Japanese instruments such as the shamisen and the sanshin (native instrument of Okinawa). These instruments are shaped like the banjo (bearing some of the same tonal qualities), yet they are fretless, with only three-strings, and are plucked with the fingers.

Saburo Watanabe has spent more than fifty years in the pursuit of bluegrass music, not only as a writer-editor for *MoonShiner* magazine and historian of the genre in Japan, but as an accomplished banjo player in his highly praised ensemble Bluegrass 45 (named in honor of the year bluegrass began, 1945). Watanabe formed the group in 1971 and has toured the United States and the world, sharing the stage with several top bluegrass artists. Growing up, he never really thought much about the banjo, though he was familiar with its crisp, twangy sound. He eventually had an experience that steered him toward the five-string banjo:

> I believe it was [the] summer of 1964, maybe '65. One day, I happened to turn on [my brother's] tape recorder when he was out, and I hear [this] unbelievable sound. It was "The Old Home Town"—not fancy, just a simple old bluegrass song, but it hit me like lightning. I still remember the sight from [the] window of my brother's room. The rice field and forest trees were all shining in beautiful green. I thought it was a perfect combination of the song and banjo at that time. I wanted to play banjo, and I did. After a while, I found out [why the] banjo is difficult to play. If you listen to the first version of "Foggy Mountain Breakdown" recorded 1949, you'll understand the difficulty of the five-string banjo and the true genius of Earl Scruggs.

Watanabe's gravitation toward Earl's banjo and bluegrass music was part of an almost counterculture response by the Japanese youth to the cultural barriers that tried to suppress the artistry of rural America. As documented in chapter 5, Flatt and Scruggs paved the way for the genre to sustain credibility when no one in eastern Asia was willing to showcase that kind of entertainment. What Scruggs brought to Japan in 1968 is still widely appreciated and copied, based on the impressive number of Japanese bluegrass bands and attendees at conferences like the IBMA and SPBGMA. Saburo confirms his country's attraction to bluegrass and their ongoing need for the fundamentals of Scruggs:

> Japanese bluegrass was mostly developed by college students. [It was never on] the mainstream media for these [past] fifty years. Most Japanese bluegrassers started to pick at college. Today they still teach Earl's "Cripple Creek" or "Blue Ridge Cabin Home" as the first tune to learn to play banjo and bluegrass. Every year, we still have a couple of hundred newcomers at the college bluegrass clubs all over Japan. In Japan, most of us understand if someone wants to play three-finger banjo, you should learn Earl first.

East Asia isn't the only foreign area to express a passion for bluegrass and Scruggs-style banjo playing. Europeans have also embraced and copied Earl's three-finger roll patterns. Some of the most notable players, such as Swiss native Jens Kruger, were produced within the borders of the transatlantic continent. The fondness for Scruggs and his banjo within Europe is reinforced by Chris Keenan, organizer of Ireland's Johnny Keenan Banjo Festival:

> Within Europe, Earl's presence is unmistakable. It's always obvious that nearly every bluegrass musician and band were influenced by the music of Earl and of Flatt and Scruggs. The majority of five-string banjo players play Scruggs style. The Eastern Europeans, who many years ago were not able to openly listen to and play music, have a particular affinity to bluegrass music. I regularly encounter musicians and fans in former Eastern Bloc countries who possess an incredible amount of bluegrass knowledge—some even able to recite whole catalogs of tunes and facts.

As mentioned, bluegrass music's worldwide appeal can be experienced every fall at the IBMA convention. Fans and musicians stretching from the British Isles all the way to New Zealand can be spotted at workshops, seminars, live shows, and band showcases. Additionally, Europe has its own IBMA counterpart, the European Bluegrass Music Association (EBMA), headquartered in the Netherlands. Good tone, good timing, good separation between notes, and drive stir people and draw them into an experience both intellectual and spiritual. Earl Scruggs epitomized all the above, and citizens throughout the world connect with it because it has all the elements of *great* music.

One of the most popular bluegrass bands in Europe today is Italy's Red Wine from Genoa, formed in 1978 by banjoist Silvio Ferretti with celebrated guitarist Beppe Gambetta. Their amazing drive, tone, and timing are second to none among American ensembles. They have toured extensively in the United States, sharing stages with award-winning artists like Alison Krauss and Union Station, Tony Rice, Ricky Skaggs, and the Del McCoury Band. Ferretti is the quintessential Renaissance man and not only plays banjo professionally but is a pediatric surgeon and a luthier who builds guitars, banjos, and quality banjo bridges. He is an articulate man of excellence, and a true disciple of Earl Scruggs.

Born in 1952, Silvio tried his hand at a variety of musical instruments, including piano, guitar, dulcimer, mandolin, autoharp, and electric bass, throughout his youth before pursuing the banjo in his early adulthood. Despite his late entry into the five-string arena, Ferretti recollects how the sound of Earl's banjo struck a chord with him years earlier:

> My first introduction to the sound of the banjo happened with *Washington Square* in the early sixties, I guess, actually, the Italian version of it, entitled *L'uomo del Banjo*, "The Man with the Banjo." It was a tenor, played very basically, so I didn't much care for it. Then I literally stole some records from my uncle, and there was some great five-string banjo on them: Pete Seeger, Doc Watson, and Earl Scruggs. I heard Earl on a Vanguard Records LP box set, recorded at the Newport Folk Festival with Flatt and the Foggies. "Salty Dog Blues" just blew my mind. I guess, like everybody hearing him for the first time, I thought, how can he do that? I thought he was the only man on earth who could play the banjo like that. Still do, by the way.

As a fan of bluegrass, jazz, 1960s and 1970s pop, and old country music, Silvio says Earl Scruggs opened the door for the banjo and expanded its repertoire:

> To me, Earl worked the magic of making the banjo sound musical and above musical genres. In his hands, the banjo has found a place in other musical genres, and that place is rooted in the *sound* that Earl got out of it, not in the notes, not in the phrasing. The *sound*. I recorded Scruggs-style banjo on pop songs, and it fit, not because I'm a monster player—I'm not—but because I learned [the] banjo sound from Earl. Not many banjo players can boast such an influence on music. Earl Scruggs was unique.

Yet when it comes to the more progressive end of bluegrass that blends various genres together, Ferretti expresses a more traditional viewpoint. "I don't even listen to jamgrass bands. I really don't care for that. I consider Scruggs style the basic foundation of bluegrass, along with Monroe-style mandolin, or derived styles of mandolin, and the kind of rhythm guitar that Flatt developed and others brought to perfection. Take those factors away and, to me, you don't have bluegrass."

In Sweden, Jens Koch grew up in a home where music was played, and his interest in the banjo began when he was around twelve years old in the mid-1990s. His uncles used to visit his house and perform Dixieland jazz on four-string tenor banjos. It was the sound of the banjo that Jens found attractive, even though they were not five-string banjos. Eventually, he told his uncle that he wanted to play the banjo, and it was at this point he was exposed to the recordings of Flatt and Scruggs. Though he claimed to his uncle that he wanted to play the tenor banjo like him, his uncle understood the difference between the four- and five-string banjos, as Koch reveals:

> He said, "Son, you need to hear this first before deciding on the tenor banjo." It was one of those moments when your jaw drops. You can't stand still. You want to know how it's done and you want more. I had loved the sound of the tenor banjo before, which made me want to play the banjo, but the sound of the five-string along with the drive that it has in the hands of Earl, that captured me totally. Since that day, I'm a true Scruggs appreciator. Later, I got to learn about his taste, as I heard more banjo players. Earl's sense of melody and choice of notes and phrasing still make me smile.

Jens is thoroughly steeped in Scruggs, but other influences can be heard in his playing from J. D. Crowe, Terry Baucom, Ron Stewart, Jim Mills, Sammy Shelor, and Sonny Osborne. He has his own technique and readily acknowledges, "We are other human beings playing banjo, created with our unique set of DNA, and sometimes I just think that we need to remember that. We're so affected by those who inspired us that we try to play like them, and I think that, often, our true voice doesn't get out as much because we try to play like others."

In 2006, Jens met up with Christoffer Olsson, Erik Igelström, Tobias Strömberg, and Jimmy Sunnebrandt at a bluegrass festival in Sweden and quickly realized they had chemistry and the makings of a great band. They decided on the name G2, meaning "Generation Two," because each of the members have fathers or uncles who play bluegrass. If Koch and Ferretti, along with others, such as Jens Kruger, are any indication of the way European bluegrass banjo players think about the impact of Earl Scruggs, then the future looks very encouraging for the banjo in Europe. The quality of the bluegrass bands rising out of Europe (as well as Asia) demonstrates an intentionality among the musicians and a commitment to learning how to play like the father of the bluegrass banjo.

EARL'S MILLENNIALS

By the 1990s the line in the sand between traditionalists and progressive bluegrass fans was less of an issue, and even to this day there's no sign that progressive musicians are in any way attempting to undermine traditional music, nor for that matter are there progressive banjo players attempting to erase the past of Earl Scruggs as the starting point for the bluegrass banjo's pilgrimage. No matter how far beyond traditional bluegrass this current generation of banjo players decide to travel, Earl's influence will always be obvious.

One such Scruggs disciple who is known for his comprehensive and creative approach to jazz banjo is North Carolinian Ryan Cavanaugh. Alongside other accomplished progressive banjoists like Béla Fleck, Matt Menefee, and Rex McGee, Cavanaugh began his banjo curriculum at the "University of Scruggs" in 1990. "My dad introduced me to Earl's banjo playing, and the album was *Will the Circle Be Unbroken*, and still to this day I think that is some of Earl Scruggs's best playing, but I met Earl years later when I went to his house in Nashville for one of [his] jams."

Most of the Scruggs disciples in this chapter speak of their banjo learning experiences as Scruggs-centric, in that they came from families that were familiar with and focused on old-time string music and traditional bluegrass. Bill Monroe, Flatt and Scruggs, and the Stanley Brothers were all that many people listened to, and it makes sense that the young banjo players, learning to pick in that kind of atmosphere, were most likely to be receptive to Earl's talent. The musical Petri dish that Ryan Cavanaugh developed in was not exclusively Scruggs-fed but included the influences of a multiplicity of musical genres, and this is to be expected, given that it was in a different place and time in history. His vast experience with other musical genres gives him an ear for connections with Scruggs, as he insightfully describes:

> I found, only through a study of [East] Indian rhythm styles, that upbeat drive, and Earl Scruggs was a very accessible American way

to hear this type of thing, and it sounds so American to us, but if you listen for it in American styles, Earl Scruggs is the only guy doing that. It was an eye-opener to hear those Indian musicians, or to hear John McLaughlin, or to hear Pat Martino play guitar. It's like, wait a minute, these guys are doing the same, but Earl was the first, and it was exciting to hear that flow of notes. Stevie Ray Vaughan had this song called "Scuttle Buttin'" where he played a bunch of really fast notes, and I related that to Earl Scruggs. I had to learn how to play that, and it sounded like something Earl would do. I learned it on the guitar first and then the banjo later.

Following in the same progressive path as Béla Fleck and others, Cavanaugh continues to be cutting-edge, experimenting with new forms of music on the banjo. It says a great deal about a banjo player when he lands a nine-year gig with the prominent jazz saxophonist Bill Evans. Most people could not have imagined in the 1950s that decades later there would be new generations of Scruggs-inspired banjo pickers playing modern jazz in notable bands (a reality once dreamed by Earl himself after his impromptu jam with King Curtis in 1960).

The longstanding belief of bluegrass purists that progressivists were diminishing the quality of the genre continues to bleed in the twenty-first century. However, with the millennial generation of musicians, that's simply not the case. Noam Pikelny is one of the latest banjo prodigies to come from the lineage of progressivism. Prior to his participation in a number of acclaimed bands, such as Leftover Salmon, the John Cowan Band, and the Punch Brothers, Pikelny was introduced to the instrument through the modernistic interpretations of Béla Fleck:

> I started playing banjo when I was eight years old. My brother was playing mandolin, and he saw a bluegrass band play at school as part of the rotating arts program. Eventually I wanted to learn an instrument. My parents thought if I learned the banjo, my brother and I could make music with each other. So they suggested the banjo, and I was fine with that. So I was just a little kid learning clawhammer, old-time banjo, and it was probably my brother's twelfth birthday, and I went to a music store to buy him a record, and the salesman there struck up a conversation with my dad and I, and [my dad] told him I played the banjo. He asked if we had heard the new Béla Fleck and the Flecktones album. We said no, we had not, and had never heard of him. So he sold us the album, and I couldn't believe the

sounds that I was hearing out of that banjo. As a little kid, I didn't believe that he was playing the same kind of Gibson Mastertone banjo as, like, Earl Scruggs, and I couldn't believe he was using the same three-finger picks as Scruggs used.

I remember going to see Béla with my family here in Chicago to see him play live and to see with my own eyes how he was pulling those sounds off. Lo and behold, he was playing a Gibson Style 75 Granada banjo and wearing three-finger picks like Earl Scruggs would have used. That's what I wanted to do. I wanted to play modern music like Béla.

The symphonic appeal for young Pikelny was reversed, compared to most banjo players who were first impacted by Earl Scruggs. Noam's objective right out of the gate was to emulate Fleck. Fortunately, there were some thoughtful people in his life to give him the proper wisdom and guidance he needed to accomplish the goal of mimicking Béla Fleck, as Pikelny elaborates:

Everybody in the community suggested that if that is what I was interested in, I should take several steps back and learn the fundamentals of Earl Scruggs–style banjo [because] all the modern players like Béla, Tony Trischka, and Bill Keith, all had cut their teeth on Earl Scruggs before they started pursuing their own exploration of the banjo. At first I just thought that was just a means to an end, and I thought, well, if I have to, I'll do it. Then I started to work out of the Earl Scruggs book, and I ordered the Flatt and Scruggs box set recordings.

So I started to learn the Flatt and Scruggs tunes, and I just really fell in love with it, with the bluegrass style. I kind of lost my focus on what the original goal was—to learn this traditional stuff in order to get back to the more modern stuff. Now I was mostly focused on the traditional stuff. I think I took for granted the brilliance of Earl Scruggs. I think, as a kid, Earl Scruggs was playing sounds so elemental to me that it's, like, you hear it and can't imagine bluegrass banjo playing sounding any different. When someone thinks of bluegrass banjo, or if you ask someone, what comes to mind when you think of bluegrass banjo? It's the sound of Earl Scruggs. I don't think it made an impact on me as a little kid like it did as I grew older and started to realize that he actually developed this style, and these musical phrases, and rolls and licks that we use right now are the result of his creativity.

Born in 2000, native East Tennessean Willow Osborne (no relation to the famed Osborne Brothers) is an astounding banjoist who's had the honor of appearing with Rhonda Vincent and the Rage on PBS and participated in a documentary on the life of Swiss banjoist Jens Kruger. As one of the youngest rising talents to emerge in the wake of Scruggs, Willow's musical skills were nurtured from the age of four when she began taking lessons from Gary "Biscuit" Davis, a four-time international banjo champion. By age ten, she was proficient enough to play professionally in live shows, and within a few short years she gained endorsements from the Deering and Neat banjo companies, along with GHS Strings and BlueChip Picks.

For as rapidly changing and tech savvy as all musical genres have become in this new millennium, Willow credits the man who pioneered a revolutionary new sound more than a half century before she was born with being at the core of her musical identity:

> Earl was very, very influential to me. I grew up listening to him, and he's one of my heroes. Honestly, he's my biggest hero. Even though I've listened to all of his stuff, I go back and listen to it and study it. I mean, he's just that player that everybody wants to sound like and I want to sound like. I look up to him definitely, and also as a person and a player. Earl's playing is just so clear and he's got such a polished tone. I mean, the way he plays, he always executes exactly what he wants and he makes it seem so easy, but whenever you try to play it, it's like, *wow!* What Earl played, like, his notes and choices of licks and clarity, is just what every banjo player really strives to be today.

Opinions differ greatly among banjoists on how long the Scruggs influence is going to last. No doubt, Earl can still be heard in the repertoire of today's emerging bluegrass banjo players. Osborne, though, offers her opinion on those willing to sacrifice the banjo's soul for pizzazz:

> Honestly, there's two groups of people in bluegrass, where if you go to, like, a bluegrass festival and you start walking around, you can hear the music that has the heart—what bluegrass really is. Earl, honestly, he put that heart into it, in the drive, and I feel like a lot of younger players are losing that because they're just kind of trying to be flashy [to] get everybody's attention. Earl was just very simplistic, yet complex, and that's just a weird way of putting it—but it's just what made him and just gave bluegrass that distinct sound.

Anyone questioning whether or not young people are supporting traditional bluegrass needs to attend the IBMA or SPBGMA conference or any bluegrass festival in the United States. The number of young kids jamming and performing in their own bands is more than impressive. You'll find these youngsters playing more progressive forms of bluegrass, yet even in that you can hear the echo of Earl Scruggs in *every* banjo solo.

Whether professional or amateur, known or unknown, fluent or just beginning, all living three-fingered five-string banjoists are disciples of Earl, proving that the current generation is not moving away from Scruggs. They continue to demonstrate the connection between what Earl pioneered and the advanced techniques that arise generation after generation. As bluegrass artist Sam Bush reaffirms, "There's a Scruggs influence everywhere for everyone who wears a thumb and two finger picks."

NOTES

1. HUMBLE BEGINNINGS

1. The origin and elements of old-time string music are documented in Neil V. Rosenberg, *Bluegrass: A History*, rev. ed. (Urbana: University of Illinois Press, 2005), esp. 6–10, and verbalized by Camp Springs Bluegrass Festival organizer Carlton Haney in the film *Bluegrass Country Soul* (Washington Film Group, 1972).

2. Descriptions of Flint Hill and its people are drawn from a 1961 radio interview with Earl Scruggs by Ernie Knight of WLOE as well as Scruggs's book, the revised and enhanced edition of *Earl Scruggs and the 5-String Banjo* (Milwaukee: Hal Leonard, 2005), 158–60, and from Cleveland County disc jockey Hugh Dover's comments in the NET documentary *Earl Scruggs: His Family and Friends* (1970).

3. On Earl's awkward positioning of Junie's banjo at an early age, see Scruggs, *Earl Scruggs and the 5-String Banjo*, 159.

4. The purchase price of Junie's banjo is listed in Earl Scruggs's first edition of *Earl Scruggs and the 5-String Banjo* (New York: Peer International, 1968), 149.

5. Scruggs, *Earl Scruggs and the 5-String Banjo* (2005), 159.

6. Scruggs recounted this argument on WSM's *Intimate Evening* program on March 26, 2007, and it was included in Eddie Stubbs's on-air *Tribute to Earl Scruggs* on WSM 650-AM on April 4, 2012, from WSM's official website (wsmonline.com). It is also described in Scruggs, *Earl Scruggs and the 5-String Banjo* (2005), 158.

7. Accounts of Earl's weeklong practice of "Reuben," Junie's visit, and Earl's mother's advice are chronicled in "Earl Scruggs Biography: Chapter 1—

The Early Years," http://www.earlscruggs.com/biography.html, and in Earl Scruggs, *Earl Scruggs and the 5-String Banjo* (1968), 155.

8. Earl's banjo/fiddle duets with Dennis Butler were recalled in an interview with Eddie Stubbs on December 8, 2002, and also featured in *Tribute to Earl Scruggs*.

9. See *Earl Scruggs: His Family and Friends*.

10. Scruggs, *Earl Scruggs and the 5-String Banjo* (2005), 161.

11. Peter Cooper, "Earl Scruggs, Country Music Hall of Famer and Bluegrass Innovator, Dies at Age 88," *Tennessean*, March 28, 2012; Bob Carlin, "Roots of Earl and Snuffy: Searching for the Banjo along the North/South Carolina Border," *Bluegrass Unlimited*, May 2009, 54–60.

12. Junie Scruggs's recordings appear on a compilation album called *American Banjo: Tunes and Songs in Scruggs Style* (Folkways Records, 1957) and on the CD *American Banjo: Three-Finger and Scruggs Style* (Smithsonian Folkways, 1990).

13. See Rosenberg, *Bluegrass*, 7.

14. Rosenberg, *Bluegrass*, 35–36, 45–46, 55–56, 59, 61, 70–72; Scruggs, *Earl Scruggs and the 5-String Banjo* (2005), 161–62.

15. Shumate recalled his meeting with Scruggs and arranging his audition with Bill Monroe at MerleFest in Wilkesboro, North Carolina, on April 30, 2005; see also Scruggs, *Earl Scruggs and the 5-String Banjo* (2005), 161.

16. Earl explained choosing "Dear Old Dixie" and "Sally Goodin" to play for Bill Monroe on *Tribute to Earl Scruggs*.

17. The Birth of Bluegrass is commemorated by a historical marker outside of the Ryman Auditorium in Nashville, which was placed on September 27, 2006, by the Tennessee Historical Commission (Marker Number 3A 209).

2. FROM BLUE GRASS TO FOGGY MOUNTAIN

1. Earl Scruggs, liner notes for *The Essential Earl Scruggs* (Sony Music Entertainment, 2004).

2. Scruggs, *Earl Scruggs and the 5-String Banjo* (2005), 162.

3. Stubbs, *Tribute to Earl Scruggs*.

4. Louise Scruggs, liner notes for *Earl Scruggs and Friends* (MCA Nashville, 2001). See also Louise's words in *Earl Scruggs: His Family and Friends* (1970); James Orr, liner notes for *Earl Scruggs with Family & Friends: The Ultimate Collection Live at the Ryman* (Rounder Records, 2008).

5. There is much debate over whether the Gibson banjo that Earl Scruggs bought from Haze Hall and later traded to Don Reno in 1949 was an RB-3 or an RB-75. Jim Mills is a recognized authority on Gibson's prewar Mastertone

banjos. He has thoroughly researched and documented this controversy in his book *Gibson Mastertone: Flathead 5-String Banjos of the 1930s and 1940s* (Anaheim Hills, CA: Centerstream, 2009), 87–95, and has certified that the banjo Earl traded to Don Reno is an RB-75.

6. The price of $37.50 is noted in the "Earl Scruggs Biography," http://www.earlscruggs.com/biography.html. Speculation exists that Jenkins may have paid a higher price (Mills, *Gibson Mastertone*, 51).

7. Mills, *Gibson Mastertone*, 57–58.

8. Scruggs, *Earl Scruggs and the 5-String Banjo* (2005), 19–20.

3. FLATT AND SCRUGGS

1. Scruggs, *Earl Scruggs and the 5-String Banjo* (1968), 153.

2. See Rich Kienzie, liner notes for *Flatt and Scruggs: Foggy Mountain Gospel* (Sony BMG Music Entertainment, 2005), and Josh Graves, *Bluegrass Bluesman: A Memoir*, ed. Fred Bartenstein (Urbana: University of Illinois Press, 2012), 60.

3. Flatt and Scruggs's first meeting with T. Tommy Cutrer was mentioned by Earl Scruggs on WSM's *Intimate Evening* program on March 26, 2007, and appeared on *Tribute to Earl Scruggs*.

4. Scruggs, *Earl Scruggs and the 5-String Banjo* (1968), 153.

5. Scruggs, *Earl Scruggs and the 5-String Banjo* (2005), 159.

6. See "Chapter 9: An Era of Prosperity," C. F. Martin & Co., https://www.martinguitar.com/about/martin-story/; interview with Roger H. Siminoff in Marilyn Kochman, *The Big Book of Bluegrass: The Artists, the History, the Music* (New York: Quill / A Frets Book, 1984), 35.

7. See "About Us," Newport Festivals Foundation, http://www.newportfestivalsfoundation.org/about-us/.

8. Louise Scruggs's liner notes for *Earl Scruggs and Friends* and Earl Scruggs's liner notes for *The Essential Earl Scruggs*. Earl spoke of the banjo's ability to "blend in" with other types of instruments from various genres in *Earl Scruggs: His Family and Friends*.

9. Curly Seckler's dismissal from the Foggy Mountain Boys was explained by Seckler's manager and biographer, Penny Parsons, via email correspondence with Gordon Castelnero.

4. THE BEVERLY HILLBILLIES

1. See interview with Paul Henning by Bob Claster for the *Archive of American Television*, September 3, 1997, http://emmytvlegends.org/interviews/people/paul-henning.

2. Paul Henning recalled employing the help of a friend who played the piano for "The Ballad of Jed Clampett" in his interview with Bob Claster for the Archive of American Television (1997) via their official website (emmytvlegends.org).

3. See *Billboard*'s Charts Archives, http://www.billboard.com/archive/charts.

4. See airdates and episode names in Stephen Cox, *The Beverly Hillbillies: A Fortieth Anniversary Wing-Ding* (Nashville: Cumberland House, 2003).

5. CHANGIN' TIMES

1. Rosenberg, *Bluegrass*, 150–51. Carnegie Hall's official program from *Folksong '59* does not identify Earl Taylor and the Stoney Mountain Boys, as they are listed third on the roster of entertainers as "Bluegrass Band."

2. Peter Cooper, "Earl Scruggs, Country Music Hall of Famer and Bluegrass Innovator, Dies at Age 88," *Tennessean*, March 29, 2012, and Cooper, "Flatt & Scruggs Crossed Cultural Boundaries," *Tennessean*, May 3, 2013.

3. Flatt and Scruggs's taping at George Washington University and their June 15, 1963, airdate was mentioned by Earl Scruggs in an interview with Ernie Knight on WLOE in May 1963 and documented in a press release from the ABC Television Network on May 23, 1963.

4. Nashville's Centennial Park crowd of more than 20,000 on July 14, 1963, was documented by the Tennessean and reprinted in Flatt and Scruggs's *Picture Album Song Book* (1965).

5. The first edition of *Earl Scruggs and the 5-String Banjo* from Peer International Corporation is copyrighted 1968. No definitive reasons have been substantiated for why it was delayed two years from its anticipated March 1, 1966, street date.

6. Ralph Emery's introduction of Flatt and Scruggs in *Country Music on Broadway*: "Good bluegrass music has been taking the country by storm. And these boys we're about to bring you are just about the best in that line. They've traveled the country more than anybody else, I suppose, singing the great bluegrass songs. They've been in New York many times—with us right now,

give a big welcome for Lester Flatt, Earl Scruggs, and the Foggy Mountain Boys" (Marathon Pictures Corporation, 1964).

7. See *Billboard*'s Charts Archives, http://www.billboard.com/archive/charts.

8. Grammy Awards for the performers of two versions of "Foggy Mountain Breakdown" in 1969 and 2002 are verified via the Past Winners Search page on the Grammy's official website (grammy.com).

9. Rosenberg, *Bluegrass*, 309.

10. Ibid.

11. Ibid., 310; Kochman, *Big Book of Bluegrass*, 34; and Scruggs, *Earl Scruggs and the 5-String Banjo* (2005), 167. Scruggs also affirmed his desire to play different types of music in *Earl Scruggs: His Family and Friends*.

12. Cox, *Beverly Hillbillies*, 27.

13. "Flatt, Scruggs Ending 21-Year Partnership," United Press International, April 11, 1969.

6. PUSHING BOUNDARIES

1. Earl's "great sense of relief" is affirmed by Gary Scruggs. See also Rosenberg, *Bluegrass*, 310; Kochman, *Big Book of Bluegrass*, 34; and Scruggs in *Earl Scruggs: His Family and Friends*.

2. NET was absorbed by PBS in 1970. See Carolyn N. Brooks, "National Educational Television Center," *Encyclopedia of Television*, Museum of Broadcast Communications, http://www.museum.tv/eotv/nationaleduc.htm.

3. Louise Scruggs mentions the *Banjoman* premiere at the Kennedy Center in her liner notes for *Earl Scruggs and Friends*.

4. Earl's Grammy for his performance on the recording of "Earl's Breakdown" is verified via the Past Winners Search page on the Grammy's official website (grammy.com).

5. The original 1974 poster for *Where the Lilies Bloom* notes that it is "filmed in color in the backwoods of the Blue Ridge Mountains." Locations and local casting verified by IMDb.com, Robert Radnitz "Where the Lilies Bloom" page on Roger Ebert's official website (rogerebert.com), and the North Carolina Film Office's official website (ncfilm.com).

6. Details of Earl's 1975 plane crash appear Graves, *Bluegrass Bluesman*, 52, and in Scruggs, *Earl Scruggs and the 5-String Banjo* (2005), 169–70. Wreckage of the plane was photographed by Owen Cartwright of the *Nashville Banner* (September 29, 1975), which clearly shows the plane's right wheel severed from the remainder of the aircraft. Most of the visible damage is on the plane's underside.

7. Marty Stuart's urging Earl Scruggs to visit Lester Flatt in the hospital is confirmed by Gary Scruggs and documented by *Country Music* magazine columnist Patrick Carr's liner notes for *The Essential Flatt and Scruggs: 'Tis Sweet to Be Remembered . . .* (Sony Music Entertainment, 1997).

8. Louise Scruggs, liner notes for *Earl Scruggs and Friends*, and Earl Scruggs, liner notes for *The Essential Earl Scruggs*.

7. EARL, EARL, EARL

1. The death of Steve and Elizabeth Scruggs was noted in the *New York Times*, September 25, 1992. Earl's eight months of mourning was documented in Louise Scruggs, liner notes for *Earl Scruggs and Friends*, and Scruggs, *Earl Scruggs and the 5-String Banjo* (2005), 171.

2. Scruggs, *Earl Scruggs and the 5-String Banjo* (2005), 171.

3. Faye Dunaway's invitation to Earl Scruggs is listed in the "News" section of Earl Scruggs's website under December 2, 2001, http://www.earlscruggs.com/news.html.

4. The Three Pickers Grammy nominations announcement is noted on the Earl Scruggs news page December 4, 2003, on Earl Scruggs's official website (earlscruggs.com).

5. "News," EarlScruggs.com, November 13, 2007, http://www.earlscruggs.com/news.html.

6. "News," EarlScruggs.com, August 18, 2010, http://www.earlscruggs.com/news.html.

7. Doug Hutchens, "The Earl Scruggs Gibson Banjo," *BITH Newsletter*, 2000; Roger Siminoff, "The Five String King: Earl Scruggs," in *Gibson Guitars: 100 Years of an American Icon*, by Walter Carter (Los Angeles: General Publishing Group, 1994), 117; Walter Carter, "Gibson Honors Earl Scruggs with the Earl Banjo Model," press release, July 19, 2002.

8. The 1999 Grammy for Best Country Collaboration with Vocals (on the recording of "Same Old Train") also went to Earl's fellow participants Clint Black, Joe Diffie, Merle Haggard, Emmylou Harris, Alison Krauss, Patty Loveless, Ricky Skaggs, Marty Stuart, Pam Tillis, Randy Travis, Travis Tritt, and Dwight Yoakam.

8. THE INFLUENCE OF EARL SCRUGGS

1. The *Frets* interview with Sonny Osborne appears in Kochman, *Big Book of Bluegrass*, 52, 54.

2. Fred Bartenstein's comments come from the DVD bonus track of *Bluegrass Country Soul*, 35th Anniversary Collector's Edition (Time Life, 2006).

3. David L. Russell, "Alan Munde: Banjo Pickin' Gentleman," *Tri-State Bluegrass Journal*, July 2005.

4. The rise of newgrass with Bill Emerson and guitarist Cliff Waldron's *New Shades of Grass* in 1968, which "emphasized 'contemporary' repertoire (particularly rock songs)"; Walter Hensley's banjo album *Pickin' on New Grass*; and the 1970 Bluegrass Alliance album *Newgrass* are chronicled in Rosenberg, *Bluegrass*, 298.

5. See "Biography," CharlieCushman.com, http://charliecushman.com/BIO.htm.

6. Ibid.

SELECT BIBLIOGRAPHY

Bluegrass Country Soul, 35th Anniversary Collector's Edition. Directed by Albert Ihde. Time Life, 2006.

Carlin, Bob. "Roots of Earl and Snuffy: Searching for the Banjo along the North/South Carolina Border." *Bluegrass Unlimited*, May 2009, 54–60.

Carr, Patrick. Liner notes for *The Essential Earl Scruggs*, by Earl Scruggs. Sony Music Entertainment, 2004.

Carter, Walter. *Gibson Guitars: 100 Years of an American Icon*. Los Angeles: General Publishing Group, 1994.

Cooper, Peter. "Earl Scruggs, Country Music Hall of Famer and Bluegrass Innovator, Dies at Age 88." *Tennessean*, March 28, 2012.

———. "Flatt & Scruggs Crossed Cultural Boundaries." *Tennessean*, May 3, 2013.

Country Music on Broadway. Hosted by Ralph Emery. Directed by Victor Duncan. Marathon Pictures, 1964. http://www.tcm.com/tcmdb/title/563284/Country-Music-on-Broadway/.

Cox, Stephen. *The Beverly Hillbillies: A Fortieth Anniversary Wing-Ding*. Nashville: Cumberland House, 2003.

Earl Scruggs: His Family and Friends. Directed by David Hoffman. Produced by Amram Nowak. NET, 1970.

"Flatt, Scruggs Ending 21-Year Partnership." United Press International, April 11, 1969.

"George Washington University." *Hootenanny*. Hosted by Jack Linkletter. Directed by Garth Dietrick. ABC-TV, June 15, 1963.

Graves, Josh. *Bluegrass Bluesman: A Memoir*. Edited by Fred Bartenstein. Urbana: University of Illinois Press, 2012.

Henning, Paul. "The Beverly Hillbillies." Interview by Bob Claster. Archive of American Television, September 3, 1997. http://emmytvlegends.org/interviews/shows/beverly-hillbillies-the.

Hutchens, Doug. "The Earl Scruggs Banjo." *BITH Newsletter*, 2000.

Johansson, Jan. "Flatt and Scruggs Interview with Ernie Knight, WLOE 1961." YouTube.com. https://www.youtube.com/watch?v=Fji4B7juZZs.

Kienzie, Rich. Liner notes for *Flatt & Scruggs: Foggy Mountain Gospel*. Sony BMG Music Entertainment, 2005.

Kochman, Marilyn. *The Big Book of Bluegrass: The Artists, the History, the Music*. New York: Quill / A Frets Book, 1984.

"Louise Scruggs Memorial Forum: Jo Walker-Meador." Country Music Hall of Fame, November 12, 2014. http://countrymusichalloffame.org/contentpages/louise-scruggs-memorial-forum-jo-walker-meador#.V4QVx15TGM8.

"The Martin Story: Chapter 9, An Era of Prosperity." C. F. Martin & Co. https://www.martinguitar.com/about/martin-story/.

Mills, Jim. *Gibson Mastertone: Flathead 5-String Banjos of the 1930s and 1940s.* Anaheim Hills, CA: Centerstream, 2009.

Orr, James. Liner notes for *Earl Scruggs with Family & Friends: The Ultimate Collection Live at the Ryman.* Rounder Records, 2008.

Rosenberg, Neil V. *Bluegrass: A History.* Rev. ed. Urbana: University of Illinois Press, 2005.

Russell, David L. "Alan Munde: Banjo Pickin Gentleman." *Tri-State Bluegrass Journal,* July 2005.

Scruggs, Earl. *Earl Scruggs and the 5-String Banjo.* New York: Peer International, 1968.

———. *Earl Scruggs and the 5-String Banjo.* Milwaukee: Hal Leonard, 2005.

———. Liner notes for *The Essential Earl Scruggs*, by Earl Scruggs. Sony Music Entertainment, 2004.

Scruggs, Lousie. Liner notes for *Earl Scruggs and Friends*, by Earl Scruggs. MCA Nashville, 2001.

Stubbs, Eddie. *Tribute to Earl Scruggs.* 650 AM WSM, Nashville, April 4, 2012. http://wsmonline.com/archives/tribute-shows/.

Stubbs, Eddie, and Earl Scruggs. *An Intimate Evening with Eddie Stubbs and Earl Scruggs.* 650 AM WSM, Nashville, March 26, 2007. http://wsmradio.libsyn.com/an-intimate-evening-with-eddie-stubbs-and-earl-scruggs.

Where the Lilies Bloom. Directed by William A. Graham. Radnitz/Mattel Productions, 1974. http://www.imdb.com/title/tt0072401/?ref_=ttco_co_tt.

INDEX

ABOUT THE AUTHORS

The idea for this book began with David L. Russell's long desire to pen a biography of Earl Scruggs. Upon hearing this from David, I suggested he may want to include a different angle. Having previously authored a book, as well as written and produced local television documentaries, I'm well acquainted with the level of commitment it takes to properly execute such a task, and I am also cognizant of the potential competition that may beat you to the marketplace.

In July 2014, I discussed with David the possibility of foregoing a traditionally narrated biography in favor of an oral history from the viewpoints of musicians and entertainers who were inspired by Scruggs. That way, he could collect numerous stories from the vast number of people he knows in bluegrass, plus he'd have a project that's unlikely to be duplicated by a competing author. David liked the idea and asked for my assistance. After a few months of inactivity, I phoned him the day before Thanksgiving to inquire about the status of the book. He said, "I haven't done anything yet, but I haven't forgotten about it either." At that moment, I suggested we get started immediately.

We got together in early December to map out our strategy and commenced with the preliminaries over the following weeks. After the Christmas holidays, our real work began in January 2015. We conducted a series of interviews for the next several months and began writing in May. This project was truly a labor of love, as both David and I share a mutual admiration for Earl Scruggs, his music, and his legend. Our journeys in discovering the five-string banjo and the magnificence

Gordon Castelnero (left) and David L. Russell. Photo by Gordon Castelnero.

of Scruggs began in our youths. David's introduction to the banjo is a multilayered combination of family heritage and a simple, inspired love for that wonderful, twangy sound, as he explains in his backstory:

> I was introduced to the banjo as a small child on trips from metro Detroit to East Tennessee, visiting my mother's relatives and vacationing in the Smoky Mountains. My first encounter with the banjo was on the streets of Gatlinburg, Tennessee, at the age of five as I watched an old man with a long beard, dressed like a mountain man, play the banjo and shuffle his feet. I can't recall how well he played, but as far as I was concerned, it was an amazing sight to behold. As I think about it, however, I do believe he was playing clawhammer style, as opposed to three-finger style. Nonetheless, I still loved the sound.
>
> Over the years I would encounter the banjo via *The Beverly Hillbillies* and *Hee Haw*, but it wasn't until 1975 that I finally decided to get myself a banjo after watching the Smoky Mountain Travelers play a live show in Gatlinburg, Tennessee, at the Riverside Motor Lodge. My father and I saw an advertisement for live bluegrass at the Riverside Motor Lodge, and he said, "Hey, let's go watch a bluegrass

show!" I was more than happy to go, and little did I realize what a life-changing decision that would be for me.

The show started with a bang as the Smoky Mountain Travelers led off with a lightning-fast version of "Fire on the Mountain," but all I could seem to focus on was the blazing banjo of Bill Chambers, a local Knoxville, Tennessee, legend. Halfway through the show, Chambers played a bluesy banjo break on a fiddle tune called "Stony Lonesome," and I turned to my father saying, "I really want to play the banjo." His body language told me that he didn't really take my statement seriously, yet in the following year his tone changed significantly when I was actually jamming with other bluegrass musicians.

My first banjo instructor, Bill Ryan, introduced me to the *Earl Scruggs and the 5-String Banjo* book, and that is when I came to realize that the banjo playing on *The Beverly Hillbillies* theme was Earl Scruggs himself. I soon learned the significance of Earl as *the* master of the bluegrass banjo, and for the next two years he was all I would study.

I was fortunate to have encountered local Detroit bluegrass musicians like Mitch Manns and Dana Cupp Jr. These guys were (and still are) devout disciples of Earl Scruggs, and I was able to glean a great deal of knowledge and experience from them. Mitch took me under his wing and put me through his Earl Scruggs boot camp. I'll never forget the first time I went to his home in Dearborn Heights for what I refer to as a banjo wake-up call. After he played a few Scruggs-style tunes on my banjo, he said, "Let me see the picks you're using." So I handed him my wimpy set of Ernie Ball picks, and he squished them into oblivion, saying, "These picks are useless!" He then handed me a set of 0.25-gauge National finger picks and a heavy National thumb pick and said, "These are the kind of picks you need to play like Earl." I came to realize that if I wanted to play Scruggs-style banjo, I needed to have the proper hardware to pull it off. Sadly, Mitch Manns passed away soon after we finished writing this book; he will be greatly missed.

I had been playing the banjo about two years when I landed my first teaching job at the Gitfiddler music shop in Northville, Michigan. I initially got the job after helping the owner, Tom Rice, sell a couple of banjos off his shelf that had been sitting there for quite a while. I remember him saying, "I need a guy like you around here, Dave. You want a job?" I jumped at the chance and eventually accumulated around twenty-five banjo students within a year or two. It was during this time, in late 1979, that I met my coauthor, Gordon

Castelnero, an eager fourteen-year-old banjo enthusiast. He was actually one of my better students, and he seemed to clearly grasp Scruggs style and catch on quickly.

The greatest thrill for me over the years has been the opportunities I have had to play with some great bluegrass musicians. I cut my eye teeth in Detroit and other parts of Michigan, having played with local bands like the Sunnysiders, John Hunley and the Kentuckians, Wendy Smith and Blue Velvet, Timberline, Fox River Band, the Mike Adams Band, Run for Cover, Lare Williams and New Direction, and Hardline Drive. I was also honored to play and jam with some bluegrass legends like Bill Monroe, Jimmy Martin, Mac Wiseman, Bobby Hicks, Alan Munde, and Frank Wakefield, with whom I had the chance to tour for a couple of weeks in 2001.

It's an honor to have played bluegrass music at a professional level a few times in my life and, even more humbling, to know that there are professional musicians at a much higher level than what I have experienced. My encounter with these pros taught me a great deal about what I did not yet know regarding bluegrass music and the banjo, and the journey continues on.

Down through the years, I branched out into other styles of banjo, including melodic and single string (or what is referred to as Reno style), yet I have always come back to Earl Scruggs. There was a time many years ago when I thought there were a number of banjo players that could play just like Earl, but my current opinion is that nobody has even come close to the master. The disciples of Earl will testify to the fact that he still leaves them speechless. His playing had a touch, feel, tone, and sense of timing that the best of the best cannot reproduce to this day.

I was fortunate to have had the opportunity to meet Earl and to talk to him on a few occasions. I played banjo in front of him one time and was never more nervous in all my life as he watched my right and left hands. That was an experience for which I am grateful, and one I will never forget.

Despite the fact that there are some incredible banjo players that followed Earl, there are two things that will never change. Earl will always be, irrefutably, the master of the five-string banjo, and no one is ever going to beat him at his own game.

As for me, growing up in Livonia, Michigan, my fascination with the banjo and Mr. Scruggs began in the spring of 1979 when I was finishing the eighth grade at Ford Junior High. I saw a classmate, Caleb Cook, pick a five-string banjo in our school talent show. Watching the fingers of his right hand move and listening to the crisp sound generated by his instrument made an impression on me. A few weeks later, I was at my uncle's house listening to a Flatt and Scruggs record on his elaborate stereo system that literally made the floor vibrate from the decibels blaring out of its mammoth speakers. The first cut was "The Ballad of Jed Clampett." Of course, I had heard the tune on television numerous times, but that was through a small monophonic speaker on my parents' black-and-white Philco television set. So when I heard the song cranking in stereo at such a high volume, it sounded amazing. It packed a punch that was so overpowering I was hooked. From that day forward, I wanted to play the banjo like Earl Scruggs.

During the summer, I worked two paper routes to save most of my money for a banjo, while spending a few dollars here and there on Flatt and Scruggs records. I was blown away by the second-string hammering in the opening lick of "Foggy Mountain Breakdown" and couldn't wait to learn it. Just before school started in the fall, I purchased my first banjo, a Hondo II, from Grinnell's music store for $120.00 (which to me seemed like a step up from the Kay banjo they had for $90.00). When school began, I was fortunate to have Caleb in my first-hour English class. I asked him to teach me the banjo, and he obliged by showing me a few roll patterns along with tablature instruction. Immediately afterward, I bought a copy of *Earl Scruggs and the 5-String Banjo* from a guitar shop near my house. Caleb and I tried to coordinate a few lessons, but as our school assignments were quickly piling up, he suggested I'd be better off taking professional lessons. One of the places he recommended was the Gitfiddler music shop.

In December 1979, I signed up for lessons and met David L. Russell. I spent every Saturday afternoon for the next few years learning Scruggs style from him. He used my Scruggs instruction book often as a teaching tool, and I was thrilled when I could finally pick "Foggy Mountain Breakdown," "Flint Hill Special," "Reuben," and "Sally Ann"—just a few of the Scruggs tunes I listened to incessantly in the preceding months as Earl had become my musical hero. By the time I reached my sophomore year at Churchill High School in the fall of 1980, I started picking with one of my classmates, Kevin VilleMonte, who played acoustic guitar, and we often called ourselves Lester and Earl. Soon afterward, I was flattered when another friend from school, Tim Sprad-lin, asked me to aid him in learning Scruggs style on the banjo.

During these years, David L. Russell and I became good friends outside of the lessons. When I was looking for a better banjo, he sold me his Iida Masterclone Model 240 (a clone of Gibson's RB-5) for $550, on a $50 monthly payment plan, and I still have it today. When he went off to college in 1982, I didn't see him again until 1991 for a brief moment when I visited the Gitfiddler and was surprised that he had returned there to teach. In 2009, I went to the Livonia Public Library to use their computer for a few minutes when a man I didn't recognize asked me if I used to take banjo lessons—it was David.

Since then we have corresponded from time to time discussing pos-sible banjo projects, and always at the center of them was Earl Scruggs. I didn't have the opportunity to become a professional musician, as life took me in a different direction, but I never forgot the ole five-string nor my love for Earl's music. He's still my favorite instrumentalist and the one whose recordings are at the top of my playlist. When I had lunch with David that afternoon in July 2014 to give him my thoughts about this book, I was flattered by his invitation to assist. At first, I was thinking of just helping him as a consultant, but the more I listened to Earl's records in the subsequent months, the more persuaded I was to coauthor with him. Unlike David, I never had the privilege of meeting Mr. Scruggs. However, in chronicling his life through the collective memories of those we've interviewed, I feel I've come to know him well and with a much higher level of respect than I ever thought was pos-sible.

Researching and writing this book has brought both of us an enor-mous amount of joy, and we hope that you've had an equal (if not greater) amount of gratification in reading about the life and legacy of a true musical icon—Earl Eugene Scruggs.